1995

Cooperative Education and Experiential Learning

Forming Community-Technical College and Business Partnerships

Jeffrey A. Cantor

*Lehman College,
City University of New York*

Wall & Emerson, Inc.
Toronto, Ontario • Dayton, Ohio

DEDICATION

The support for completing this book comes from my wife Ruth, and children David, Julie, and Adam. To them I dedicate this book.

J.A.C.

Orders for this book may be directed to:

Wall & Emerson, Inc.	*or*	Wall & Emerson, Inc.
Six O'Connor Drive		8701 Slagle Rd.
Toronto, Ontario, Canada		Dayton, Ohio 45458
M4K 2K1		

Or by telephone or facsimile:

Telephone: (416) 467-8685 Fax: (416) 696-2460

Canadian Cataloguing in Publication Data

Cantor, Jeffrey A.
    Cooperative education and experiential learning

Includes bibliographical references and index.
ISBN 1-895131-14-6

1. Education, Cooperative.   2. Experiential learning.
I. Title.

LB1029.C6C35 1995   373.2'8   C95-930554-8

Printed in Canada.

1 2 3 4 5 6   04 03 02 01 00 99 98 97 96 95

Table of Contents

List of Figures

Introduction

The idea of sharing responsibility for the preparation of America's workers and leaders is gaining more and more acceptance as we witness profound change in both our education and economic systems. At the focal point of these changes is the concept of cooperative education—the sharing of responsibility and resources by these two systems, education and business, for worker education and training. Through cooperative education, future workers are provided with opportunities for experiential learning—learning by doing.

Why Such a Book?

Yes, America is at the crossroads of a revolution in its system of education. As we approach the 21st century we must face several indisputable facts about the educational condition of our nation. First, our schools are not adequately meeting the goal of producing literate young adults, capable of functioning as responsible workers and citizens. Perhaps this is partly because, for too long, public education and business have operated in isolation from one another and from the community in general.

Second, many of the education and training programs, which are geared specifically to produce technically trained workers for our nation's businesses and industries, are seriously out of touch with the very businesses they serve.

American business is also facing serious problems—including a shortage of qualified potential workers and a current workforce that lacks the literacy and technical skills necessary to function productively. It is estimated that the American business community has spent $40 billion in education, 75 percent of which goes to basic skills remediation. Both educators and business people recognize this dilemma and are seeking solutions.

The Approach

This book is a practical guide to cooperative education and experiential learning in community and technical colleges. It can also be useful for educators at the secondary level, as well as for business people responsible for training and development; or for community leaders sponsoring programs to link people (including youth) with employment opportunities, thus promoting economic development through better use of human resources. A solution to our educational dilemma is to establish partnerships and coalitions of public education and business and industry to provide training, education, and re-education of our nation's youth—both within the high school and technical institute or college, and on the job in the community. Today, this activity, termed *cooperative education* and *experiential learning*, is expanding in scope and practice. Cooperative and experientially based education as discussed in this book includes various kinds of partnerships consisting of different organizational arrangements and players. Firms or companies, municipalities, the federal government, organized labor, professional groups or civic organizations etc., can make a difference when they join forces with public education. Experiential learning takes place through many new and innovative approaches and activities within partnerships. These include: community-sponsored mentoring programs; clinicals; practicums and internships; and business-sponsored activities such as apprenticeship programs.

Through experience (as a corporate training director and currently as a consultant to government, and business and industry) in developing training and education partnerships and coalitions, this author has found that one of the biggest obstacles to effective linkages is a lack of understanding of the other organizations, including their roles, resources, constraints, and abilities. Such misunderstandings create communication barriers. To overcome these barriers, the business community needs information on what community colleges can and cannot do when joining into partnerships. Similarly, educators need to understand business operations as they relate to training. With this information all can effectively plan to make the best use of their collective available resources. When all parties to a coalition know the mutual constraints, resources, and limitations with which they are working, very creative configurations can be developed to maximize mutual benefits. The material for this book is drawn from this author's experiences on "both sides of the fence," and on research conducted into educational linkages and partnerships carried out for the US Department of Labor and Education and US Navy. These experiences are described. Therefore, through an analysis of lessons learned and resources available, this book will provide the educator, business person, and community development worker with an overview of the various kinds of cooperative education and experiential learning arrangements that can and do work elsewhere.

A Practical Guide

The goal of the book is to highlight what works, and why, in cooperative educational partnerships of community colleges, technical schools, businesses, and the community, and to provide guidance to professionals in these areas so that they may replicate, develop, and conduct programs of their own. The book is designed to be practical— therefore language common to all parties concerned is used and specialized terminology defined, as well as ample graphic illustrations provided. By actually citing and describing successfully operating cooperative experiential learning programs, highlighted by discussions of underlying concepts and ideas, readers will be able to visualize the benefits and applications of these concepts and ideas and adapt them to their own needs and situations.

J.A.C.
Danbury, Connecticut
January, 1995

Chapter 1

Cooperative Education and Experiential Learning: An Overview

Cooperative education consists of planned programs of experiential learning that combine formal classroom study with career-related work experiences in the community or business and industry or government. Thus, cooperative education includes both academic and professional training. Cooperative education enhances traditional classroom or academic instruction by providing practical work- or community-based experience (experiential learning), relevant to learners' educational and career goals.

The community and technical college (hereinafter referred to as "the community college") is the institution of higher education uniquely able to plan, arrange, and provide the structured workplace learning experiences that complement various educational programs and serve differing learner populations. Community colleges were specifically established to provide their community constituencies with easily accessible college-level programs, as well as occupationally oriented education and training. Today these institutions are the primary sources of training and technical assistance for a community's businesses and industry (Bowsher, 1989) and centers of cooperative education.

Cooperative education programs by their very nature involve linkages of employers, and/or the government, oftentimes the community-at-large, and the community college (Heermann, 1973). For cooperative education programs to work well, the instructors and administrators responsible for these programs need to know how to communicate among their various institutions and organizations (see Figure 1–1). They need to be able to interact with training and human resource development professionals in business and industry. This book is a resource of information and ideas on how to design, implement, and promote cooperative education and experiential learning activities in partnerships of education and business and industry and community.

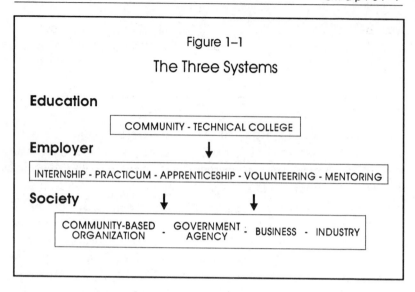

Figure 1-1

The Three Systems

Education

COMMUNITY - TECHNICAL COLLEGE

Employer   ↓

INTERNSHIP - PRACTICUM - APPRENTICESHIP - VOLUNTEERING - MENTORING

Society   ↓   ↓

COMMUNITY-BASED - GOVERNMENT : BUSINESS - INDUSTRY
ORGANIZATION   AGENCY

Why Cooperative Education?

The Changing Workforce

National demographic trends confirm what is already apparent—the traditional workforce of the past, once composed largely of white males, no longer exists as such. Instead, in the United States, many more workers are now older, female, and come from more socially diverse and economically disadvantaged backgrounds (Johnston and Packer; 1987). Today, more than ever, cooperative educational partnerships are essential in order to maximize the social and economic potential of these special populations (Boyer, 1983).

Let's take a closer look at the changing workforce.

Older workers

Due to declining population growth a shrinking pool of younger people is now available to enter the workforce. The average age of people in the workforce will soon increase from 36 to 39 years. Second career training will become more necessary and, therefore, more common.

Female workers

More women are entering the labor force. Between now and the year 2000, women will come to comprise two-thirds of new entrants into the workforce. By the end of the century, it is projected that nearly 61 percent of working-age women will be employed, many in non-traditional occupations where the employment needs are critical—health technologies, public services, and high-technology service professions.

Minority group workers

Members of minority groups will comprise 29 percent of new entrants into the labor force between now and the year 2000, a figure that is twice the current share. The current workforce will have to adjust to working with people from many cultural backgrounds, and vice versa.

Immigrant workers

An increase in the number of immigrants into the workforce is also projected. For the rest of this century it is estimated that approximately 600,000 immigrants will enter the United States each year; almost two-thirds of these will attempt to enter the labor force with limited English and social customs that differ from those of the existing workforce (Johnston and Packer, 1987, pp. xix–xx).

Illiterate workers

Literacy problems are increasing to crisis proportions in today's workforce. Business leaders and educators point to an alarming lack of basic literacy and computational skills among our nation's workers. As a result, on-the-job literacy education has become a necessity (National Commission on Excellence in Education, 1989).

Together women, nonwhites, and immigrants will make up more than five-sixths of the new additions to the workforce by the end of the century. The overall effects on business and industry of such dramatic changes in workforce composition are exacerbated by the fact that increasingly technical skills are now required in the workplace (Johnston and Packer, 1987). American business is starved for qualified workers. Cooperative education serves as both a recruitment tool for employers and an entry to the workforce for learners.

The Community College and Structured Workplace Learning

The use of the term 'community' in the designation of the two-year college reflects an important reality. Today, much more than in the past, society believes in the need for and value of community involvement in our public educational systems: the community college exemplifies this goal.

Experiential learning opportunities through cooperative education are consistent with the goals and functions of the community college and, therefore, should be an integral part of all community college programs. Through various experiential learning activities, such as credit for life experience or cooperative work-and-learn internships, adult and non-traditional learners can optimize the time and resources they invest in college study.

In their efforts to meet the needs of their learner populations, community colleges serve many functions. They typically offer some of the following programs (Monroe, 1972).

Transfer curricula

College-parallel or transfer (liberal arts) curricula is a basic part of a community college's mandate. Many learners enroll in liberal arts courses as a means of exploring their interests and broadening their horizons, or in search of a career or major area of study. Or they may have as a longer term goal the desire to earn a four-year, or baccalaureate, degree. Liberal arts courses also constitute some part of most occupational programs of study. Business and industry leaders usually support making these courses a required part of occupational programs in order to produce well-rounded workers prepared for and capable of the kinds of more complex tasks they will face.

General studies

General studies are courses taken by learners without a specific transfer or occupational goal in mind. These courses are, for the most part, in the humanities and are held to be an essential part of any complete liberal arts program.

Occupational training

The community college is the primary agency able to meet the job training needs of its community. Business and industry, government, and social and health care institutions look to community colleges for effective and up-to-date occupational training. These programs are often offered for credit towards terminal or Associate degrees, and also on a non-credit and/or contract training basis.

Adult and continuing education

Programs and courses also are provided for mature learners and workers seeking either continuing education of an avocational nature or specific technical training. This adult and continuing education division of a community college is often the place where the business community first looks to develop contract programs to meet their corporate human resource needs.

Developmental and compensatory programs

These programs are designed to help learners overcome learning deficits and raise learning potential. Community colleges by design offer these kinds of services and readily admit learners who seek higher education and/or technical training, but who do not meet basic admissions requirements. Often, through experiential learning activities, community colleges provide the supportive services necessary, such as mentoring and volunteer programs, for learners to succeed in realizing their higher education and training goals.

Counseling and guidance

Community colleges offer a variety of educational and psychological counseling and guidance services to their learners. Included are vocational aptitude batteries, career counseling, job development, and job placement services. Access to counseling and guidance is very important to community college learners as this varied and multi-faceted student body often has special needs.

"Goal finding" or "cooling out"

By providing accessible educational opportunities—accessible both geographically and financially—community colleges provide services to very diverse student bodies. Through cooperative education opportunities, community colleges offer learners maximum freedom and support to select appropriate careers and the time and opportunity to explore different educational programs—much more so than in a typical four-year college or university. This is termed the "cooling-out" or "goal-finding" function (Monroe, 1972). A typical statement of purpose of a community and technical college is presented in Figure 1–2 below.

Figure 1–2

Purpose of the College

In seeking to increase opportunities for further education within its region, Tunxis Community College is committed to a program of learning and services that provides:

- a stimulating, effective and economical education for qualified students who wish to attend college within commuting distance of their homes;

- career programs leading to the Associate Degree for those students who desire employment after two years college;

- liberal arts and pre-professional education leading to the Associate Degree for those who plan to transfer to baccalaureate programs in senior colleges or universities;

- certificate programs for those students who desire a short period of specialized study;

- counseling to aid students in the development of their educational, vocational, and personal goals;

- opportunities of continuing education through part-time study;

- a spectrum of extra-curricular activities designed to enhance student awareness of social and cultural values and of community issues.

Tunxis Community College

Salvage

The attempt to "salvage" potential drop-outs is closely related to the remedial and the counseling functions, and is one of the aspects that separates community colleges from their four-year college or university counterparts. In addition to giving aid to the learner with limited academic abilities, spoken language problems, or other learning deficits, community colleges offer guidance and inspiration to non-motivated but intellectually able learners. Cooperative education and experiential learning instructional strategies are designed to provide this kind of support.

Benefits to the Learner

The value of cooperative education becomes clear when we consider the nature and needs of the community college learner. Experiential learning improves the educational environment for a learner. Through practical job- or career-related experiential learning and/or hands-on training in a chosen field, formal classroom learning is clarified, reinforced, and made relevant. In addition, by participating in cooperative education a learner has an early opportunity to experience and test a potential career choice before investing significant time and effort in formal education and training. Thus, cooperative education bridges classroom theory and job practice and allows the learner to experience the excitement of doing the real job. And early accomplishment on the job is a powerful motivator for future effort.

The employer or supervisor, as an instructor, is best able to provide the learner with a role model for appropriate worker performance. Learners gain real feedback in on-the-job situations to ensure eventual job competence, thus increasing self-confidence. Whether or not the cooperating employer becomes the full-time employer for a learner, valuable contacts and entrées into the industry can be made through cooperative education.

An important ingredient of career education is learning to work alongside all kinds of people. As our nation's population changes, more immigrants, minorities, females, single heads-of-household, and unemployed people will look to cooperative education as a means to learn-and-earn. Learners and instructors alike benefit from using the workplace as a laboratory for developing interpersonal skills, as well as for instruction and learning. By working together for a shared purpose, people entering our society from different cultures become more understanding of and understandable to other peoples. To achieve this rapport is often not possible in the classroom alone.

To summarize, cooperative education offers the following benefits to the learner (Wilson, 1987):

- clarification of career interests and goals to make sure appropriate educational and/or occupational choices have been made;
- motivation for study through greater appreciation of the relevance of classroom learning;
- improvement in self-reliance, self-confidence, and leadership and managerial skills;
- development of cognitive and attitudinal skills central to successful job performance;
- practice in interpersonal relations skills; and
- decreased isolation of culturally and economically disadvantaged learners.

It also provides:

- financial assistance for disadvantaged learners;
- valuable on-the-job learning experiences, not available in the classroom, aimed at acquiring marketable job skills;
- feedback through performance assessment;
- exposure to working role models in real situations;
- opportunities to establish contacts in the field and begin networking for future employment; and
- higher starting salaries after graduation due to the acquisition of actual work experience.

Benefits to the Employer

Participating (cooperative education) employers benefit from the opportunity to recruit and pretrain future employees, which can reduce labor costs and improve overall business and community economic development (Brown, 1984). Community colleges always screen learners prior to placement on any job site, thus ensuring employers that the selected learners are willing and able to learn and work successfully on the job. Thus, participating employers benefit by having the college serve as a source of entry-level workers in markets where the supply of qualified entry-level labor is often tight.

Research demonstrates that those learners who participate in cooperative education programs ultimately become more satisfied and productive workers for any employer. These learners are immediately exposed to work ethics and responsibilities, acquire appropriate behaviors, and develop realistic expectations. Employers can observe individual learners' work habits on the job and decide whether or not they would make good employees. The employer is *never obligated* to continue a learner in employment past the cooperative education period.

Participation with cooperative education also offers the following benefits to the employer:

- opportunities to influence the college curriculum design and content where it relates to the firm's employee training needs;
- assistance with worker recruitment, screening, and selection;
- better access to women and minorities as potential employees;
- higher employee retention and productivity;
- lower training costs;
- potential employees who have gained, as learners, a realistic picture of what to expect when working; and
- improved community public relations.

Grossman et al., 1988

Benefits to the Community College

Business and industry soon recognize that the community college is a valuable partner in job training and economic development. And the community college derives many advantages from such recognition. To carry out cooperative education programs close liaison between the college faculty and the employer is required. Faculty/business exchanges often begin through exposure to these programs, enabling college faculty to keep their skills current. The college's course of study is updated and verified as "job congruent." The worksite becomes a kind of college laboratory, complementing and supplementing the college facilities. And cooperation can lead to further tangible benefits, including equipment donations, loans, and scholarships.

In addition, cooperative education programs make it easier for colleges to both recruit and retain learners. For example, Pace University has documented, through surveys and interviews with faculty, students, and employers, that at least one-half of its incoming learners were influenced to attend Pace because of the existence of its cooperative education programs. The retention rates of cooperative education programs are reported at 96 percent, compared to the university-wide rate of 52 percent (Dube and Korngold, 1987). Thus, the advantages gained by the college include:

- closer relationships with business and the community;
- better community public relations;
- access to additional potential sources of financial aid and prospects for fund-raising;
- access to state-of-the-art employer facilities (often without cost or at lesser cost);
- better use made of college facilities;
- increased learner enrollment;
- better learner retention and graduate placement;
- workplace-tested curriculum; and
- opportunities to update and train college faculty, thereby ensuring that information, etc., is current.

Polking and Cannon, 1981

The Community Also Benefits

Finally, the community-at-large benefits from the college cooperative education program as well.

- A pool of college-educated workers is provided for business start-ups or expansion, thus ensuring continued economic development; and
- There is an increased likelihood that learners will stay in the community to work and live after graduation.

Experiential Learning in Action: Cooperative Education Methodologies

There are several kinds of experiential learning activities or methods that community colleges often use in conjunction with business and industry and the community. These include the following:

- fieldwork, the practicum, or on-the-job work experience;
- internships and clinicals;
- apprenticeship programs in cooperation with unions and industry;

- the awarding of community college degree credit for life experience, work experience, or military education and training;
- volunteerism and mentoring; and
- Tech Prep and articulated 2+2+2 programs run in cooperation with secondary education and business and industry.

Approximately 200,000 post-secondary students were involved in these various kinds of cooperative education programs at about 1,000 colleges and universities during the late 1980s and 1990s. These programs are described below.

Traditional Cooperative Education Programs

Traditional cooperative education programs place learners on the job with participating employers off-campus, sometimes on a full-time basis in alternating semesters, or sometimes on a part-time basis for 10–20 hours a week, while attending college. Learners are usually paid for their work by the employer. As these cooperative education experiences are generally part of the college program in which learners plan to matriculate, they thus receive college credit for their work on the job. Cooperative education courses are offered in technical and career, as well as liberal arts/transfer, curricula.

For instance, American River College in California offers this typical Work Experience course:

98 Work Experience (1–4 units)

Prerequisite: Drafting 51 and permission of the instructor/coordinator.

Students will be provided with practical and developmental experiences while receiving on-the-job training. These experiences will be determined on an individual basis according to employer's need and the student's capability.

1992 Catalog, p. 112

At Dundalk Community College in Maryland, this course offers a part-time paid work experience:

Cooperative Education I: Industrial Electricity Electronics Maintenance Technology (181–1 credit; 182–2 credits, 183–3 credits, 184–4 credits) Work experience to be arranged.

Prerequisite: 12 college credits, 2.5 grade point average (in major), and consent of academic advisor.

Through Cooperative Education, you will earn both academic credit and pay for knowledge derived from advanced work performed on the job. If you qualify, you will be placed in a part-time position related to your program of study, where you will perform a variety of work-related functions. You will be assigned to a faculty coordinator, who will assist you in the development of performance objectives and monitor your progress. If you meet the prerequisite requirements for Co-op and an appropriate placement is available, the College Co-op Director, your faculty coordinator, and your work supervisor will work with you to identify an appropriate placement, develop your personal employment goals, and direct you in acquiring new skills. To apply for Cooperative Education, see your academic advisor or the College Co-op Director for the necessary forms and information.

1989–1991 Catalog, p. 106

Experiential learning is not only to be found in the occupational curricula, however. These kinds of activities are also appropriate in college parallel and general education programs. For instance, at Mohegan Community College:

ENG 298: Work experience in English:

This course allows students to apply their knowledge of English in a practical setting, such as tutoring or publications. The numbers of credits, course requirements, and means of evaluation are specified in a contract between instructor and student.

1990–1991 Catalog, p. 133

And in the Music Department at Sacramento City College this experiential learning course is offered:

MUSM 48: Work experience in Music 1–4 units

This course includes a one-hour lecture each week and 75 hours of related, paid work experience or 60 hours of volunteer work experience for one unit; and, 75 or 60 hours of related work experience for each additional unit. The course may be repeated when there is new or expanded learning on the job.

1992–1993 Catalog, p. 139

Hence, experiential learning courses may also serve to promote volunteerism and mentoring and the other civic and social goals of the community college. On-the-job experiences are discussed in Chapters 6, 7, 8, and 9.

Internships and Clinicals

Internships are another form of experiential learning. Used to convey more complex or technical skills, the internship is a formal part of a particular college program. Credit is granted for the internship, which can range from one semester to a year or more and is usually the culminating or skills-perfecting activity in a program. Whereas on-the-job activities are usually paid experiences, internships may not be. As an incentive to the employer to participate, the learner is often *not* compensated for services performed in the employer's workplace during an internship. Supervision by the college faculty is always required as part of the employment agreement.

Northcentral Technical College in Wisconsin offers learners in the Data Processing Program opportunities for internships.

INTERNSHIP/FIELD STUDY (Data Processing) 4 Hours 2 Credits

Internship requires a job in an approved data processing installation for a minimum of 80 hours for one semester. A job interview with résumé, analysis of a job position evaluation from the employer and a write-up by the student are required. Field study students will complete an industry project using college equipment. For third/fourth semester Data Processing students.

1990–1992 Catalog, p. 85

And in a Paralegal Studies program at Dundalk Community College in Maryland:

LAW 273/LAW 276 Legal Assistant Internship (3–6 credits) Work experience to be arranged.

Prerequisite: 18 credits in Paralegal Studies curriculum or consent of instructor.

This is an elective legal specialty course for all students in the Paralegal Studies curriculum. This course is designed to provide you with practical experience in the function and responsibilities of a paralegal and to give you an opportunity to employ the skills acquired in required courses. You will work at least 120 hours for 3 credits and 240 for 6 credits.

1989–1991 Catalog, p. 118

At Manchester Community-Technical College in Connecticut the following clinical course is offered in the Medical Laboratory Technology Program.

MLT 201 Clinical Microbiology 4 credits

An introduction to the basic theories of clinical bacteriology and mycology, aseptic techniques for handling specimens and preparing media, primary specimen inoculation, subculturing, colony-count techniques, processing anaerobic and microaerophilic cultures, staining techniques, and antibiotic susceptibility testing.

1992–1993 Catalog, p. 207

Internships, as well as other forms of cooperative education and fieldwork experiences, require close planning and coordination between faculty and industry. Considerations of liability, publicity, certifications, etc., must be discussed and planned for. Supervision of learners, grading policies, preparation of calendars, and so on are all major concerns. The impact of business cycles and layoffs, as well as the role of union involvement, must be considered and provided for as well. Chapter 6 will treat all of these issues.

Apprenticeships

The apprenticeship, an age-old employer-based training method, is now the subject of renewed interest. The on-the-job portion of the apprenticeship is delivered by the employer; related technical education is often provided by community colleges. Many colleges and employers are now expanding the apprenticeship to include formal on-the-job training courses with college credit awarded towards an Associate degree. Many businesses and unions register a dual-enrolled (via the state departments of labor) apprentice into college programs.

Dundalk Community College offers apprenticeships to provide structured work-based training in several technical and occupational areas of study, and also awards Associate degree credit for completion of the apprenticeship portions of the program. For example:

Apprenticeship Training

Satisfactory completion of an appropriate training program registered and recognized by the Maryland Apprenticeship and Training Council may make you eligible to receive up to 15 college credits for such training.

1989–1991 Catalog, p. 12

Industries such as Toyota Motor Corporation, unions such as the International Brotherhood of Electrical Workers, and public services such as the International Association of Firefighters all have successfully operating programs as described in Chapters 7 and 9.

Life Experience Recognition

Community colleges recognize the value of the experiences brought by learners to the classroom by offering programs and activities that capitalize upon mature learners' prior life and work experiences (Simosko, 1985). To gain college credit learners develop a portfolio which describes and documents these experiences. College faculty evaluate these experiences for appropriate credit award towards a specific college program. Careful organizing, structuring, administering, and promoting of adult life experience and experiential learning determines the success of these programs.

Dundalk Community College administers prior learning through a formal course in Portfolio development. Dundalk's course reads:

> *Assessment of Prior Learning Portfolio Development* (3 credits)
> Three hours of lecture a week, one semester.
>
> Prerequisite: Consent of Coordinator of Assessment of Prior Learning.
>
> This course is designed to assist students to examine their past experiences, and to identify and clarify college-level learning in a format that can be evaluated by a faculty assessor for possible credit awards for existing DCC courses.

1989–1991 Catalog, p. 22

This three-credit course enables learners to develop portfolios in which learning outcomes that have been met through prior experience are described. Appropriate documentation must be provided. An assessment committee reviews and evaluates the portfolio and determines the number of credits appropriate for the experience. Most colleges stipulate that the prior experience must be in an area related to the degree pursued; typically the maximum number of credits can not exceed 50 percent of the credits needed to earn the degree.

Chapter 11 describes in detail how to incorporate learners' life experience into community college programs.

Mentoring and Volunteerism

Community colleges offer learners the opportunity to grow socially and professionally through structured service-oriented experiences. By helping others, we all grow and learn. Mentoring and volunteerism build a learner's sense of self-worth and identity, and develop civic responsibility in all who participate. Mentoring and volunteerism—whether on campus or in business and industry—is often used as a means of supplying a formal cooperative educational experience.

Colleges work cooperatively with community-based organizations, as well as businesses, to place learners in positions where they provide workers or citizens with literacy education or other kinds of skills training. The learners receive college credit for the volunteer work.

Mohegan Community College recognizes the value of mentoring and volunteerism to a learner's overall development and offers formal courses to prepare the learner for these activities, such as:

COUN 211 Peer Counseling 3 semester hours

Prerequisites: Completion of at least one semester at Mohegan with a minimum of 6 credits and 2.5 GPA. Successful completion of PSY 111 or equivalent course, training or experience, or consent of instructor.

This course is designed to help prepare and develop skilled, empathic Peer Counselors for placement in positions at the College and in the community. The techniques, methods, and functions of peer counseling will be explored and integrated with theoretical concepts to be applied in a variety of settings.

COUN 212 Peer Counseling Practicum 1–3 semester hours

Prerequisites: COUN 211 and consent of instructor.

Students who have successfully completed COUN 211 will apply peer counseling skills and methods through supervised placement in a College or community setting.

1990–1991 Catalog, pp. 126–127

Chapter 10 will highlight what works and why in mentoring and volunteerism programs and how to develop and implement programs to meet the unique needs of a community and its students.

Articulated Secondary and Post-Secondary Programs

Another innovative cooperative education and experiential learning activity is the federally legislated Tech Prep or 2+2 articulated program carried out under the auspices of secondary schools and business and industry. Tech Prep programs are articulated (or combined) programs of study whereby learners gain college credit and career experience for study done while in high school. These programs are useful in both general and technical education. They attract learners to the college by providing an early taste of college work. Thus, motivation through early successes is provided for learners who otherwise might not attempt higher education.

Community colleges are beginning to operate these programs in significant numbers. Many are developing consortia arrangements for cooperative education Tech Prep programs with their area high schools, and oftentimes business and industry. Teachers and administrators in both the high school and community college agree on a specific body of knowledge and skills within a course and/or program which is common to both institutions.

The State Center Community College District in Fresno, California is a pioneer in this area. Working with local area high schools, it has developed programs in high technology areas which permit a learner to begin preparing for a career while in high school, progressing through a sequence of planned and conducted learning experiences leading to an Associate degree from the community college and then onto the California State University—Fresno to complete a Bachelor's degree. These programs exist in several areas of technology and education. Fresno City College stipulates:

Articulation with High Schools (2+2+2)

Fresno City College has entered into course-specific articulation agreements with a number of local high schools whereby students may gain college credit for articulated courses taken in high school once they have successfully completed 12 units on campus.

If you have completed one of these articulated courses at the high school, you should have received a certificate acknowledging that fact. The certificate should then be turned in to the college registrar or to a member of the college's counseling staff.

1992–1994 Catalog, pp. 28–29

Tech Prep programming has as its objective structured education and training in high technology, science-oriented subjects. Tech Prep development is often underwritten by the Perkins Applied Technology and Vocational Education Amendments of 1990, the "Tech Prep" Act. Tech Prep program development and administration is described in Chapter 12.

Chapter References

Bowsher, J.E. (1989). *Educating America: Lessons learned in the nation's corporations*. New York: John Wiley & Sons.

Boyer, E.L. (1983). *High school: A report on secondary education in America*. New York: Harper & Row.

Brown, S.J. (1984). *The influence of Cooperative Education on first job after graduation*. Boston: Northeastern University. (ERIC No. ED 254 663).

Dube, P.E., & Korngold, A.F. (1987). Documenting benefits and developing campus and community support. In *Cooperative education: A new era*. San Francisco: Jossey-Bass.

Grossman, G.M., Warmbrod, C.P., & Kurth P.K. (1988). *Post-secondary education cooperative education: An examination of survey results and policy implications*. Columbus: Center on Education and Training for Employment, The Ohio State University.

Heermann, B. (1973). *Cooperative education in community colleges: A sourcebook for occupational and general educators*. San Francisco: Jossey-Bass.

Johnston, W.B., & Packer, A.H. (1987). *Workforce 2000: Work and workers for the 21st Century*. Indianapolis: Hudson Institute. (ERIC No. ED 290 887).

Monroe, C.R. (1972). *Profile of the community college*. San Francisco: Jossey-Bass.

National Commission on Excellence in Education. (1989). *A nation at risk*. Washington, DC: U.S. Department of Education.

Polking, K., & Cannon, C. (Editors) (1981). *1981 Internships*. Cincinnati: Writer's Digest Books.

Simosko, S. (1985). *Earn college credit for what you know*. Washington, DC: Acropolis Books.

U.S. Department of Education. (1991). *America 2000: An education strategy sourcebook*. Washington, DC: Author.

Wilson, J.W. (1987). What students gain from cooperative education. In *Cooperative education a new era*. San Francisco: Jossey-Bass.

Wilson, J.W. (1989, Winter). Assessing outcomes of cooperative education. *Journal of Cooperative Education, 25*(2).

Chapter 2

Planning and Designing
Experiential Learning Programs

This chapter describes the formal cooperative education planning processes which must be carried out for experiential learning to be effective. Instructional systems design (ISD) procedures complement experiential learning program planning and development. ISD as an ongoing and a closed-loop process (see Figure 2–1) begins by examining the needs of the learner, occupation, business and industry, or community. However, this examination and analysis of needs does not end when training begins; paying attention to the on-going needs of the audience or organization is critically important if instruction is to be kept relevant.

ISD enables college faculty to identify:

- specific learner needs and learning styles which can be best met through cooperative education;
- the requisite knowledge and skills (e.g., course content) for successful career and life performance;

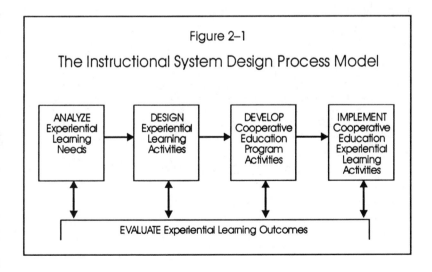

Figure 2–1

The Instructional System Design Process Model

| ANALYZE Experiential Learning Needs | DESIGN Experiential Learning Activities | DEVELOP Cooperative Education Program Activities | IMPLEMENT Cooperative Education Experiential Learning Activities |

EVALUATE Experiential Learning Outcomes

- the manner in which learner needs and course content may be matched through experiential learning (e.g., cooperative education in alternating semesters with on-campus courses);

- the best instructional methodologies (e.g., internships; apprenticeships) to deliver course or program objectives; and

- how best to evaluate cooperative education programs and experiential learning outcomes.

It is essential to consider each of the above items when planning specific experiential learning activities. As well, these activities should be planned as an integral part of overall course and program development. To guide planning and development, the Experiential Learning Planning Model described here is comprised of three phases which are parallel to ISD. These are: (1) an input phase; (2) a process phase; and (3) a product or outcomes phase.

The Experiential Learning Planning Model: An Overview

Figure 2–2 presents the Experiential Learning "Planning" Model. This chapter will deal primarily with the first two phases—Input and Process—which parallel the Analysis and Design steps of ISD for curriculum planning. The last phase—Product—is also briefly discussed.

During the first *Input Phase*, using data analysis procedures, the following are examined:

- learner needs, including the special instructional needs of adults (e.g., need to work part time or need for hands-on training), or the need for language training for learners with limited English and upgrading for non-traditional learners;

- course and program content requirements, including the need for environmental simulations and hands-on training which are most appropriately carried out through experiential learning;

- college needs for laboratory facilities, equipment, and/or adjunct faculty and specialized expertise not available at the college.

To conduct this analysis, faculty should collect and review data from various sources, including the college's student personnel office, and business and community leaders.

Figure 2-2   The Experiential Learning Planning Model

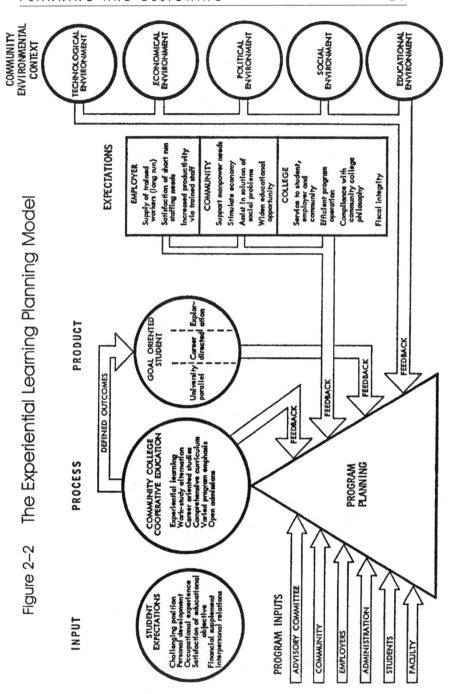

From Barry Heermann, *Cooperative Education in Community Colleges.*
Reprinted with permission of Jossey-Bass.

When all of these above needs have been identified, the next *Process Phase* begins with the selection of experiential learning activities to support the college course or program. The following steps are part of this second phase:

- drawing up experiential learning performance objectives;
- identifying experiential learning activities complementary to each performance objective;
- planning and designing experiential learning instructional strategies; and
- designing evaluation strategies.

Now the chosen experiential learning activities are developed and implemented. This involves the following processes:

- training and orientation of faculty and staff;
- identification of potential worksites;
- recruitment and orientation of employers;
- development of cooperative education agreements; and
- promotion of the program.

Finally, in the instructional model's last or *Product Phase*, a total program evaluation and review are conducted.

The Experiential Learning Planning Model: Input Phase

Now, for a fuller discussion. The Planning Model's *Input Phase* includes all of the steps normally performed in an instructional analysis (see Figure 2–3). It begins with an analysis of the targeted adult learner population, includes the collection of as much relevant data as possible, and concludes with the analysis of programs/courses.

Understanding Adult Learners

A recognition that adult learners have special characteristics is essential to selection of appropriate instructional methodologies for experiential learning. Each learner population has specific characteristics and needs that should be considered in program planning (see Figure 2–4) (Cantor, 1992). To examine these factors is termed an audience analysis. Adult learners seek and expect challenging learning opportuni-

Figure 2–3

The Model Input Phase

INPUTS

✓ Course/Program Syllabi and Associated Materials

✓ Occupational Advisory Committee Advice

✓ Learner Needs, Feedback and Advice

✓ Alumni Feedback and Advice

PROCESS

✓ Cooperative Education Coordinator Assembles all Data

✓ Advisory Committee Assists Faculty and Cooperative Education Coordinator to Analyze Data

✓ Identify Required Knowledge, Experience, Skills and Needs for Instructors, Facilities and Equipment

OUTPUTS

✓ List Experiential Learning Needs

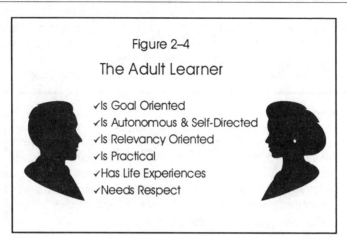

Figure 2–4

The Adult Learner

✓Is Goal Oriented
✓Is Autonomous & Self-Directed
✓Is Relevancy Oriented
✓Is Practical
✓Has Life Experiences
✓Needs Respect

ties. They need opportunities for individual personal development towards their ultimate career goals. They also seek occupational experience in their chosen fields. Today, many also need the financial support offered through cooperative work-and-learn experiences. As outlined in Figure 2–4 the adult learner displays the following characteristics.

- *Is goal oriented*—Adult learners like to work toward personal goals that they themselves establish. For non-traditional learners, such as first-generation college attendees, who may be unsure of career and life choices, the opportunity afforded by community colleges to examine possibilities and receive additional support is extremely important. This is often done by providing practicum or fieldwork opportunities early in programs of study. Learners begin to hone in on a career choice through these early preliminary experiences.

- *Is autonomous and self-directed*—Adult learners want to make their own decisions. They should be guided to make appropriate experiential learning activity choices commensurate with their best learning styles. Some adults are more cerebral or academic and thus like the formality of classroom study and reading. Others prefer a "hands-on" approach or more physical activity. Experiential learning allows for individual flexibility.

- *Is relevancy oriented*—Adult learners need to see how formal learning relates and contributes to their goals. Experiential learning activities, such as work-experience, practica, field work, internships, apprenticeships and/or clinicals, provide this relevance.

- *Is practical*—Adult learners want learning to have practical value. They should immediately apply new knowledge and skills to derive benefit from their learning. Internships, clinicals, and apprenticeships permit a close integration of theory and practice.

- *Has accumulated personal life experiences*—Adult learners bring their accumulated life experiences to community college programs. This is especially true today of the many mature workers who find themselves involuntarily displaced from their jobs. Cooperative education can recognize the value and relevance of their life experiences and thus can avoid repetition of learning which costs the learner time and money.

- *Needs respect*—Adults need to be treated as adults. Experiential learning recognizes the learner as an individual with his or her own needs and best learning style. This attitude separates community college learning from other forms of higher education and makes it unique. For example, many minority learners currently entering community colleges have faced a lifetime of prejudice. As learners, they are now treated with respect, which bolsters self-confidence and encourages mutual understanding. In addition, these programs help to develop interpersonal relations skills needed by learners in order to effectively participate in society.

Thus, experiential learning is designed to accommodate adult learners' special attributes and provide them with the opportunity to gain the satisfaction of meeting their personal educational objectives.

Data Collection

Input Phase planning data comes from several sources (e.g., community, business, and government representatives, faculty and administration, and formal advisory committees), who can provide information concerning academic and/or job requirements. These people also can suggest opportunities for cooperative education in business, government, or the community.

Employee groups and unions can be useful sources of information about job requirements and can become extensions of the college program through their participation. By being an integral part of program planning, their ultimate participation as worksite providers is practically guaranteed. If they are not part of the planning process, later participation may be more difficult to achieve. Together they can also assess the quality

of a college program from observation of on-the-job performances of workers.

Other community-based groups are also useful in the cooperative education planning process. Civic groups can provide information about opportunities for volunteer work in the community suitable for learners in various academic disciplines. For instance, a League of Women Voters might recognize that some citizens need tutoring in the basic reading/literacy skills required for voter registration. Civic leaders can also promote and publicize the cooperative education program to various other community constituencies, thus opening doors for the college. Likewise, industry associations, business groups, chambers of commerce, government leaders, and alumni groups all can offer similar kinds of feedback and assistance.

Faculty and administration provide useful input to the planning process on such matters as curriculum development, facility sharing needs and arrangements, budget limitations, credit award possibilities for experiential learning, and contractual and legal requirements.

Learners and alumni are also a necessary part of the planning process. Their comments and reports provide useful indicators of program successes and the need for change. Alumni can share which experiences were valuable to them for career exploration and skills development, what hardships and barriers they faced, and what changes or improvements they believe are necessary.

An open and honest dialogue among employers, advisory committees, and college staff should take place. Roles and responsibilities must be made clear through this planning process; each party should know exactly what their expectations, duties, and responsibilities are. Figure 2–5 is a questionnaire useful for this purpose. Chapter 3 describes procedures for effectively working with these groups to identify, plan, and develop experiential learning opportunities.

Course/Program Analysis

Next, planning must analyze specific course(s) and/or program requirements to discover where experiential learning would be appropriate and effective (see Analysis Step in Figure 2–3). College faculty and program coordinators should work with various groups (advisory committee members, learners, employers, employees/labor, community

Figure 2–5

Learner Follow-Up Questionnaire

Name_____ Date_____

Address_____

Sex_____ Marital Status_____ Number of Children_____

1. Did you transfer to another college or university after graduation? Yes___ No___
   If so, where did you transfer to?_____ What was your
   major?_____ When did or will you graduate?_____
   What was your cooportunity cluster and major at the community college?
   _____

2. Are you employed by a firm with which you co-oped as a student at the community college? Yes_____ No_____

3. Who is your present employer?_____
   What is your job title and responsibility there?_____
   What is your salary?_____

4. List employment you have had since graduation, beginning with the most recent
   position.
   Employer   Job Title   Dates   Salary   Reason for Leaving
   _____
   _____
   _____
   _____

5. Are you employed full time in your present position? Yes_____ No_____
   Did you purposely seek out that employment because of a personal or family
   need? Yes_____ No_____ If yes, what is that need?_____

6. Are your current personal needs and goals similar to those you experienced as a
   student? Yes_____ No_____ If not, why?_____

7. Do you believe you were hired because of your community college education?
   Yes_____ No_____ If yes, what aspect of your college education was a primary
   influence in your employment?_____

8. Do you feel your cooperative education was important to your college success? If
   yes, how?_____

9. Which courses and work experiences were most valuable to you in your process of
   career development?_____
   _____

10. If you could have changed some aspect of the cooperative education experience,
    what would it be?_____

11. If cooperative education had been optional and you were to do it all over again,
    would you have selected the program? Yes_____ No_____

12. Additional comments or recommendations: _____
    _____
    _____

From Barry Heermann, Cooperative Education in Community Colleges.
Reprinted with permission of Jossey-Bass.

members, and college faculty and administrators) through an Experiential Learning Planning Committee. Together they should identify:

- the knowledge and job skills which should be presented formally to the learner in an academic setting, and/or the experience and exposure which should occur in a work or community-based environment;
- the need, if any, for instructor talents not readily available within the college; and
- the needs of the instructional facility external to the college, including work environments, equipment, tools, etc.

Most course and program syllabi and associated curriculum materials can be used for purposes of experiential learning review. This assessment should produce a comprehensive list of experientially based knowledge and/or job performance requirements. For instance, when considering occupational or career curricula, it is important to identify those tasks that learners should be able to do upon course or program completion which require practice in or exposure to a workplace or community. The level of higher education appropriate to the program should also be considered or reviewed. Some programs are appropriate for one year of study (a certificate); others require two years of study (an Associate degree). Some programs can be contained in two formal years of study by using summers for internship or practica. More about this in Chapter 3.

The planning committee can now analyze all available data, together with their own various knowledge bases, perceptions, experiences, and insights, in order to decide what are the needs for cooperative education and experiential learning. It is important for faculty to ensure that this occupational needs data be updated on a regular basis. Additionally, tasks which will require specialized equipment or instructor talents, additional kinds of facilities, and other specialized environments otherwise difficult to acquire or replicate should be noted. When these aspects of a course/program have been considered, it can be decided whether cooperative education has a role to play.

Course/Program Development

Alternatively, a planning committee may decide there is a need to develop new experiential learning courses. If this is the case, an occupational analysis is first carried out. Standards of performance and workplace requirements for each job and task must be clearly identified so as to match them to appropriate instructional strategies. Will the job be performed under conditions which must be simulated because of safety considerations, such as nuclear power plant control room operations? In such a case, cooperative education linkages with business and industry become essential for instruction. Does the job require special worker personalities or tolerances, such as in the case of emergency room nurses or nursing home workers, where early exposure to working conditions is important? It is important to conduct a comprehensive occupational analysis that identifies the required knowledge, as well as the criticality, difficulty, and frequency of various skills.

Thus, occupational analysis is: (1) a listing of necessary job performances; and (2) necessary environmental considerations. Central Piedmont Community College uses a system of measurable learning objectives (MLOs), which are recorded and agreed upon by employer, learner, and college prior to commencing a cooperative education experience. (Central Piedmont Community College Catalog, 1990–1992)

There are several ways to identify the requisite tasks performed in an occupation. One way is to observe workers on the job over a period of time and record the tasks performed. A second, and more commonly used method, is to meet with a group of workers from an occupation and, together, identify the tasks to be performed. Using advisory committee members, together with other employers and/or program graduates, a program or course development committee can be formed. However, it is not the intention of this book to provide comprehensive information on course development (for that see Cantor, 1992; Cranton, 1989). Rather, it is intended to provide an overview of the process of course analysis for appropriate decision-making uses in cooperative education.

The Experiential Learning Planning Model: Process Phase

The Planning Model's *Process Phase* begins with a review of *Input Phase* findings to determine where providing experiential learning activities would best meet learner needs. Once such possibilities have been identified, actual program design can begin.

Course/Program Design

The focus of the Design Step in the *Process Phase* (see Figure 2–6) is to:

- determine experiential learning-based performance objectives;
- select experiential learning methods and instructional activities appropriate to specific courses/programs; and
- develop strategies to evaluate experiential learning.

Determine performance objectives

The development of performance objectives must be carefully carried out. Every performance objective should specify an observable behavior to be performed to a measurable standard of performance (see Cantor, 1992). Furthermore, a performance objective should indicate the specific environmental conditions under which the behavior should be performed. For instance:

> When presented with an anxious injury victim in an Emergency Room, the nursing student will demonstrate an ability to calm the patient while taking a medical history according to Hospital procedures.

These kinds of performance objectives cannot be met without clinical experience. Such experience should aim to ensure competent performance by a learner upon completing cooperative education and acquiring a job. Performance objectives become even more important as more community colleges are providing learning warranties to business and industry by guaranteeing the competence of the learners they have trained. The listing of performance objectives becomes the blueprint for experiential learning instructional strategy selection.

The next steps to follow include:

- grouping and sequencing performance objectives for experiential instruction; and
- listing worksite requirements.

Often it is more administratively efficient to provide experiential learning opportunities through a single specific course rather than as a part of several courses in a program. Therefore, the experiential performance objectives should be grouped: (1) by topic and content; and (2) by performance sequence. In this way, it becomes easier to make decisions about incorporating experiential learning into individual courses as opposed to creating specific courses called practica or work experience.

Figure 2–6

The Design Step

INPUTS

 List experiential learning needs

PROCESS

 Identify learner expectations for experiential learning

✓ Develop experiential learning instructional methods and activities appropriate to a course/program

✓ Develop experiential learning-based performance objectives

✓ Devise evaluation strategies for the desired experiential learning

OUTPUTS

✓ Cooperative education and experiential learning course and program plans, including:

    (1) numbers of learners anticipated
    (2) numbers of faculty needed
    (3) potential employers at worksites

For example, a program in Justice Administration at Hillsborough Community College, Florida, initially redesigned in 1983, offers a single 3-credit practicum, which includes all of the performance objectives deemed appropriate for experiential learning.

The Automotive Technology Program at Montgomery College, Maryland, first designed in 1978 when dealers needed entry-level technicians, offers a practicum worth one to three credits as part of the two-year degree requirements (Figure 2–7). This practicum course, taken concurrently with the major area technical courses, provides complementary work experience.

Consider the relationship of the performance objectives to the various other community college functions, such as general education, transfer curricula, guidance and/or cooling out functions. Community colleges will often list cooperative education (e.g., work-based study) as a general degree elective so that learners may use this course to explore careers, firm up career decisions, fulfill social or civic goals, or develop academically allied or avocational skills. For instance, Harford Community College in Maryland offers "Community Experiences Courses" (CE 291–CE 294), variable credit (1–4 credits) to enable learners to earn academic credits for direct service to the community. (Catalog, 1989–1991) Faculty and learners agree upon performance objectives in individual learning contracts. These courses motivate learners to give something back to the community while pursuing their specific learning goals.

Match activities to objectives

Once experiential learning objectives are developed, faculty (and experiential learning program committees) should consider appropriate cooperative education activities to deliver the learning. Figure 2–8 describes the various experiential learning activities and their instructional relationships to learning goals and the needs of learners. For instance, if the performance objectives indicate a need for short-term exposure to a particular environment (e.g., a court room for a legal assistant introductory course), or for simple skills development (e.g., a parts department inventory department for an automotive service parts management course) then a practicum or work-experience course is indicated.

A practicum can be integrated into an existing course without need for additional faculty coverage. It can be administered less formally than

Figure 2–7

The Montgomery College Program

THE DEGREE PROGRAM

The associate in arts curriculum provides the instruction to enter the industrial and commercial fields of automotive technology, including automotive maintenance and repair, parts supply, service, sales, and administration. It includes study and practice of all automotive systems, supplemented with the study of communication with the public, management, and industry. Elements of practical business and personnel management are introduced. Students will also acquire a broad foundation in general education.

First Semester

AT 101	Introduction to Automotive Technology	3
AT 105	Automotive Science	3
AT 115	Automotive Electricity I	4
CH 109	Chemistry and Society*	4
EN 101	Techniques of Reading and Writing I*	3
HE 100	Principles of Healthier Living*	1

Second Semester

AT 107	Internal Combustion Engines	4
AT 116	Automotive Electricity II	4
AT 221	Automotive Fuel Systems I	4
EN 104	Technical Writing*	3
	Mathematics foundation*	3

Third Semester

AT 222	Automotive Fuel Systems II	4
	Automotive electives (2)**	8
	Humanities distribution*	3
	Social Sciences distribution*	3

Fourth Semester

AT 251	Automotive Technology Practicum***	1(3)
	Arts distribution*	3
	Automotive elective	4
	Group II foundation†	3
	Humanities or Social Sciences distribution*	3
	Total credit hours	**68(70)**

*General Education requirement.

**Includes choices of AT 109, AT 110, AT 225, AT 227, AT 229, AT 231.

***AT 251 Automotive Technology Practicum may be taken any time after AT 101 and AT 115. Students should consider taking AT 251 during the summer.

†General Education requirement; Group II foundation: CA 120, CS 101, or SP 108 recommended.

Reprinted with permission of Montgomery College.

those experiences requiring extensive faculty visits to worksites. However, many colleges do operate separate practicum courses within programs which service a number of different courses; faculty coverage then is split between faculty who have learners participating in the course. A faculty member may be awarded fractional credits (e.g., 0.5 semester-hour load) for supervising one or a few learners participating in the practicum course. Alternatively, larger enrollments in a practicum experience for a particular program may warrant a separate practicum course or course section.

Internships and clinicals are appropriate experiential learning situations when specific blocks of performance objectives require structured workplace instruction. For instance, learners in a second-year machine tool program requiring on-the-job instruction by a master technician in a shop using numerically controlled machines would benefit from internships or clinicals. Another example is offered by a learner of a foreign language who wants to acquire both job experience and language interpretation skills in a dynamic and demanding environment, such as the United Nations. Or, an internship would suit a dental assistant learner who needs a clinical experience in a dental office to complete the program requirements and earn a licensing certificate. In all cases, the college must have access to community-based facilities, and the help and participation of employers and skilled worksite supervisors. The learners need the exposure to the work environment in order to polish their skills and test their occupational choices.

Internships and clinicals require faculty supervision and coverage. Usually, faculty points for "load purposes" are as few as 3 or 4 learners for 1 semester hour credit load. Thus, they are very expensive courses to operate. (Chapter 6 will discuss internships.) Additionally, when operating clinical experiences, costs associated with the salaries for professional adjuncts and liability insurance must be planned and budgeted for. (Chapter 9 will discuss these in more detail.)

Our student bodies are becoming more conscious of the need to participate in the community in which they live and learn. They are demanding that their formal courses for study provide credit-bearing activities to formalize civics education in new and innovative ways. Volunteer activities in AIDS clinics undertaken by social work or family counseling students, or mentoring primary and secondary school students by pre-education majors are the kinds of activities in experiential learning which might be indicated by the performance objectives.

Figure 2–8

Experiential Learning Activities

Experiential Learning	Meets Learner Needs For:	College Course Requirements	College Need
Practicum / Work Experience	• Exposure to career • Specialized learning • Work & Learn	• Overview exposure to discipline • Access to technical skills of employers	• Access to work environment • Access to equipment
Internship	• Acquisition of work experience in field • Skills development	• Overview exposure to discipline • Access to technical skills of employer	• Access to work environment • Access to equipment
Apprenticeship	• Structured workplace learning & earning	• Skills portion of trade training	• Access to work environment & master craftsmen
Clinical	• Work experience with patients & other health care practitioners	• Skills portion of health care education	• Access to health care facility
Academy	• Structured public service training	• Education & skills portion of public service program	• Access to facility and officers
Volunteer	• Civic & social skills • Emotional & social development	• Meet civic & social goals	• Partnership with community
Mentoring	• Learners help learners	• Tutoring • Literacy development within courses	• Tutors link with community
2 + 2	• Builds learner confidence • Recruits non-traditional learners	• Recruitment into programs • Interface with feeder institutions	• Link with community schools
Credit for Life Experience	• Maximize past experiences • Avoid repetition		• Community goodwill

In some cases the performance objectives can be met by other non-traditional forms of experiential learning. This book will also deal with these activities. For instance, a college might sponsor a training academy or other business and industry training for which college credit can be awarded. (Chapter 9 will describe these arrangements.) While these learning activities are structured and formalized, they often do not require faculty supervision or engender costs!

Some colleges recognize the parallel nature of some secondary school work to performance objectives stipulated in their programs. Therefore, linkage arrangements are made with these secondary schools to award credit for mastery of these performance objectives upon entry to the college program by a high school graduate. (These 2+2 programs will be described in Chapter 12.)

And, of course, experiential learning program planners want to recognize the past experiences of learners, thus avoiding duplication of experiences and demoralizing learners. This is achieved by permitting credit for life experience (as described in Chapter 11). This planning will help match performance objectives to experiential learning activities.

Other factors that must be considered when developing programs are described below.

- *Numbers of learners anticipated*—College faculty need to estimate numbers of learners within courses or programs who will participate in experiential learning activities once these activities are approved. This information then is useful to determine requirements for work-stations and faculty supervision.

- *Faculty resources for supervision*—The need for faculty supervision in turn affects budgeting and must be taken into consideration. Cooperative education becomes costly when faculty must be compensated for worksite visitation. This will be discussed in the following chapters.

- *Potential employers in the community to serve as worksite sponsors*—Finding employers, and coordinating program and job training takes time to carry out. Faculty work closely with advisory committees to accomplish this. Succeeding chapters will describe this process in detail.

The final output of the Design Step will be a plan for and list of the appropriate kinds of experiential learning activities for a program and/or course.

The Experiential Learning Planning Model: Product Phase

Development and Delivery of Programs

The final phase is the *Product Phase*—designed to achieve meaningful cooperative education opportunities for all learners, regardless of their particular goals. The Development Step of the Product Phase operationalizes the experiential learning activities. Included are counseling and supervising learners on the job, and general program and worksite administration. The Product Phase also includes program evaluation. (Chapter 14 will describe evaluation activities.)

A major part of the development step is working with advisory committees to develop, negotiate, and implement training in worksites. The college and the employer share in the training of learners as workers. By working closely with the college, the employer can ensure that the overall training program, as well as the related classroom content, matches job requirements. By providing worksite training, the employer ensures that the on-the-job training exactly matches the firm's needs. Identifying worksites in business and industry, community-based organizations, and/or government will be discussed in Chapter 5.

A plan for learner cooperative education recruitment, screening, and worksite placement now should be developed. This plan should include:

- an initial screening process to establish basic qualifications for cooperative education learner enrollment relative to each learner's needs for, and ability to profit from, worksite training;

- a process to identify each learner's career interests, basic aptitudes, and vocational interests through psychological testing and other means; and

- a process for examining learners' school records to identify academic strengths and weaknesses, attendance, discipline, peer relationships, and attitudes. (This will be described in Chapter 5.)

As a result of the college's outreach and access to women and minorities, participating employers are able to work cooperatively with and ultimately recruit these populations.

To assess program outcomes, feedback loops throughout the planning process are essential. These loops must be capable of collecting data from participating cooperative employers about learners' work efforts and requirements, feedback from learners on goal attainment, expectations from employers, the community and the college, and information from the community about what is happening in the outside world.

Chapter References

Cantor, J.A. (1992). *Delivering instruction to adult learners*. Toronto: Wall & Emerson.

Cranton, P. (1989). *Planning instruction for adult learners*. Toronto: Wall & Emerson.

Heermann, B. (1973). *Cooperative Education in community colleges*. San Francisco: Jossey-Bass.

Keeton, M.T. (Ed). (1980). *New directions for experiential learning* (No. 9). San Francisco: Jossey-Bass.

Chapter 3

The Organization and Administration of Experiential Learning

The way in which a community college is organized will play a major part in how its cooperative education and experiential learning programs are planned and developed. This chapter describes and discusses the typical ways in which the administration of cooperative education is organized at the community college, and identifies and outlines the roles and responsibilities of cooperative education coordinators, advisory committees, faculty, and employers for the planning of experiential learning.

Administrative Organization

How community colleges organize to plan and administer cooperative education differs depending upon the size of the college and its emphasis on cooperative education. But, whatever the structure, to serve as a principal contact every cooperative education program should have someone who is known to the community and familiar with the academic disciplines offered at the college. This person, usually termed the cooperative education coordinator, can be assigned to either the student services division, the office of the chief academic officer (dean or vice president), or the academic and occupational program divisions of the college.

The Organization of the Position of Cooperative Education Coordinator

Heermann (1973) describes several community college organizational configurations for cooperative education which are still found today. Generally, colleges administer cooperative education with:

- a centrally based coordinator in the student services division;

- a coordinator based in the office of the dean of academic affairs;
- a coordinator at the divisional level;
- a coordinator at the specific program level; or
- a coordinator reporting directly to the president.

These configurations are discussed below.

A centrally based coordinator in the student services division

This structure permits close working relationships with the placement, counseling, and financial aid offices, but does limit identification with specific academic programs. Under this arrangement central cooperative education coordinators primarily focus their attention on recruiting new worksites, placing learners with cooperative employers, and helping learners develop good work habits and work relationships. As a centrally based cooperative education coordinator usually cannot represent each and every instructional program at the college, an active cooperative education advisory committee, whose members represent all academic programs at the college, must be in place to ensure close ties to the specific programs.

A coordinator based in the office of the dean of academic affairs

A person working in this structure usually has closer ties to and contact with the various instructional programs of the college. This organizational structure facilitates the coordination of actual course and curriculum instructional programming. The coordinator can work closely with faculty and advisory committee members to develop experiential learning instructional objectives and associated activities. In addition, this coordinator can act as an informational interface between the program and business and industry. Program chairpersons who involve this coordinator in divisional instructional meetings and program planning activities ensure that their programs will be well represented in cooperative education courses. Individual program advisory committees should be in place and active so as to provide this coordinator with the necessary information to facilitate experiential learning activities across the college.

A coordinator at the divisional level

This configuration places the cooperative education representative close to the various academic programs operating within a division. In this arrangement, the coordinator usually has a subject matter background closely connected to the division's programs (e.g., industrial technologies or health careers), and therefore can better articulate its nature. This coordinator can get closely involved in the academic aspect of the cooperative education activities. For instance, at this level, the coordinator can become personally involved in evaluating experiential learning portfolios for college credit. This person also can well represent these programs to the appropriate businesses in the community which do or could use their learners. However, when several cooperative education coordinators are working within a single college in its various divisions, a mechanism must be in place for ensuring that coordinators interact and share resources, employer leads, placement opportunities, etc. Divisional program advisory committees can provide this opportunity.

A coordinator at the specific program level

Cooperative education instructors can serve collaterally as coordinators at the specific program level. These coordinators are naturally very knowledgeable about and concerned with their own programs and represent them well. However, where such a system is in place as the sole method of cooperative education organization, there is virtually no uniform college-wide coordination. Typically, in these situations, program survival and longevity depends on the enthusiasm and efforts of individual faculty members.

A coordinator reporting directly to the president

Cooperative education coordinators reporting directly to the president are becoming more commonplace as structured workplace training and Tech Prep programs gain in popularity. Tech Prep funding has facilitated hiring such coordinators; in fact, many programs which are externally funded by federal grants support such coordinators.

A coordinator based in the office of the president has maximum visibility and credibility in the business and civic communities. Such a person also has the authority to commit college resources. However, this structure is removed from close contact with both student services and academic programs. Therefore, a communications mechanism must be in place within the college to facilitate cross-divisional information transfer so that this coordinator can properly represent the college programs. Generally, a person in this configuration primarily "opens doors" to faculty to find further placements for their students. Once a partnership with a firm has been created, another coordinator closer to the program assumes supervisory responsibility for the learner on the job.

The Organization of the Advisory Committee

Collectively, the various advisory committees described in this chapter are essential to the smooth planning and delivery of quality cooperative education programs. Clearly, having input from as many knowledgeable sources as possible will lead to improved education. Community leaders, management officers, industry representatives, etc., all of whom are recruited to serve on these programs, can provide up-to-date information that helps determine goals, curriculum, and instruction. As is also apparent, these committees, especially the members of the cooperative education advisory committee, as individuals, create initial linkages to business and industry to secure employer participation and learner placement.

The structure of the community college advisory committee is of paramount importance in how efficiently its objectives are met. Typically, a community college has three levels of advisory committees:

- a central committee;
- occupational and/or program committees; and
- a cooperative education and experiential learning committee.

These are described below.

A central college advisory committee

This central or general committee functions at the executive administrative level. Depending on the state/local structure for community college governance, this committee provides advice to the college president and/or district board of trustees on matters of a general nature, including cooperative education. This committee generally is comprised of people at senior levels in business and industry, and prominent members of the community. These people use their contacts and influence to create new cooperative educational opportunities for the college.

Occupational and career program advisory committees

Several of these committees usually are created to represent local business and industry and government, and advise the program's faculty and college administration in matters relating to the operation of a specific instructional program. Members of these committees provide access to firms and businesses in occupations included in cooperative education programs.

A cooperative education and experiential learning advisory committee

This committee includes community business and industry leaders, college faculty, learners, and administration, and also members drawn from the other two committees. The functions of this committee involve planning and directing program operations, and linking the college and community.

Figure 3–1 below is a sample letter than can be used to recruit advisory committee members.

How the advisory committee works

These committees should have charters that spell out in detail their responsibilities and the procedures by which they operate. It is the responsibility of the college cooperative education administrator and each of the cooperative education faculty coordinators to ensure that the committee(s) meet(s) at least once each semester or as often as necessary to plan and develop effective experiential learning activities. At these meetings, program coordinators should arrange for:

- presentations and overviews of cooperative education activities during recent semesters;
- information on numbers of learners participating in cooperative education, job sites, and employees; kinds of activities learners are engaged in; and other pertinent data;
- discussion of new programs and opportunities for expanding experiential learning at the college; and
- identification of needs for worksites in the coming semester.

College program advisory committees should be actively maintained as they provide the impetus and direction for experiential learning program development. Keep minutes of the activities of all meetings and include

Figure 3–1

Sample Letter to Recruit Cooperative Education Advisory Committee Members

Cooperative Education Community College

Dear Mr./Ms. _____

It is with great pleasure that we invite you to participate in the Community College's Cooperative Education advisory committee. Your appointment, should you accept, has been approved by the Board of Trustees of the Community College District for a period of three years.

Because of your acknowledged expertise as a practitioner, the college looks forward to the potentially important contributions that you can make to the cooperative education program. Your input is essential to the development of community ties and the formulation of objectives, policies, and procedures for the program.

The first meeting of the committee will be held in room _____ on _____(date) at _____(time) in order to consider the broad aims of the cooperative education program and the function and authority of this committee. The agenda for the meeting is enclosed.

Sincerely,

_____

College President

Enclosure: Agenda

detailed descriptions of the roles and responsibilities of committee members. These records can serve as a mechanism to monitor past activity and facilitate future action.

Administrative Responsibilities

Now, let's take a closer look at the roles and responsibilities of various members of cooperative education team.

The Cooperative Education Program Coordinator

This coordinator is an important contributor to the success of any cooperative education program and is usually a member of the college faculty, often (though not always) with academic rank, who serves in a multi-faceted role of placement officer, student personnel counselor, salesman, instructor, and administrator. This person is also an educational recruiter, troubleshooter, and disciplinarian (Heermann, 1973). The cooperative education program coordinator is often the principal professional community college educator responsible for the development step of the Experiential Learning Planning Model. (Figure 3-2 describes the development step of the Experiential Learning Planning Model.)

In carrying out the responsibilities of cooperative education program coordinator, the individual selected must fulfill several roles and perform several functions. These include the development of:

- course/program goals and objectives;
- processes and procedures for worksite selection and administration;
- learner recruitment and screening procedures;
- counseling procedures; and
- effective public relations.

However, the cooperative education coordinator's actual job responsibilities will depend upon the administrative structure in which she or he works. In a decentralized model some of the tasks listed above and described below may actually be carried out by faculty coordinators.

Figure 3–2

Development Step of the Experiential Learning Planning Model, Process Phase

INPUTS

✓ Cooperative education and experiential learning course and program plans, including:

    (1) numbers of learners anticipated
    (2) numbers of faculty needed
    (3) potential employers at worksites

PROCESS

Working with advisory committee

✓ Develop course goals and objectives to be delivered through cooperative education and experiential learning

✓ Develop processes and procedures for worksite selection and administration

✓ Develop learner recruitment and screening procedures

OUTPUTS

✓ Goals and objectives for experiential learning and cooperative education

✓ Worksite selection and administration procedures

✓ Learner recruitment and screening procedures

Developing goals and objectives

As an instructional designer, the cooperative education program coordinator works with others to develop course/program goals and objectives. This involves establishing, in conjunction with employers, specific and defined objectives for work experiences, based upon the overall course or program goals and objectives. Depending on the organization of cooperative education in the college, the coordinator may work across academic disciplines with other faculty and staff in educational planning activities, or may carry out the planning role as a line function for the administration. The coordinator also organizes the advisory committees and facilitates their contribution to the development of appropriate goals and objectives. He or she designs a formative evaluation process to monitor continuously the total program, and, as well, conducts follow-up studies of graduates. These evaluative functions should be carried out in conjunction with the institutional research officer of the college.

Developing processes and procedures for worksite selection and administration

As an administrator, the cooperative education program coordinator identifies suitable employers and worksites, develops policies and standards for program operation, and draws up employer agreements. In addition, the coordinator assists with budget development and program scheduling. She or he coordinates in-class instruction and on-the-job experience, meets with employers at regular intervals, and visits learners at their places of employment.

Developing effective public relations

As public relations representative, the coordinator engages in program promotional activities and personally represents the college in the business community and the community at large. The coordinator should be highly visible both inside and outside the college in order to develop a successful cooperative education program. The aim is to enlarge and strengthen the ties between college and community.

Developing learner recruitment and screening procedures

As a recruitment officer, the cooperative education program coordinator establishes procedures for attracting learners to the program, and initiates processes for screening learners in order to determine appropriate placements for them. The coordinator determines the readiness of learners for an experiential learning program, which often involves assisting them to obtain further educational certificates and/or other required documentation. He or she arranges for learners to be interviewed by employers and placed with suitable firms, as well as determining the suitability of employers for cooperative learning in general and specific learners in particular.

Developing counseling procedures

As a student counselor, the cooperative education coordinator confers with learners about personal and program problems and assists them in exploring and/or reviewing career options.

The College Faculty

Members of faculty are also pivotal to the success of community college cooperative education. In such programs, faculty are asked to take on three areas of responsibility. First, they must incorporate work-based activity for all learners into their instruction. Second, they also must be involved in the Input Phase of the Experiential Planning Model. And, third, they must approach these tasks enthusiastically in order to sell them to learners and employers.

Developing appropriate teaching skills

As structured experiential learning expands and the cooperation of business and industry and education in workforce development grows, a new perspective and some different skills are required of classroom teachers in order to effectively integrate work with study. College faculty, therefore, must recognize the need to take on an important part of the responsibility for providing successful cooperative education programs and incorporate new ideas into their teaching methodology when necessary.

For example, good instructional practice dictates that academic faculty should relate the content and style of their teaching to the experiences and activities their learners are undergoing on the job. Instruction should be developed that, as much as possible and feasible, incorporates classroom instruction with work-based activity. To do this, one must constantly place emphasis on linking theory and practice. Hands-on learning makes the conceptual come alive to many learners.

Class instruction in occupational courses must be used to motivate and prepare learners for the work assignments they will be undertaking. When they return to the classroom, discussion can clarify and reinforce the experience and reveal the relationship between what they learned and what they did. The purpose of classroom instruction can be made much clearer by such comparison.

For example, after each work experience learners are usually required to hand in a work report in which they describe the job and what was learned. To link instruction and work again, the completion of these reports can be presented as part of the English course at the college. They can provide the instructor with a real-life avenue for effective application of what is studied in composition to what is required on the job. In such actual situations the teaching of writing skills can be more effective.

Academic subjects, such as English, sociology, or history, should also emphasize that the concepts being taught can and are to be applied to real life situations. Awareness of the wider world of ideas should be made exciting by showing how these ideas operate in circumstances learners will encounter.

As well as teaching in new ways, instructors in cooperative education must acquire or sharpen up their interpersonal skills. Because their learners come from many dissimilar backgrounds and bring with them varying levels of abilities and skills, faculty members must be aware of these differences and search for ways to make cooperative education meaningful and effective for all. In addition, the instructional process must take into account not only the academic and career requirements, but also the personal needs of all learners.

Experiential learning enables faculty to develop in their learners those affective competencies so necessary for life and work. Constructive work attitudes, community pride, civic responsibility all come with positive experience gained in the real world.

Although asking faculty to rethink their teaching methods may impose some strain, cooperative education has very concrete advantages to offer. For example, grants may be available to those who enter into cooperative relationships with business and industry. In addition, faculty often gain access to community and business resources, such as state-of-the-art facilities (e.g., laboratories) and the latest equipment. And faculty/business exchange programs expose instructors to the most recent methods and practices, allowing them to upgrade their knowledge and skills. In presenting their programs to the community, faculty also become much more familiar with and closer to the content of their subject.

Planning

Faculty also need to be included in the planning aspects of experiential learning. Through direct contact with business and industry members of cooperative education advisory committees in the initial stages of program planning, the faculty of specific programs will become more comfortable with experiential learning as a bona fide instructional process, and begin to interweave on-the-job training into their particular courses. Faculty will begin to involve themselves in worksite selection, learner on-the-job supervision, and integration of class work with worksite experiences. Chapter 5 describes in detail the process by which this happens.

Marketing

In addition, faculty must be involved with the marketing of cooperative education across the college and the community. They can become an integral part of the marketing efforts in a teamwork approach with the cooperative education coordinator. For example, staff members can play their part by including cooperative education activities in the agendas of community-based and professional association meetings, by preparing displays and presentations, and, of course, by making cooperative education a requirement within their courses of study.

The Employer

Participating cooperative education employers are a key ingredient in successful experiential learning. While the benefits of a cooperative education partnership are usually the main attraction, the achievement of the stipulated educational goals must be as important to these employers as to the colleges if the programs are to succeed. Hence, employers must be fully informed and involved in all three phases of the Experiential Planning process. The more they know, the better their understanding will be, and the more completely they will support all the aims of programs.

Why do employers participate? First, they stand to gain. They will be the future recipients of community college graduates as workers. By participating with the college in the educational process, they are in a position to influence positively the learning outcomes for these graduates. In effect, they become partners in the educational planning and delivery of the subject material. Thus, employers often are able to shape what will be taught and learned with their own particular business or industrial needs and demands in mind.

Next, the employer is able to try out learners before making any commitment to hire them. In these times of government regulation of hiring practices, the opportunity to view and assess a learner for some time without legal commitment is an important inducement to participate. And, of course, those participating employers are able eventually to select the best learners that the college has to offer. In fact, some employers believe that taking part in cooperative education is an excellent method for recruiting new employees. After all, the college does much of the canvassing, screening, and testing, and employers can often actually participate in the interview process. In addition, cooperative education partnerships offer employers a valuable source of part-time, seasonal, and contingent labor.

Often, a further benefit is technical assistance offered to the firm's regular employees in the form of remedial or advanced skills training, sponsored by the college and using their faculty. As all of the above gains ultimately save participating firms money, they are cost-effective.

However, the benefits and advantages of these educational partnerships do not provide the only reasons for employer participation. Many employers see participation in cooperative education as a civic responsibility. They wish to give something back to the community in which they live and work, and see this as a way of contributing to the making of the future leaders of that community. They take this responsibility very seriously and provide the best educational opportunities they can to learners.

Basically, the tasks of cooperative education employers are threefold and involve:

- providing the necessary background and knowledge for learners to perform the task(s) efficiently;
- supervising learners during the work period; and
- evaluating learners' accomplishments.

In 1970 the Cooperative Education Association offered guidelines, which still hold true today, for employers entering into a partnership with a college in a cooperative education program. Here are those guidelines.

(1) A realization on the part of the employer that Cooperative Education is first and foremost an educational program integrated with practical experience. From an educational viewpoint, the employer should give considerable importance to the meshing of particular academic experiences with practical factors at the working site; a series of coordinated experiences for the learner as he returns to the employer in succeeding employment periods; the placing of the student in those areas of employment which will be most conducive to the learning process; and the consideration of the long-range objectives of both the student and the employer.

(2) A genuine interest in integrating and developing the cooperative learner as a 'team member' in the organization.

(3) A top-level management commitment that the Cooperative Education program will be an important program in the personal development of the corporation.

(4) The appointment of a well-qualified company coordinator who understands and is in agreement with the objectives of Cooperative Education. He must have a good knowledge of the colleges and universities with which he will be working and of their academic programs. He should have a recognized position that will enable him to develop the program throughout the corporation.

(5) Close attention to the supervisor of cooperative learners, with emphasis on placing the learners under supervisors who can see their roles as "educators" as well as supervisors.

(6) Establishment of a separate budget for salaries paid to cooperative learners, enabling the learner to be placed in any appropriate department. This avoids the imposition on normal operating budgets and tends to be a financial safeguard for the program.

(7) A philosophy within the organization that the program will be sustained to a reasonable degree through normal fluctuations in economic conditions.

(8) A well-planned series of experiences for the learner, creating an attractive and viable program which will cause a favorable reaction and contribute to his personal development.

(9) The payment of a salary to the learner which is fair and competitive.

(10) While the granting of fringe benefits is not a requirement for participating in a cooperative program, it is desirable to give the learner as many advantages as possible. The more "he looks like" a permanent employee, the more likely he is to think in terms of permanent association with the employer.

Hunt and Knowles, Handbook of Cooperative Education, 1971, p. 172.
Reprinted with permission of Jossey-Bass.

Employer development is crucial, and the college should provide orientation and assistance to employers and supervisors to encourage excellent on-the-job experiences.

The manner in which cooperative education coordinators and employers communicate is extremely important to effective experimental learning activities and programs. Therefore, Chapter 4 will be devoted to describing the promotion of effective linkages through communication and articulation.

Chapter References

Heermann, B. (1973). *Cooperative Education in Community Colleges.* San Francisco: Jossey-Bass.

Hunt & Knowles (1971). *Handbook of Cooperative Education.* San Francisco: Jossey-Bass.

Chapter 4

Developing Linkages for Experiential Learning

This chapter is about communication, the single most important ingredient in the development and operation of successful experiential learning activities. The effectiveness of the next process in the Experiential Learning Model's Planning Phase, the *Development Step* (the establishment of working relationships), depends on communication. Clear communication promotes cooperation between the community college faculty and administrative staff, participating employers, and other community members. A special form of communication is called "articulation."

What is Articulation?

Articulation is simply a planned process for inter-organizational communication. In cooperative education it is particularly necessary because cooperative education planning is a process that involves many individuals and groups. It begins with communication between faculty and advisory committees, and then extends out to employers and the community. As the network of communication widens, the process becomes more and more complex, and the contact mechanisms must become more and more carefully maintained.

Eight Principles for Effective Communication

Effective linkages require clear communication, which results from a sound understanding of articulation. The following are eight principles that lead to successful articulation (Dornsife, 1992):

- promote open, clear, and frequent dialogue;
- build relationships based on respect and trust;
- assure leadership and commitment through clearly stated goals;

- focus on mutual rather than individual goals;
- guarantee mutual benefits to all parties;
- promote faculty involvement;
- initiate performance-based curricula;
- develop written cooperative education agreements.

Each of these principles is now discussed in detail.

Promote Open, Clear, and Frequent Dialogue

Communication must be open, clear, and frequent. Unless all involved participants know about and support the development of an experiential learning program and establish close linkages among each other, setting up such programs and maintaining the necessary contact either won't happen or won't be successful. Program and cooperative education advisory committee meetings are excellent environments for this communication to take place (U.S. Department of Labor, 1992; 1989; 1988).

What action should be taken?

Communicate widely and honestly

Ensure that communication occurs among counterparts in all participating organizations and internally among all members of the same institution. This can take place through informal discussion on the telephone or by fax, as well as in meetings. The most successful experiential learning partnerships are characterized by open and candid communication at all levels, often on a daily basis, regarding all aspects of program activity and policy.

Encourage contributions from all participants.

Routinely foster new ideas. If an idea is rejected, urge (expect) partners to rework it, describe the difficulties with it, and offer suggestions about how it could be made useful. This behavior produces feelings of ownership, contribution, and commitment within all collaborating organizations. It encourages partners to speak freely about the program and share credit for its success.

Allow sufficient time

The creation of stable and lasting partnerships inevitably requires a great deal of time. Most of this is *expensive* time, because significant involvement and commitment is required of the senior management of the firm and college, especially during the initial phases of implementation. Moreover, continuous readjustments and/or redesign will be required throughout the life of the partnership in order to keep it operating efficiently. A good college-to-work partnership may take as long as a decade to develop to maturity, with occasional ups and downs along the way.

Strive for accountability

Someone must be assigned the responsibility for communication. Everyone else must know who that person is. As described in Chapter 3, some community colleges or college districts jointly fund a single coordinator, or a college can assign a separate person at each program level to perform this role. Instructional staff must have clearly defined responsibilities, and those who are coordinating the effort must clearly understand these responsibilities.

Build Relationships Based on Respect and Trust

Solid relationships are built on respect and trust. And respect begins with involvement, which usually takes time and is developed through the process of actually working together on common goals. Fostering a climate of negotiation and cooperation in business/college partnerships, in which all points of view are heard, will pay dividends (Cantor, 1990).

What action should be taken?

Establish separate bodies to oversee partnerships

Respect and trust are reinforced by working together and maintaining regular communication. Frequently, in order to further cooperation, partnerships create independent entities to oversee programs (e.g., joint program advisory committees) or seek the assistance of outside organizations (e.g., economic development groups) to function as brokers (Cantor, 1990). These third-party players can foster a win/win situation and correct the impression that any one partner is serving only a vested interest. Generally, the broker's role is to see that focus is held on two issues—learner needs and expected outcomes. By continually emphasizing needs and outcomes, and by maintaining open dialogue so that compromises and solutions always support the stated mission, all partners inevitably look beyond their own self-interest. In some localities, non-profit foundations comprised of members of all participating organizations foster this initial trust. Chapter 13 will discuss this further.

Assure Leadership and Commitment through Clearly Stated Goals

Effective communication and leadership from the very top of the organization, whatever its structure, is a key element for the success of program development. Presidents and college boards, as well as college trustees, must take some leadership responsibility for communicating institutional goals and expressing support for experiential learning, and should commit institutional resources toward that effort. Program coordinators, department chairs, and faculty members also must provide leadership in cooperative education programs. These college policy makers and leaders must make sure that the goals and values of cooperative education and experiential learning are understood, disseminated, and supported.

What action should be taken?

Secure employer commitment

In the best cooperative education programs, employer commitment typically is demonstrated and expressed by the chief executive officer (CEO) or at least by a senior vice-president within the organization. Likewise, top elected officials in the public sector, and superintendents or presidents of other community colleges must exhibit a "front-office" presence. A genuine commitment to making the learning experience more meaningful, relevant, and effective for all concerned must originate from the top levels of partner organizations and should grow both horizontally and vertically within all organizations if partnerships are to be truly successful. This top-level commitment is necessary to bring status and visibility to the cooperative education partnership. For example, at Montgomery County Community College in Pennsylvania, this commitment is demonstrated by business, college, and public school memberships in a Tech Prep consortium.

But while decision-making authority rests at upper levels, the responsibility for maintaining contacts, generating support, and making operational decisions must be extended to the program operators—faculty and employers/supervisors—if programs are to grow. In this way, ownership of the program and pride in its outcomes are experienced by all, and so commitment is further extended and solidified.

Communicate the goals

Before anything happens, there must be a comprehensive understanding among partners regarding desired program goals and expected outcomes. When drawing up these goals and objectives, it is important to serve the short- and long-terms "customer" needs of every participating partner. These expectations should, in fact, be written and formalized through employer/college agreements. Samples of such agreements will be displayed in the following chapters.

Follow basic principles

Cooperative education program partnerships should be guided by these basic principles:

- *Create Motivation*—Experiential learning activities should motivate learners to complete degree programs and become productive workers and citizens.

- *Ensure High Standards*—Experiential learning activities should be designed to ensure that learners attain high academic goals.

- *Link Work and Learning*—Experiential learning activities should link college classroom curriculum to worksite experience and learning.

- *Focus on Employment and Careers*—Experiential learning activities should enhance the learners' prospects for immediate employment after leaving college and/or entry on a path that provides significant opportunity for continued education and career development.

Focus on Mutual Rather than on Individual Goals

By emphasizing shared rather than separate objectives, trust and respect are further enhanced, and the likelihood of cooperation between partners is increased.

What action should be taken?

Start with issues that all participating institutions can agree upon and build on these

Make the learner the top priority. Focus on goals, not on turf. Participants must be willing to work for the common good instead of their own advantage. If problems occur, concentrate on the common goals and the good of the learner. Compromise is the key. Compromising does not mean losing; everyone wins through dialogue.

Develop modest initial goals

Start small and build. Often the easiest place to start is with a single college program involving a practicum or work-experience course. Or consider instituting a Tech Prep or 2+2 technical program if faculty members are open to change. Concentrate administrative efforts and resources towards only one or two programs at a time to do the job well. The success and benefits from that first established program will convince other departments to participate.

Include employers in planning

Employers of all sizes and types should be included in planning these partnerships. Large employers are usually better able to handle the added supervisory responsibility associated with cooperative education programs and generally have more on-the-job training slots to offer. Small businesses, on the other hand, often see partnerships as a source of part-time workers and are eager to participate. And while learners might not receive as much structured training with small employers, they generally gain more varied work experience. Smaller businesses also gain from partnership involvements by extending their influence and networks. They therefore tend to speak favorably about the program and share credit for its success.

Appoint one person to be the common point of contact for all programs

Sometimes developing the partnership around a single umbrella cooperative education program eases the burden of administration. While partnerships can function effectively with any number of employers, it is advisable to limit participation to a single organizational program so that only one individual is the point of contact for all partners. This facilitates communication tremendously, and a single set of books and administrative procedures makes the program far easier to administer than those involving multiple systems. For instance, if a particular partnership involves 16 programs, only one person should administer and operate it.

Guarantee Mutual Benefits to All Parties

To be successful, communication efforts must ensure that all parties benefit. Each business concern and the college must clearly recognize the advantages to be derived from cooperative action. Unless both parties thoroughly understand how they will gain, they will not be willing to commit the time and resources necessary for meaningful articulation.

What action should be taken?

Adopt the perspective of the private sector

Evidence clearly indicates that the educational partners in the successful programs tend to develop, or at least understand, what may be termed a "private sector perspective" that emphasizes learner-as-worker performance (Dornsife, 1992). They readily accept their role as a service-provider on a community partnership team with responsibility for carrying out instructional mandates established by the partnership. They do not assume total control. They demonstrate a readiness to deal with issues of accountability and a willingness to negotiate and seek consensus when problems arise.

Accept the importance of deadlines

One important aspect of this performance perspective is a commitment to *timelines*. In successful programs, colleges responded quickly when bringing education and training on-line, generally by making decisions more rapidly and keeping their calendars more flexible than the typical community/technical college.

Promote Faculty Involvement

In order to ensure a successful program, involve faculty at the earliest opportunity. Invite as many faculty members as possible (representing all programs which will have experiential learning components) to participate in the meetings to plan program and develop curriculum. This helps all parties get to know, understand, and respect one another. Rotate meetings between any and all facilities so that instructors can better understand the "other guy's" program and facilities.

What action should be taken?

Figure 4–1 provides ideas to promote faculty involvement.

Initiate Performance-based Curricula

Programs are easier to understand and describe when coursework and learning activities are built around the performance objectives to be learned and/or developed. Working with such a performance-based

Figure 4–1

Twenty Things to do to Increase Faculty Involvement

- Continually inform faculty about experiential learning.
- Act as a go-between to link faculty from different departments.
- Organize informal discussions.
- Find out the concerns of people to be involved.
- Work through supportive opinion leaders on campus.
- Establish a faculty committee on experiential education.
- Have students affirm the value of experiential education.
- Conduct workshops or sponsor speakers on campus.
- Stress excellence in order to win faculty support.
- Ensure that academic advisors understand/promote experiential learning as an integral part of the curriculum.
- Arrange faculty internships.
- Help key faculty members arrange sabbaticals that involve experiential learning.
- Set up a summer study group of faculty, focusing on experiential learning.
- Create a rotating faculty position in the central office for experiential education.
- Take faculty on worksite visits.
- Encourage faculty to design and implement research projects related to experiential education.
- Establish Field Study Coordinatorships (similar to Teaching Assistantships) for graduate students or advanced undergraduates.
- Establish a collection of resources on experiential learning for faculty.
- Invite faculty to professional meetings for experiential educators.
- Offer senior faculty opportunities to take on leadership roles in experiential education.

Reprinted from Strengthening Experiential Education within Your Institution, ed. by Kendal & Associates, 1986, with permission of National Society for Experiential Education, 3509 Haworth Dr., Suite 207, Raliegh, NC 27609-7229 (919-787-3263).

course, instructors and curriculum people can better coordinate the educational experiences for learners. A performance-based course ensures that instructors have a common approach and a common language for planning (U.S. Department of Labor, 1992; 1989).

What action should be taken?

Develop measurable learning objectives for cooperative education programs and specify these on learning contracts

See Chapter 14 for more information on carrying this out.

Develop Written Cooperative Education Agreements

It is important to prepare cooperative education agreements to ensure that all participants understand what is expected of them and what can be expected from others. Most organizations with cooperative education agreements institute them at two levels: at the institutional level and at the learner/program level. Chapter 5 will discuss and display examples of learner/employer agreements.

What action should be taken?

Put the agreements in writing

All agreements should be carefully drawn up in detail and recorded. These formal written agreements should be signed by the chief executive officer of the schools and colleges, and the businesses or firms. Presidents and directors/superintendents usually sign the agreements at the institutional level, and department or program heads sign at the program level.

Publicize the agreements

The written cooperative education agreements need to be publicized both inside and outside the institutions involved. In this way everyone involved in program planning and delivery is fully informed of the final form this educational experience will take.

Now, Begin the Process

The question "who's in charge?" doesn't matter according to California community college educators who have been successful in developing cooperative education and experiential learning articulation agreements. Sometimes the lead is taken by the community college; in other cases the employers or secondary schools take the first step in exploring possible joint efforts. Either way, someone has to consider these questions.

- What businesses, organizations, and learners will benefit from these discussions?
- Who are the key players in each organization?

Step 1: Schedule a planning meeting

The agenda for a planning meeting can be relatively simple, but should at least include the following essential items.

- Identify organizations who might benefit.
- Establish broad goals.
- Determine annual program goals (requires at least a two-hour meeting).
- Develop a timeline and list tasks.

Step 2: Secure the endorsement of chief executive officers

Again, successful cooperative education articulation ultimately requires the policy-level approval of the chief executives at each institution (college and business) and the endorsement of each board of directors or trustees. Including a formal policy statement from each organization gives credence to all remaining steps. Even colleges that have taken a more informal approach to articulation usually choose eventually to have a set of written policies to guide staff who follow them in the future (U.S. Department of Labor, 1992; 1989).

Step 3: Develop coordinating mechanisms

A program coordinator begins the process of building and developing cooperative education partnerships. The following actions should be taken.

- Identify one person to serve as the coordinator of a single program.
- Identify those courses or programs that will be tackled first. (See cooperative education planning committee decisions described in Chapter 2.)
- Select the faculty to receive release time for program development (e.g., identifying desired competencies that

learners should master in the respective experiential learning activities).

- Develop formats for a prototype agreement that will fit the local situation (see Chapter 5).
- Establish the mechanisms for ensuring and maintaining consistent communication.
- Document all meetings and decisions to maintain a formal record of progress.

Step 4: Orient staff members of participating organizations

It will be up to the "middle managers" in each institution to inform their staff of the possibilities and potential of cooperative education and experiential learning.

- Emphasize the policy-level commitment of the chief executives and the respective boards or advisory committees.
- Describe the proposed instructional activities (e.g., practica, internships, apprenticeships, clinicals, mentoring, 2+2s, life-experience credits).
- Provide adequate and detailed instructions and models to follow.
- Select a facilitator or chair to run meetings.
- Clarify how faculty initiative enhances the possibility of success.

Step 5: Arrange interagency work sessions

Cooperating instructors (and employers) will need to work out details of curriculum, course sequences, competencies covered, and standards of performance. Provide opportunities for visits to each other's firms and campuses, hold joint meetings to review goals and objectives, and undertake discussions of instructional strategies and resources.

Step 6: Complete draft agreements

Upon completion of the draft agreements, the committee and program coordinator must decide if these will be presented to the board of trustees for approval or if administrative approval will be sufficient.

Step 7: Implement the process

All participants who work to implement the articulation of programs should frequently and regularly gather and share important information.

- Encourage each faculty member to become an enthusiastic advocate for the process that has been developed.
- Give particular attention to sharing the new program options.
- Accumulate data on the learners who begin to take advantage of the system for program refinement and reporting.

Step 8: Review the process annually

Chapter 14 describes in detail the review and evaluation process.

Overcoming Barriers to Effective Linkages

Plan effectively

Since successful program implementation requires careful planning which takes a great deal of time, the planning process is a particularly important stage of program development. It must be given enough emphasis and scope in order to involve fully all participants, but, at the same time, it must be efficient and effective so that their time is well spent.

Corporate partners in successful partnerships provide a most precious resource—*time*. The time that individuals devote to the development and implementation of cooperative education partnerships is generally uncompensated and given at significant personal sacrifice. Faculty members and administrators, for instance, often spend many evenings developing networks, promoting programs, working on placements, and providing personalized services to learners. A direct correlation exists between the extent of the personal investment each individual within the partnership makes and the continuing success and growth of that partnership (Cantor, 1990).

It is during the initial planning phase that partners must come to terms with the large amount of time required for the development of successful programs. Partnerships often take two to three years from concept stage to actual start-up, another two to three years for implementation, adjustment, and revision, and two more years to reach full maturity and generate significant outcomes.

The *clarifying process* of considering options, forming plans, and writing reports provides a vital forum for airing and resolving the many inevitable differences between partners. It binds all to a common mission and helps to close the gap between private- and public-sector perspectives.

Make sure that planning is *market-driven*. It cannot be too conceptual in nature. It must deal directly with the realities of existing circumstances and allow for rapid adjustment to changing conditions. For example, during a downturn in economic circumstances, internships in which learners are not compensated for their services are easier to market than work-and-earn programs. Always consider the program's effect on the productivity of the partners.

Partnerships should always *formalize their plans* as a way of assuring ownership among all participants and maintaining program continuity as leadership of the organization evolves.

Finally, in all plans include a means of assuring *accountability*. Assess outcomes frequently to determine progress in regard to both student and program goals. In the program's publicity include a commitment to hold the entire program accountable to the taxpayers, who support a good portion of the costs.

Specific planning techniques

When planning and developing cooperative education programs, certain measures will avoid community-instituted barriers (Cantor, 1990; Kendall et al., 1986).

- Establish a single contact for the program—one person who is authorized to provide an official public position on all issues and answer requests for information.

- Convene *regular and frequent* meetings of the cooperative education advisory committee. Establish and hold to an agenda that sets time parameters and specifies relevant issues for discussion.

- Be sure representatives of all business and community groups stay actively involved in ongoing planning and revision. These people must be authorized and ready to represent the views of their respective partner groups. Moreover, all must contribute substantively in order to generate feelings of ownership.

- Develop formal planning documents that all representatives sign. These should list responsibilities, timelines, activities, resource needs, and assignments. Write a *separate* policy document that lays out the rules under which the program operates; again, have it signed by all participants.

• Make sure the structure of the program reinforces the mission to which each partner has agreed. The mission statement should facilitate fulfillment of individual organizational objectives.

• Consider establishing the partnership as an independent entity, separate from its college, school, and business partners (e.g., a not-for-profit corporate entity). Select a director and establish budget and policy on the basis of program needs. Be sure accountability is directed only to the board of the program. The Tech Prep and School-to-Work Transition programs can assist in this process.

• Maintain the involvement of upper-level management of partner organizations both in cooperative education policy operation and planning activities—but decentralize decision making over time so that people at every level contribute and feel ownership for the program's activities and outcomes. The combination of top-down support and decentralized decision making not only helps maintain priority and commitment, but also guards against the tendency to rely solely on one or two key players.

• Record goals and objectives for all experiential learning activities. Be sure they are reasonable; assess progress toward their accomplishment on a regular basis (e.g., quarterly). Provide ample opportunities for revision along the way. Incorporate employer needs, wage levels, and skill requirements in the statements of objectives.

Expect problems

All experience to date indicates that every cooperative education program will encounter numerous difficulties and frustrations along the way. The most successful programs simply anticipate problems and develop contingency plans for dealing with them. The cardinal rule for handling difficulties is to confront them openly, fairly, and creatively. Always bring them before the entire partnership team, even if they are to be assigned to a sub-group or committee for resolution.

Solve organizational conflicts

"Turf battles" can occur even within the most exemplary programs, arising within individual partner organizations, among programs, faculty, or other partners, and occasionally between the partnership and the larger community.

To avoid these problems, spread decision-making responsibilities among many people within partner organizations. Indeed, a key characteristic of successful programs is *decentralized* decision making and broadly distributed responsibility for maintaining contacts among partner organizations.

Signed memos-of-understanding help to maintain program continuity by extending "ownership" among all partner organizations. Also, public awareness of the partnership, generated through local media exposure, helps to codify external (and therefore internal) expectations for the program, even though officials in partner organizations may change.

Interestingly, problems seem to occur more often *within individual partner organizations*, especially as programs mature. Internal battles often arise over issues such as the use of equipment or facilities, broken or mistreated equipment, scheduling or rotating students through the work processes, workloads, time demands, etc.

When dealing with these problems keep the following points in mind.

- A strong top-down commitment to the partnership is the best antidote. The success of the partnership *must* remain a priority concern of the top leaders within each partnership organization.

- If possible, establish the program as a separate entity with its own point of contact, schedule, facility, and independent cost center.

- Get other partners to determine in advance how partnership activities will affect and fit into their respective operations, with particular attention to the introduction of students into their workplace.

- Build a strong community constituency for the partnership so that it is viewed positively in the larger public arena and thereby contributes favorably to the reputation of each partner organization.

Difficulties *between partner organizations* often arise when introducing the program to new organizations. In one instance, when attempting to recruit contractors and union representatives, one partnership promoted itself as a way to overcome "deficiencies" in their affirmative action hiring practices. Rather than winning the contractors over, this approach generated a defensive reaction regarding their "deficient" status!

Learn enough about potential partners to determine how the partnership complements each organization's mission. Then push *benefits* rather than problems, and follow with a discussion of the proposal as a win/win opportunity.

When dealing with day-to-day problems among partner organizations use these techniques.

- Focus on a single mission for the program; subordinate all other objectives or needs to that mission.
- Recognize and accommodate the needs of each participating partner.
- Work for equity for each participating partner.
- Draw advice and resources from every partner so that each feels ownership for the program.
- Give credit for success among the partners—offer frequent "thank you's."
- Establish clear-cut rules about how partners should discuss the program and its problems in public.

Two strategies are useful when dealing with conflict *between the program and outside organizations.*

- Draw representatives from outside organizations into the planning process and onto curriculum review committees.
- And continue to enhance the program's public image by emphasizing its *success*; publicize its progress, particularly that which complements the objectives of external organizations.

Deal with demographic and economic change

Problems frequently arise because of economic or demographic changes in a region, such as the varying number of learners from year to year, the growth of non-English speaking populations, and shifts in the local economy from manufacturing to service-based industries.

Usually the best way to deal with any of these factors is to "stand the problem on its head." That is, view the necessity of dealing with such changes as an opportunity for revitalizing the partnership. These challenges often prove useful—particularly within mature programs—for not only do they stimulate new ideas, but also lead to the rekindling of efforts within the partnership.

When confronted with economic or demographic changes, established programs have drawn upon lessons learned during the early development of their partnerships to forge fresh relationships with new partners. Inevitably, this effort has resulted in a broadening of their programs to include many more learners than had been served.

Bring it all together through work-based learning

A guiding principle for successful cooperative education partnerships is that *the more faculty link their lessons and materials to actual worksite experiences, the more likely it is that programs will be successful.* This demonstrates clearly to business and industry how important their contribution is to the achievement of program goals.

The best instructional strategy incorporates actual or highly simulated job-site operations into normal course content. Not only is student motivation to learn increased, but also higher level academic and thinking skills are generated.

Actual or simulated work environments teach learners about working under supervision and achieving viable production rates and quality levels. Learners see the effects of various peer interaction patterns, the significance of such matters as appropriate dress, attendance, and punctuality, and the importance of attaining high levels of academic skills.

When learners become involved in work contexts, they tend to aspire more seriously to their chosen career roles. Their self-esteem grows as they face adult responsibilities and solve adult problems.

Funding Cooperative Education Programs

When it comes to funding, successful cooperative education programs combine and maximize resources from both public and private sector sources. They refuse to allow lack of money to become an excuse for lack of action and use seed money to plan and implement start-up activity.

In fact, at most institutions, funding is rarely seen as a major problem. This is not to say that resources are plentiful or easy to find. However, the prevailing attitude within programs is that—given the partners involved, the importance of the mission, and the resources available within the greater community—the job can *always* be accomplished.

What follows are general comments on seeking and considering grants or outside funding resources to underwrite experiential learning. The "red tape" associated with various funding sources is often burdensome. Businesses and private sector participants seem especially sensitive to this factor and, in some instances, have counseled their co-partners to refuse public money because of it. It is often more useful to designate a specific person, usually the community college educational partner, to handle the paperwork associated with securing and using government funds. The "paperwork partner" carries the funds on its books and handles accountability requirements. The institutional resource director should explore grant possibilities to offset some of the expenses. Likewise, some employers and corporate organizations continuously sponsor experiential learning programs. The matter of finding and allocating resources, however, should be shared by *all* partners. In this way successes, and setbacks too, are shared by everyone. The efforts and contributions of the respective partners are kept roughly equitable and are appreciated by other partners.

Partners inevitably benefit from collaborative funding efforts, even when funds are not secured. Their attempts help cement relationships and leverage resources that come from within partner organizations. Even if their primary funding targets are not met, partners share ideas and clarify their views on the program's mission. Such collaborative efforts offer one additional advantage—partners inevitably learn from rejection and *do not get discouraged*. Routinely, they rework proposals and resubmit ideas to the same or new sources; their persistence is usually rewarded.

It is important to view all contributions—not just the dollars—as resources. While dollars are certainly necessary, successful programs display an entrepreneurial attitude—if the product is worthwhile and the effort is worth making, the resources can be found.

Develop your resource base

- Actively consider, pursue, and accept all appropriate resources.
- Think of *time, energy, and commitment* as resources. Often these elements are even more important than dollars.

- Don't allow a lack of resources—especially dollars—to become an excuse for inactivity or lack of success.

- Develop a budget that deals realistically with resource needs. Avoid duplicating services and keep all partners informed about the importance of their continuing support.

- Seek seed money to initiate programs and then build a record of achievement; promote successes to acquire *more* money. Local grants, philanthropic sources, and economic development agencies are good sources of seed money.

- Use your resource base as leverage to raise additional resources. Set up matching programs with private industry; sell training slots to other educational institutions or employers who are not partners. Conduct fundraising drives that include large amounts of regional publicity for contributors and their contributions.

Overcome size inefficiencies

Many start-up, experiential learning programs are simply too small to be maintained effectively. Once under way, sometimes a partnership can be formed with other programs to expand the original program. Work with employers, local governments, and social service agencies to broaden support and the resource base.

The strategy of forming *regional* partnership associations has been used effectively to overcome problems of size in numerous situations. As will be seen in the chapters on internships, clinicals, and cooperative apprenticeships, professional alignments with other institutions and/or colleges can help overcome size problems. Programs are bound to change as new expectations arise. Again, memos-of-understanding that confirm expectations and delineate responsibilities among partners are strongly recommended. Clear contacts must be established within each partner organization.

A Final Note

In summary, effective communication is essential for cooperative relationships to work. Community college faculty and staff must be able to relate to business and industry in order for cooperation to take place and for experiential learning to happen. This chapter has presented the fundamentals of effective communication for linkages of community college cooperative education programs with business and industry and the community. Subsequent chapters will describe how to apply these principles to various kinds of experiential learning activities.

Once lines of communication have been established, memos-of-understanding or agreements drafted, and specific competencies identified for which experiential learning is appropriate, the next step involves selecting worksites and matching learners to worksites. Chapter 5 will now describe this step in detail.

Chapter References

Cantor, J.A. (1990). Job training and economic development initiatives. *Educational Evaluation and Policy Analysis.*

Dornsife, C. (1992, February). *Beyond articulation: The development of Tech Prep Programs.* Berkeley, CA: National Center for Research in Vocational Education.

Kendall, J.C., Duley, J.S., Little, T.C., Permaul, J.S., and Rubin, S. (1986). *Strengthening experiential education within your institution.* Raleigh, NC: National Society for Internship and Experiential Education.

Montgomery County Consortium for Vocational/Technical Education. (1990, January). *Final report: Strategic plan for collaborative and articulated vocational/technical programs.* Montgomery, PA: Author.

U.S. Department of Labor, Employment & Training Administration. (1988). *Building a quality workforce: A joint initiative of the U.S. Departments of Labor, Education, and Commerce.* Washington, DC. Author.

U.S. Department of Labor, Employment & Training Administration. (1989). *Work-based learning: Training America's Workers.* Washington, DC. Author.

U.S. Department of Labor, Employment & Training Administration. (1992). *School-to-work connections: Formulas for success.* Washington, DC: Author.

Chapter 5

Selecting Worksites and Matching Learners to Them

Once college faculty and advisory/planning committees have decided upon appropriate experiential learning activities, the next *Development Step* in the Experiential Learning Planning Model, Process Phase, involves identifying and recruiting employers and worksites (see Figure 3–2). The term "worksite" as used in this chapter and throughout the rest of the book includes any and all work for an employer and, in addition, mentoring and volunteer assignments.

The Process of Worksite Selection

Identify Suitable Worksites

Faculty coordinators are responsible for discovering and recruiting worksites in order to provide suitable cooperative education opportunities for learners at their institutions. There are several ways in which this can be done. The program advisory committee and/or the cooperative education advisory committee can be helpful in suggesting potential firms and influential in securing the participation of businesses, and can ask their members for suggestions and recommendations. Another valuable source of sites may be the local telephone directory, particularly the Yellow Pages. Don't overlook community business development agencies, chambers of commerce, committees of 100, and other similar organizations that maintain mailing lists of members. The local chamber of commerce also may be able to help by making available business or industrial studies related to industrial development projects. Restrict the list of possible worksites to those firms or organizations that can meet the occupational needs of the college program and/or the interests of selected learners. However, include for further study *all* places of business representing approved occupational areas.

Figure 5–1 shows a sample letter of introduction that can be used to elicit employer participation in cooperative education.

Now, once as many places as possible have been identified, continue the selection process by purging the list of obviously inadequate firms as they are interviewed and reviewed. Before presenting tentative lists of potentially participating sites, certain information should be gathered on the proposed sites for consideration by the advisory committee members. This chapter will discuss what this information should include and how to gather it.

Develop Standards for Worksites

Establishing worksite standards is a joint responsibility of the faculty coordinator and the Cooperative Education Advisory Committee, with the goal of guaranteeing acceptable on-the-job educational experiences for all learners. Accordingly, faculty coordinators must develop criteria for use in the tentative selection of worksites prior to presenting these sites for approval to the advisory committee.

In drawing up standards and criteria, the following aspects should be considered:

- the reputation of the firm;
- the experiences that can be offered by the firm to the learner;
- the previous experience of the firm/mentor in cooperative education internships/practicums;
- the willingness of the firm to accept the responsibility of an educational partnership;
- the availability and ability of a mentor/preceptor to supervise the learner on the job;
- the learner's needs and desires;
- the location of the worksite with respect to the college;
- the terms of compensation, if any, for the learner;
- the length of assignment for the learner;
- the safety provisions in place for the assignment.

The following discussion of worksite characteristics should be helpful in deciding on and developing standards by which to judge potential worksites.

Figure 5–1

Sample Employer Promotional Letter

Cooperative Education Community College

Dear "Chief Executive Officer":

Cooperative Education is an important part of our community college education program. This form of education provides on-the-job experiences for our learners, providing them with necessary work skills and attitudes, and allowing them to "test out" classroom theories and concepts.

In order to carry out cooperative education programs we strive to create a partnership composed of business/industry, the community, and the college. This partnership is based on a firm understanding that provides mutual benefits to all. Our college faculty and learners receive needed resources and superior training. Your firm could also gain from such an association with our college: you will meet eager learners who may be potential employees who you can train to meet your needs and requirements. Thus, your benefits include:

- A pool of college-trained workers for your long-range employment needs.
- An on-going training program which the college will attempt to individualize to your needs, making it available to your current employees (and counting their work experiences toward filling the requirements of the program).
- An opportunity to provide a community service.

I will call you shortly to discuss this opportunity further. Enclosed are some descriptive materials about our program(s). Thank you for your consideration.

Sincerely,

Director of Cooperative Education

The reputation of the firm

Particularly for those learners who are in competitive fields, such as business, computer science, health care, etc., the reputation of the firm or organization to which they are sent can be an important consideration. These learners will want and need to build their résumés by including impressive placements to give them a competitive edge in job hunting upon graduation. And for all learners, firms with solid reputations usually can offer excellent education.

However, smaller and perhaps younger firms are often more willing to participate in cooperative education partnerships, so don't overlook them. Their lack of an established track record may be offset by the extra enthusiasm and effort they put into the relationship.

Experiences offered by the firm

Of paramount concern in selecting a site for experiential learning are the activities that the learner will perform in the course of the job. Basically, these experiences should parallel the learner's course material. The firm and the person who will supervise and mentor the learner (the preceptor) should be able to provide work-and-learn experiences that will complement the formal course of study. Often, this involves rotating the learner through several workstations on the job. If necessary, the faculty coordinator should request this kind of supervision and experience. Before making a final decision on the firm, ensure that there is in place a written stipulation of the kinds of tasks that the learner will perform and a description of the full range of experiences that will be provided.

Firm's / mentor's experience in internships / practicums, etc.

One way to help ensure that a learner encounters a positive experiential learning situation is to place that learner with a firm and mentor or supervisor that has been involved previously in a cooperative education venture. Over a period of time, as more such firms are added to the list, community college faculty develop closer working relationships with them. Learners who need more supervision then can be placed in these experienced worksites.

Willingness of firm to accept the responsibility of the educational partnership

To enter into a cooperative education partnership represents a serious commitment and responsibility for a firm or business. This partnership demands a great deal of time and personal effort, a supportive attitude and behavior, and sufficient allocation of resources. A firm must be willing to commit to all necessary efforts and resources before the relationship begins, and must realize that accepting an intern is not just a means of acquiring inexpensive labor. The faculty coordinator should specify all that will be required of the firm before any agreement is signed. If this is not done, the relationship will not start off on a clear basis, and the learner may suffer.

Availability and ability of mentor/preceptor to supervise the learner on the job

All too often, a learner is placed in a worksite at a large firm, only to become lost as he or she is ignored or overlooked in the complexity of that environment. This occurs when care has not been taken to ensure that a single person has overall responsibility for the day-to-day supervision of that learner. It is essential that a learner be assigned to one person who will supervise tasking, oversee progress, and ensure safety on the job. This person and the responsibilities involved in such supervision must be specified in the written agreement.

Thus, in considering and selecting employers, it is important that a qualified supervisor be available to serve as an on-the-job instructor for the learner. An employee is frequently chosen to provide this instruction. The faculty coordinator must be fully satisfied that the potential on-the-job instructor, whether an employer or an employee, understands his or her responsibilities and that the learner will receive the necessary education and attention. If the employer does not want to be the on-the-job instructor and if there is no employee qualified for the task, eliminate the place of business as a worksite. A satisfactory learning situation cannot occur without a qualified on-the-job instructor. Under such circumstances the learner's work experience would be of doubtful educational value.

When on-the-job instructors are considered as adjunct members of the college faculty, as is the case in some colleges, they must be informed of their function and responsibility in this role.

In addition, the ability of the firm to provide the necessary training often depends upon the availability of appropriate and sufficient equipment. Ensure not only that enough equipment is provided, but also that it is not old or obsolete.

Learner needs and desires

Consideration of the needs of the learner is a vitally important aspect of worksite selection. Knowing what each learner expects and should gain from experiential learning will enable you, as a faculty coordinator, to identify and secure the requisite firms. Therefore, at the same time that worksites are being selected, you or a counselor must be working with your learners to determine what they need and want from their placements.

Location of the worksite relative to the college

Always consider the location of the firm. It should not be too far from the college, causing learners to spend too much time traveling. Proximity to the college is also important so that coordination of program and supervision of learners are facilitated.

Worksite stability is another aspect to consider. Is the learner expected to report for work at the same time and place each day? Such situations are usually more desirable. However, in some placements worksite location varies from day to day according to the nature of the work. This may be unsatisfactory if the college and the employer find it too difficult to coordinate and supervise the on-the-job experience of the learner. But some very desirable experiential learning activities take place in such situations. For instance, some colleges work with such programs as the Washington Internship Program, which places learners in political science and pre-law programs into internships in congressional offices. In this case other means of faculty coordination are necessary.

In any event, the faculty coordinator must make sure that the learner can report for work daily at a time and place that will coordinate with his or her college program.

Terms of compensation

Ideally, financial compensation is not what experiential learning is all about. However, more and more, we are finding that learners must "learn-and-earn" if they are to be able to learn at all. Therefore, the kinds and rates of compensation offered by a firm become a matter of some importance, and one which certainly must be considered in worksite selection.

There are probably as many variations in compensation to learners as there are worksites. Some firms will provide monetary compensation through an hourly wage, slightly above but near to the minimum Federal wage. Other firms, such as hospitals and health care facilities, have established training salary schedules. Still others make available training grants to qualified learners. For example, some motor vehicle manufacturers offer grants to minority and underpriviledged learners. These grants cover hourly wages, college tuition, tools, and books.

The faculty coordinator should maintain a list of those firms that provide compensation and/or grants, and reserve these placements for those learners who most need them in order to continue their studies.

Length of the assignment

The faculty coordinator also should take into consideration whether or not the learner can be retained and employed for the duration of the experiential learning course. Some employers are unwilling or unable to guarantee enough employment for learners, especially if their businesses are cyclical with periods of relative inactivity. Inform employers and supervisors that laying off learners during the academic semester or year presents a serious problem to both the learners and the college. The employer must be able and willing to provide the specific learning experiences required for training learners. If the firm finds it necessary to lay off a learner for one or more periods during the course, then this placement should be avoided. This action may be simply an indication of what the business can support, or it may indicate a more fundamental rejection or misunderstanding of what the program is intended to accomplish.

Again, these requirements should be included in the written agreement. It must be made clear that training worksites are expected to provide on-the-job experiences for the entire course or the agreed-upon portion thereof. However, it always must be recognized that circumstances can change in such a way that learner employment must be discontinued. In this case, the college faculty coordinator simply must make the best possible adjustment.

Safety considerations

The wise faculty coordinator realizes that cooperative education involves leaving the safety of the classroom and entering a very different arena. Whenever a learner becomes involved in "hands-on" activities as part of the learning experience, a concern for safety must be paramount. The possibility of injury is no reason to avoid experiential learning, but rather is an indication for caution. Faculty coordinators need to look around potential worksites to ensure that the firm puts into practice prudent and realistic safety measures for all its employees. Discuss matters of safety that will affect the learner with the employer and preceptor. Also, specify the responsibilities of each of the parties, college and firm, for purposes of liability insurance coverage. This stipulation is particularly important in the area of health care where learners will be working with patients and exposed to disease.

Visit the Worksite: Preliminary Contacts

Making contact with prospective firms to establish cooperative education partnerships is really a marketing venture. After all, you are selling your college program and its benefits to an employer, and asking for assistance in the form of a partnership for training and education. To effectively present your program you will need to communicate the following:

- goals and objectives of the program;
- needs of the learners for experiential learning;
- benefits to the firm to be derived from cooperating.

In choosing worksites there is absolutely no substitute for personal contact between the faculty coordinator and the employer of the firm. Whether you make the first visit alone or in collaboration with other faculty members depends on whether you are making contact for your own program or working as a college coordinator for several programs. In either event, certain basic steps should be followed.

- Initially, contact the firm by phone or mail. Introduce yourself (or your colleagues) and the program (or programs). Before your visit mail ahead any informative materials that would be helpful to the firm and would arouse interest in a dialogue.

- Always make an appointment prior to a visit. Make contact with the principal executive of the firm; speak to the person or people who can commit the firm to the cooperative education relationship. If the top executive is not available, request an appointment at a later time. Allow the principal person time to make the necessary connections with others in the firm with whom you actually may be working. Often, when dealing with a large firm or organization, it is advisable for a member of the advisory committee who has high-level connections, or the college president, to make the first contact.

* Always keep your appointment or call to reschedule if necessary. First impressions are vitally important. If you expect the firm to be serious about a cooperative educational relationship, then you, as the representative of the college, must demonstrate firm commitment.

* Bring prepared literature which describes the program in sufficient detail. Make sure this literature is professionally designed and produced so that it is attractive and appealing. These are, in effect, marketing brochures for your program and must look the part.

* A formal presentation which has been prepared and rehearsed in advance should be offered. This again reinforces the serious and professional nature of the undertaking. Informality should be saved for later discussion.

* During your visit pay careful attention to the employer's reactions, including non-verbal signals. Does this person seem interested in what you are saying? Does the response generally seem favorable? Is there any evidence of a desire to cooperate with you? Of course, not every visit will result in a sell. Therefore, if there is a strong indication that this firm is not in a position to work with you, or if you decide through initial observation that the environment is not right for learning, politely terminate the visit at the most opportune moment.

* Take advantage of any offers for a tour of the facility. Depending on the nature of your program, you might see a laboratory, manufacturing plant, office, ward of a hospital, and so on. During this tour look over the organization and assess its teaching and learning possibilities, including the kind of training available, the state of the equipment, and employee morale.

* Try and determine what the attitude toward and acceptance of a learner in this facility would be. For example, in union shops, cooperative education partnerships often are viewed negatively by the workers who see them as an opportunity for their

employer to hire non-union help at lower wages. Learners should not be placed in such undesirable environments.

* It is obviously impolite to check off a prepared evaluation sheet during the interview or tour of facilities (take notes instead), but record your reactions as soon as possible after leaving.

* Make subsequent visits or phone calls if additional information is required.

Select the Final Worksites

Advisory committee recommendation

After the findings on all potential worksite firms have been summarized by the faculty coordinator, a meeting of the advisory committee should be called to discuss them. This committee may raise valid concerns or present new information that will cause some worksites to be rejected or, at least, postpone acceptance of them. In this case, follow the recommendation of the advisory committee as its members, because of their position, presumably will have extra direct knowledge and information that may not be accessible to you. Advisory committees must endorse worksites and should assist in monitoring learner progress. The advisory committee also should be consulted frequently so that it can provide guidance to new potential firms.

After the committee has made its recommendations, compile a tentatively approved list of firms for submission to administrative officers (if needed) for final approval before placements are made. Maintain a permanent file on each firm. Be sure that information recorded in the evaluation process becomes part of this file, including any selection/evaluation forms devised by your college and filled out by you.

The Process of Matching Learner Needs to Employer Worksites

Selecting and placing learners in suitable worksites is the next challenging task for the cooperative education coordinator. Community colleges with cooperative education programs must develop and implement plans for learner recruitment, screening, and worksite placement.

Assess Learners

- Conduct an initial interview and screening to establish a learner's basic qualifications, need for, and ability to profit from cooperative education.

- Identify each learner's career interests, basic aptitudes, and vocational interests through psychological testing and other appropriate means.

- Examine each learner's school records to discover academic strengths and weaknesses, pinpoint discipline problems, check attendance, examine peer relationships, and identify attitudes towards school and work.

Assist Learners to Make Career Decisions

During the process of matching learners to worksites, their personal inclinations, abilities, and career goals must be considered. Through the process of selecting a career learners acquire important life skills that are needed both during their education and in later life if they change occupations. Indeed, one of the goals of cooperative education is to enable learners to make personal career decisions. To younger learners the task of choosing a career is often difficult and sometimes seems overwhelming. But the process of examining the possibilities and making choices is an important part of matching learner to worksite and must precede such placement. Experts suggest a multi-phase approach to career decision making (see Figure 5–2).

First, know thyself

From the beginning of formal schooling and throughout life, we continually learn more about who we are and what we need. The "cooling-out" opportunities provided by community college cooperative education (see Chapter 2) allow learners more time to reflect on potential careers. And participating in cooperative educational experiences help learners discover more about their:

- interests (what you enjoy doing);
- skills (what you do well); and
- values (what is important to you).

Before making an appropriate and successful initial career choice—or, for that matter, a second, third, or fourth career choice (as many

Figure 5-2

A Multi-Phase Approach to Career Decision Making

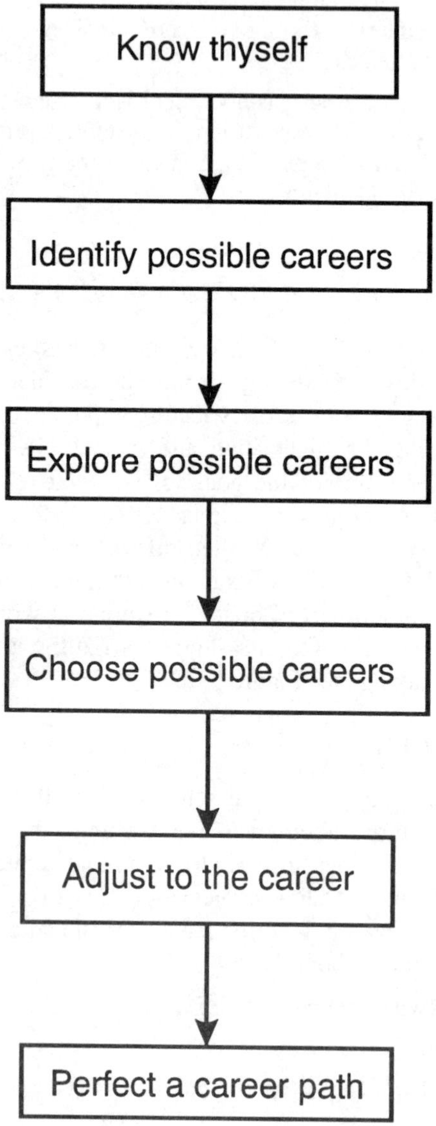

Know thyself

↓

Identify possible careers

↓

Explore possible careers

↓

Choose possible careers

↓

Adjust to the career

↓

Perfect a career path

community college learners are mature people returning for new skills)—one must know what one is good at, and likes to do; and what is important, thus valued by oneself. Thus, faculty, counselors, mentors, friends, parents, significant others, etc., should assist learners to answer these specific questions:

- What do you enjoy most?
- What abilities do you have?
- What kinds of activities do you like best?
- What skills would you like to use in your work?
- What do you want from a job?
- What kinds of things are most important to you in a job?

Identify possible careers

Community colleges offer numerous career possibilities from which to choose. In fact, new learners often become overwhelmed by the wealth of interesting opportunities. The presentation of possibilities, of course, is part of the guidance function. However, faculty and counselors must help to match a learner to a potential career path, based on the answers to the questions posed above.

Explore possible careers

Some learners have fairly definite plans and can use cooperative education to gain work experience that will provide them with a competitive edge in order to get the best job possible upon graduation. Other learners need cooperative education experiences to test the work environment or their abilities and interests in a particular career choice. Whatever the individual situation, a second phase of the process of choosing a career is to identify potential career options.

Cooperative education faculty and counselors can explain careers to learners through the use of various software programs such as DIS-COVER™. This is a career guidance program which helps assess a learner's interests, abilities, and values and then links these to possible occupations. The Armed Services Vocational Aptitude Battery (ASVAB) is also useful to select trade and technical occupations.

Choose possible careers

With a basic understanding of themselves, their unique interests, strengths, and values, and the existing career options, learners are now in a position to make career choices. These choices can be related to each other or not. They need not be carved in stone; learners do change careers while in college! However, once a career decision is made, learners can begin to strengthen job skills through internships, apprenticeships, and more higher education.

Adjust to the career

This phase of working into an occupation or career occurs during long-term, structured work-based experience. Through learning to work with peers, supervisors, and people of different backgrounds and skills, and through perfecting skills, a learner adjusts to a career.

Perfect a career path

We all learn continuously as we work and grow. Learning to learn should happen early in a career. We, as trainers, need to realize the importance of showing our learners how to benefit from experience in order to progress successfully through a career.

Chapter 6

Internships

An internship is a period of time spent in a working environment under supervision for college credit. It is usually a final or culminating activity arranged near the end of a program when many skills have been taught and mastered. It is a learning experience that helps learners translate what has been learned within the college—in the classroom—to the world of work. Interns work together with both the faculty of their academic program and the on-the-job supervisor to apply their academic learning to job practice. These experiences give learners a new perspective to bring back to the classroom and help round out their education.

The internship also offers learners an opportunity to "try out" a job. This enables learners, as college students, to try out their career choices in real work environments prior to graduation and/or investing much time and money in formal study. For a limited period, without fear of choosing the wrong career, learners can find out firsthand about an industry, company, and/or a specific job. Simultaneously, they can earn college credit. Thus, through hands-on experience learners gain academic credit for learning that takes place outside of the classroom. And, as many internships are paid positions, some financial support may be afforded.

Most community colleges offer various forms of internship experience. Figure 6–1 displays a cross section of these college offerings.

Normally, the internship experience is handled administratively by having the learner formally enroll in a credit course. For instance at Sacramento City College a typical course description reads:

Real Estate Internship: 3 units. One hour lecture, 10 hours per week.

In cooperation with the Sacramento Association of Realtors, this course provides supervised, structured, hands-on experience in a real estate sale or real estate lender or appraiser office for students seeking a career in real estate. Application for the program is through real estate instructors. Admission is competitive with finalists interviewed prior to each semester and selected by Real Estate Brokers. The California Department of Real Estate recognizes the course as a substitute for Real Estate 82, Real Estate Practice for the

Figure 6–1

Internship Opportunities at Selected Community/Technical Colleges

College	Programs	Credits Awarded
Sacramento City College (CA)	Administration of Justice Business Early Childhood Education Human Services Journalism Political Science Real Estate Recreation Sociology Technology	4 units
Porterville College (CA)	All programs	up to 16 units
Northampton Community College (PA)	Funeral Service Office Administration Early Childhood Education	4 credits 3 credits 8 credits
Northcentral Technical College (WI)	Accounting Secretarial Science Data Processing Marketing Insurance Legal Secretary Medical Secretary	3 credits 2 credits 2 credits 3 credits 3 credits 2 credits 2 credits
Tunxis Community College (CT)	Criminal Justice Human Services	3 credits 3 credits
Dundalk Community College (MD)	Legal Assistant Media Technology Ornamental Horticulture Elementary Education Electronics Technology Chemical Dependency Counseling Business Office Careers	3 credits 3 credits 4 credits 3 credits 3 credits 3 credits 3-4 credits

purpose of fulfilling the nine-unit requirement for real estate licensure.

1992–1993 Catalog; p. 153

At Northcentral Technical College, the procedure for internship credit award reads:

> Internship Study: Internship requires a job in the program area for a minimum of 8 hours a week for ten weeks. Program of activities planned with instructor and intern sponsor. Student attends a one-hour-per-week instructor-planned class as well as individual conferences with the instructor. Employer and instructor evaluate performance at mid-term and end of semester.

1990–1992 Catalog; p. 85

Internship Program Development

The development of internships is an ongoing process which continually changes and/or evolves as: (1) programs change in content; (2) learner populations change; and (3) the need for cooperation between college faculty and business and industry increases. Often, internships are culminating experiences. Therefore, internship activities must be developed to answer the specific needs of learners in the final stages of their programs, satisfy cooperating employers, and meet the requirements of the college program.

The acquisition of specific competencies, designed to satisfy the requirements of a specific course or group of courses, is the objective of an internship. Hence, these cooperative work experiences should provide focused practical experience.

Recruit Worksites for the Program

Chapter 5 described worksite identification and evaluation in detail. However, to identify cooperating employers and worksites for internships the following promotional strategies will complement the previous information (Armstrong, Bieber, and Heitner, 1985).

Contact adjunct faculty

Most colleges employ many part-time faculty to supplement and complement their full-time faculty. View adjunct faculty as primary resources to help with internship development since they are active in the business community, as well as in the academic program. Plan orientation meetings for the internship program and invite the program's adjunct faculty to attend. Integrate them into the planning for the program. Perhaps an adjunct faculty member can sponsor a learner's internship directly at his or her worksite. Or, alternatively, an adjunct can provide an entrée into the firm in the form of an interview for an internship position.

Contact alumni

Many alumni may stay involved with community colleges via the alumni association or college development office. The college cooperative education program planning committee should involve alumni in the planning process and make contact with those alumni who can hire learners as interns. Many alumni themselves have benefitted from such programs and will be willing to afford opportunities to other learners.

Contact professional organizations

Professional groups offer excellent opportunities for reaching specific types of employers. Presentations by the cooperative education planning committee to these groups not only foster an awareness of the benefits of the internship experience, but also can suggest further possibilities by conveying the entire scope of the cooperative education program. Representatives from these professional groups can "seed" future internship opportunities through informing possible firms and industries about the program.

Hold an open house

College administration and faculty can host open houses for cooperative education and/or academic programs. Invite potential employers to hear about these programs. Inform them of the needs for and benefits to be derived from sponsoring interns. In this way, firms and organizations can learn about internships and other cooperative education work/study programs and opportunities in a pleasant setting and situation. This approach removes the possibility that participants may feel pressured to make an immediate commitment.

Send recruitment packages

A professional recruitment package is an absolute necessity for an internship program. Send this material in advance of any visits to prospective employers to inform them about the overall program and college goals and expectations. Include in such packages the following (Armstrong et al., 1985):

- a brief history of the college;
- an individual brochure on each major program in the curriculum;
- a current cooperative education calendar;
- articles on the college and its various internships;
- informational pamphlets and fact sheets on internships;
- guidelines for internship supervisors;
- a list of current employers sponsoring internships;
- résumés of learners who are available for internships during the next quarter or semester;
- a sampling of graduate positions held by alumni of such programs;
- a report offering statistical data on the numbers of employed graduates and the fields they have entered; and
- a press release on any new feature of the college (a new microcomputer laboratory, for example) which might be of interest to a particular employer.

Conduct personal visits

Another important aspect of any development strategy is the one-to-one session with a potential employer, as described in Chapter 5. Be sure faculty coordinators convey the positive benefits to the employer. Such benefits include:

- highly motivated and experienced workers;
- cost-effective labor;
- the availability of help during peak times;
- a placement office to recruit workers at non-internship times; and
- a full-time liaison between employer and interns.

Send direct response letters

Another technique for developing internships is direct mail. A mailing can consist of a promotional letter, a brochure, and a response device to generate qualified leads. The advantages of this approach are many.

- The mailing is an excellent public relations tool, offering a further opportunity to tell the internship and cooperative education story.

- It contains material which the company can keep on file for future reference and use.

- It can be targeted to specific fields (data processing, accounting, etc.) in which the college has a pressing need for placements.

- The mailing may be followed up easily by internship coordinators.

Publicize the Internship Program

After making initial contact, the next step is to organize strategies to publicize the internship position. Try some of the following ideas.

Include the program in the college catalog

A section of the college catalog should include a description of the internship program, together with pictures of learners at worksites and in class. This will help to project the correct image of the program.

Write a newsletter

Internships, as well as other cooperative education work opportunities, depend on business linkages. As described in Chapter 4, it is wise to create a means for maintaining communication with present employers and reaching potential recruits. A newsletter can serve this purpose. It also helps develop worksite opportunities by educating employers about the internship/cooperative education program and the college itself. Be sure to recognize in its pages employers who do participate. And solicit involvement of new employers.

Retain and Expand the Internship Program

When it comes to strategies for retention and expansion of the existing base of employers, here are five ideas:

Hold employer receptions

Host an employer reception, open house, or annual luncheon at which awards are given to recognize and honor those companies that have provided ongoing internship opportunities for the learners.

Issue credit vouchers

Establish a credit voucher system whereby employers may take courses in return for supervising a given number of learners on a yearly basis.

Begin networking

Organize a joint networking activity to which both current and potential employers are invited. Encourage employers to share general, as well as internship-related, information. In this way you may expand your internship program within existing companies while developing new internships from the pool of invited guests.

Encourage feedback

Ask for and share employer feedback with the appropriate faculty. Only if learners continue to be trained in the most current methods and procedures in their fields can we expect employers to continue to hire them. And employers' sense of commitment will grow if they see that they are contributing directly to program development and improvement.

Update information

Remember to develop more internships at existing companies during on-site visits. Inform current employers of new college departments or needs. Find out about and be sensitive to their needs as well.

Internship Program Administration

Successful internships depend on open communication between three partners—the learner, the cooperating employer and/or worksite supervisor, and the college faculty. After the initial agreement to employ or accept an intern, the terms of the activity must be specified in writing for these three parties. At a minimum, the following items should be covered (Armstrong et al., 1985).

Terms of the relationship

Will this be an unpaid or paid experience? Some internships are not compensated by wages—some employers provide only a stipend for travel or lodging. If the position is to be paid, how much and for what purpose should be stipulated.

Kind of work or job responsibility

Specify in the written agreement the kind of work to be performed by the intern. In some cases, an outline of the assignment may be all that can be provided, as employers may not know what will actually be done until a period of adjustment passes and the intern and supervisor become acquainted with each other's skills and needs. In other cases, detailed responsibilities may be listed.

Period of the relationship

Specify the length of the relationship. Will the intern work for the equivalent of one semester—one year—one summer—or some period of months? This is important for assigning credit by the college faculty advisor.

Work schedule

Specify the hours per day, days per week, etc., that the task will entail. And don't forget to specify a supervisory contact with whom the faculty member must keep in touch.

In some colleges, internship credit is awarded based upon length of internship experience. For instance, at Long Beach City College, the development of measurable personal objectives and end enrollment in a minimum number of units for each semester of cooperative education is required. Their schedule:

Hours Worked for Semester	*Units*
75–5 hours per week:	1
150–10 hours per week:	2
225–15 hours per week:	3

1984–1984 Catalog; p. 66

Communication mechanism

Finally, discuss how the college interface will take place. In what form will the employer permit site visits? How often will such visits occur and which personnel will be involved? If possible, draw up a schedule of visits.

A typical Training Agreement is displayed in Figure 6–2 below.

Learner Preparation and Placement

Chapter 5 describes learner recruitment and placement into cooperative education in general. But, internship experiences are capstone or culminating activities, and as such are pursued only after the learner has demonstrated significant academic achievement. A typical requirement for participation in internship and related work experiences at Sacramento City College appears below.

Cooperative Work Experience Education courses are for learners who want to earn college credits for volunteer or paid work. You may enroll for credit for a job you already have.

Work Experience credits are transferable as elective credits to California State Universities and Colleges when the learners' work is related to their major or program, or when the work is related to a course the learner has or is taking.

Learners can earn one unit for every 60 hours unpaid work or one unit for 75 hours paid work.

Prerequisites for Work Experience credit:

1. For a Paid Job:

(a) Be working 20 hours per week or more. (b) Be enrolled in a total of 7 units, including Work Experience units. (c) All questions will be answered by the instructor in first class session.

2. For a Volunteer Job:

(a) Be working 14 hours per week for 4 units; 10 hours per week for 3 units; 7 hours per week for 2 units; 4 hours per week for 1 unit.

Figure 6–2

Typical Employer Internship Training Agreement

Name_____Phone_____Date_____

Address_____

Social Security Number_____

Cooperative Employer_____Phone_____

Address_____Training Supervisor_____

Employer Agrees To:

1. Provide a schedule of agreed-upon work experiences for the learner and cooperate in helping the learner meet job performance objectives.
2. Provide adequate supervision for the learner.
3. Periodically evaluate the learner's progress on the job.
4. Endeavor to employ the learner for the entire agreed-upon training period.
5. Follow all federal and state regulations regarding the employment of students.

College Agrees To:

1. Assist the learner and employer to meet the objectives of the training program.
2. Visit the worksite or consult with the training supervisor on a regular basis.
3. Coordinate the learning activities on the job with those in the educational program at the college.
4. Evaluate the learner's progress on the job periodically throughout the academic year.

Learner Agrees To:

1. Maintain regular attendance on the job.
2. Show honesty, punctuality, courtesy, a cooperative attitude, proper grooming habits, good dress, and a willingness to learn.
3. Consult with the training sponsor, employer, and program coordinator about any difficulties arising at the work assignment.
3. Conform to all the rules and regulations of the employer.
5. Furnish the coordinator with all necessary information and complete all the necessary forms and reports required in the program.
6. Devote his or her best effort to fulfilling the work assignment and accomplishing the objectives outlined in the training plan.

Employer's Signature_____

Coordinator's Signature_____

Learner's Signature_____

(b) Be enrolled in a total of 7 units, including Work Experience units.

Steps to enroll in a Work Experience Course:

1. If work is related to declared major or program, enroll for Work Experience 98 or the Work Experience Course in your major listed below, that fits your schedule.

2. If work is not related to your major, enroll for General Work Experience 97 that fits your schedule.

3. All other questions will be answered by the instructor in the class.

Placement Information:

1. Placement assistance in a volunteer or paid job related to the learner's major or program is possible on a limited basis from the Cooperative Work Experience office.

2. Many employers require completion of one to three semesters in the major before the learner is eligible for job placement.

3. A number of State agencies have volunteer programs that may lead to paid Learner Assistant jobs.

4. All jobs are open to all learners without regard to race, color, creed, age, sex or handicaps.

1992–1993 Catalog; p. 55. Reprinted with permission of
Los Rios Community College District and Sacramento City College

Internship Seminars

Many community college academic programs offer a seminar that runs concurrently with the internship experience in order to guide learners with the on-the-job work experience. Lehman College provides such a couse which includes the following typical topics:

- development of work-related learning objectives;
- selection of internship experiences;
- how to benefit from the experience;
- resolution of work-related problems;
- preparation of long-range career goals.

Figure 6–3 below displays a typical syllabus for a career orientation course. Discussion follows on each of the points listed above.

Figure 6–3

Seminar Syllabus

Course Schedule:

Date	**Class Themes**
1st week	Cooperative Education: overview of course. Why this is a valuable course.
2nd week	Focusing your career plans. Goal setting.
3rd week	Developing a long-range career plan. Career opportunities and how to locate them.
4th week	Human relations and successful employment; on-the-job training.
5th week	Preparing the résumé and letter of application.
6th week	Successful networking.
7th week	How to conduct an effective interview with a prospective employer.
8th week	Presentations by learners currently in coop programs concerning their experiences on the job.
9th week	How to make the most of your cooperative education experience. Meeting your career goals.
10th week	Examination; final lectures.

Figure 6–4

Approved Learning Objectives

INSTRUCTIONS: Record your approved learning objectives on this sheet. Be sure to review these again with your job supervisor/manager and to obtain his/her signature. Then, return a copy of these approved learning objectives to your college cooperative education/internship coordinator.

1. *become familiar with patient care management*

2. *develop clinical interview skills*

3. *practice patient counseling*

4. *orientation to dental records management*

5. _____

Supervisor's Signature_____

Develop work-related learning objectives

Together with the faculty supervisor, a learner should develop a list of learning objectives appropriate to his or her immediate and long-term goals. Figure 6–4 is a typical format for this activity.

A plan for accomplishing each task on the job can also be developed as in Figure 6–5 below.

With these goals in mind, a learner now can begin to identify and select an appropriate internship employer.

Select the internship

The first step for learners who wish to enter an internship is selecting the correct experience, one from which they will benefit. How to do this? There are a number of factors to consider (Boeder, 1981).

Money matters

Salary should not be the primary reason for either accepting or rejecting an internship. While pay is often necessary, some very good internships are offered by employers who cannot compensate learners.

Figure 6–5

Learning Objectives Worksheet

Learner_____*Mary Smith*_____Quarter___*Winter*___19_*95*_

Faculty Coordinator_____ Date_____

INSTRUCTIONS: In each of the four major areas listed below, write at least one objective you can accomplish this quarter through your on-the-job training.

1. *Career Orientation* (Identify how you plan to earn a promotion, develop different aspects of your career area, or work on something else that concerns your career growth.)

Task to be accomplished:_*become familiar with patient care*_ _*management and interview procedures*_

How to accomplish task:_*work along side of dental assistant*_

Measurement/Evaluation: (How will you know when you have met your goal?) _*Dental assistant will review my work.*_

Date Completed:_____Supervisor_____

2. *Skills and/or Knowledge Acquisition* (Identify a specific skill that you wish to acquire during the quarter.)

Task to be accomplished:_*Patient interview in dental clinic.*_

How to accomplish task:_*work along side of dental assistant*_

Measurement/Evaluation: (How will you know when you have met your goal?) _*Dental assistant will review my work.*_

Date Completed:_____Supervisor_____

3.*Skills Application* (Identify some skill or knowledge that you want to improve upon or become more proficient in using.)

Task to be accomplished:_*learn how to enter information on*_ _*patient chart.*_

How to accomplish task:_*Supervised practice in dental clinic.*_

Measurement/Evaluation: (How will you know when you have met your goal?) _*Medical records technician will review my work.*_

Date Completed:_____Supervisor_____

4. *Human Relations Skills* (Identify one way in which you want to improve your ability to work with supervisors, fellow employees, others that you associate with, and/or customers.)

Task to be accomplished:_*Patient support and counseling.*_

How to accomplish task:_*Supervised practice in dental clinic.*_

Measurement/Evaluation: (How will you know when you have met your goal?) _*Dental assistant will review my work.*_

Date Completed:_____Supervisor_____

One learner at Lehman College interned at an AIDS clinic. As a social work major, this unpaid experience really helped her decide on this kind of work as her career.

A stipend, tax-free, can often be worth more than a minimum wage. Other kinds of rewards, such as transportation, tuition reimbursement, etc., can also be negotiated. Consider the cost of clothes, lodging, etc., in a final decision.

What will be done?

The other big cost of an internship is harder to value—the learner's time. But what is time worth? At a minimum, any internship will cost the time which could have been spent otherwise and whatever else might have been learned, earned, or done. In fact, a learner is paying tuition for the privilege of working.

Learners are not really in a position to bargain, but in choosing among the internships, they should remember that they will expend a great deal of time and effort, and should get a great deal in return.

What they get may be of intrinsic value (learning and personal growth) or extrinsic value (academic credit, a line on a résumé, and whatever prestige comes with the internship) or both. To seek mainly extrinsic value in an internship is like taking primarily easy courses in college—it's a short-sighted strategy. Very little is gained in the short run and a great educational opportunity is lost in the long run (Boeder, 1981, p. 5).

Some internships will give learners personal contacts even if not much else. An internship should provide a learner with future employment contacts. At Lehman College one learner ran errands for a US Senator and another worked on clerical tasks in a city councillor's office. From these experiences and the contacts made through them, these learners were able to gain letters of recommendation that culminated in law school admission and scholarship opportunities. While the tasks performed and the skills gained may have been minimal, in the long run, the experiences paid very substantial benefits.

If developing skills and ability is of greater concern, seek internships offering more meaningful work. Look for those situations that are real short-term jobs in a field, rather than those that just offer the chance to be around where real work is done. Ask not only what one does in the internship, but also what one, personally, will be expected to get done— what will be accomplished. For instance, consider the previously mentioned Lehman College intern who worked as volunteer intern (in social work in a shelter for homeless AIDS patients in the Bronx, New York City). Responsibilities included helping clients with health, financial, and personal matters. In this case the intern was expected to to carry out very important and difficult work and thus gained invaluable skills.

Learners should be realistic about the experience and their qualifications and proven abilities. They should not set their hopes too high regarding what they can expect to accomplish in the internship.

Learners can't expect to do anything that requires skills and experience they do not have. With two years of marketing courses, no one will be entrusted with designing or running a large business. Interns must expect a certain amount of routine and/or menial work. But try to find jobs where tasks will actually be performed by the interns, even if they do them wrong at first: that is a much better experience than working as an assistant to an expert who always does them right. Does the internship offer learners worthwhile opportunities? Will they merely observe professionals work or will they do it themselves? Will they only participate in important decisions or will they actually make them, at least some of the time? Will they only be exposed to all aspects of the office or will they actively be involved in them in ways that matter? Will they work closely with the pros in the office or will they learn to be pros themselves? In short, will interns be treated as kids or as young professionals (albeit lacking in experience)?

A good guide is whether or not interns will have the chance to fail. If they are not allowed the opportunity to make mistakes, then they will not have the opportunity to make decisions or take actions that matter.

Except for a few high-prestige programs that are well known, most internships will not look particularly good on a résumé. How is a prospective employer to know whether the applicant practically ran the operation by filling in for a line executive on vacation or merely ran the copying machine and went for coffee? All interns must sell future employers on the value of their internship, if it was the former type. In general, learners should be wary of internships where they are expected to function as an assistants to executives. The good positions are those where learners will have responsibility for an area or task, where they will accomplish something they can cite in a future job interview. Find out who is selecting the interns and who will be the supervisor if one of them is accepted. Avoid jobs that involve working under the "intern supervisor" or some personnel assistant whose task is to be a "den mother" for the interns. If the immediate supervisor is not responsible for getting anything done in the organization, the interns will not be either.

Resolve work-related problems

Organize formal college seminars to provide an opportunity to discuss the various issues and problems which instructors/coordinators detect during worksite visits and/or individual counseling (see Chapter 14). The kinds of issues which may arise include:

- working and fitting into an organization;
- employer expectations of employees;
- understanding salary and benefit structures of an organization; and
- negotiating an employment offer if it comes.

Prepare long-range career goals

Also include topics relating to long-range career planning as part of the seminar. Learners need to understand contemporary issues of career-path planning, such as networking, professional affiliations, résumés, continuing education, knowing when to change jobs, and salary and benefits plans.

How to Obtain an Internship

A learner wants an internship. So usually she or he checks with the placement center early in the term and finds at least a dozen appealing programs. This potential intern now puts in long hours filling out and mailing forms to many faceless internship coordinators. Assuming the learner is typical, he(she) has worked at some labs or campus clubs and paid some dues at Burger King. Yet with dozens—sometimes hundreds—of qualified learners competing for each intern slot, the learner definitely needs an extra edge.

A learner can always try to beat the odds by scattering résumés to dozens of employers. This ever-popular method, however, is usually the least effective way to land a good internship. A better strategy is to limit the search to a maximum of five or six programs. Then, before typing a single line, consider a few key points about the internship system.

Most employers realize that internship candidates do not have a lot of job experience and that they do have a lot to learn. For that reason, an organization tends to scan applications for some clear proof that the potential intern (1) also realizes that he(she) has a lot to learn, (2) is strongly motivated to learn some of it through that organization's program, (3) will probably learn quickly enough to be worth the organization's trouble, and (4) at least knows how to act like a pro (Lowe, 1981).

Applying for an internship

With a fairly simple three-step strategy learners can meet these requirements and stand out from the collegiate herd (Lowe, 1981). The first step in the process is figuring the angles—determining how one's specific skills can meet an employer's needs. The next step is polishing one's presentation—crafting application forms, résumés, cover letters, and interview techniques that display one's qualifications in the most impressive way. Third on the agenda is following through—using tactics that politely remind the organization of who the potential intern is and why he(she) would make a good intern.

One can spin off countless variations on this basic method: it works for both formal programs and internships one creates oneself. Here are a few specific ways that Lehman College intern students have put the strategy to work.

Step one: Goal setting

In times of tight job markets many student interns are in search of internships each semester. How to put your learners at the "head of the line" should be the objective of the astute faculty coordinator.

The key to making the learner a successful candidate is to research the firms or organizations that do or may accept internships. Researching an organization and its internship program will show how to make all application materials more persuasive.

It is important to know enough about the firm to be able to ascertain its rationale for using interns. This information then can be used to formulate a gameplan for selling the intern candidate to the firm. Potential sources of information include:

- former interns on the campus;
- former interns contacted through the program's internship coordinator;

- professors familiar with the program;
- the internship announcement, the program's coordinator, or staff members;
- professional organizations in the areas involved; and
- published material on the organization's operations and structure, available from such sources as Moody's Manuals, College Placement Annual, Standard & Poor's Register of Corporations, or the Federal Career Directory—most of which can be found in the university library or placement center.

The goal of this research is to find out why and how the organization uses interns. In turn, this information tells the potential intern what approach to take in his or her application materials.

Some of the motives for sponsoring internships include:

- Public relations—the firm or organzation uses the college relationship as a means to create a positive community image.
- Cost containment—the firm or organization is under financial strain and needs to turn to less skilled labor to maintain profitability.
- Altruism—the firm or organization wants to help aspiring career-minded students get off to the right start in their careers.
- Future benefits—the firm or organization recognizes the advantages of attracting and training young professionals who may stay to eventually become managers and leaders.

Thus, the reasons for establishing internship programs vary widely. In some organizations, the public relations (PR) element of the program is most important: employers get considerable mileage out of giving the best and brightest minds a boost up the career ladder. Many publishing and legislative internships fall into this category. Other organizations, including many low-budget service and political groups, rely heavily on interns to perform semiskilled tasks. Still others use their internship programs to field potential new recruits. If the primary purpose of an organization can be determined, potential interns can pitch their own qualifications more precisely and effectively.

For example, a new business, a small bookkeeping service, in need of professionals in accounting and general management might take on interns with this kind of course training. The firm might assign these interns to general accounting functions under the supervision of a firm principal or key manager. The cost savings in maintaining a number of interns yearly is substantial, yet the firm is able to function effectively because the interns bring the needed basic accounting and general management skills. Those interns making a good impression during their internship may be offered part-time work while completing their degrees, and eventual full-time work upon graduation. In the meanwhile, the intern learns the firm's operational style and business.

A nonprofit community service organization in the Bronx, NY, uses Lehman College interns with majors in social work, health careers, nursing, and business administration on a regular basis. Social work students work with troubled youth, immigrants, and the elderly; health careers and nursing students with the infirm; and business administration students with aspiring entrepreneurs. The organization advertises its services to its community constituency through the students who reside within the community. In effect, the students are giving back to their own community through their internships and applying their learning in a practical manner.

Step two: Marketing the student

In the final analysis, obtaining an internship largely depends on the impression made by the candidate, either on paper with the application or in person in the interview. This is the chance to stand out by a polished presentation of skills, abilities, and character traits. Much of the time in our Lehman College seminar on internships is devoted to getting students ready for their internship interviews. This is time well spent as their initial job interviews after graduation also will require these skills. Learners need to discover and appreciate what "sells" in a job interview. And that "sale" begins with the résumé and cover letter—the first impression the learner makes.

The learners in the seminar review a large cross-section of résumés and cover letters amassed over time. These range from very well-prepared packages to hand-written (and poorly, at that!) samples. After reviewing these samples, they clearly can see the need for effective presentation. We inform them that it is estimated that the average employer spends about ten seconds looking at the average résumé. Therefore, an intern candidate does not have much time to make an impression. We then provide learners with access to wordprocessors and editors, who are volunteers from the secretarial studies program.

There are many career manuals that give a basic formula for putting together a résumé. (Two of the better sources are *Guerilla Tactics in the*

Job Market by Tom Jackson (Bantam Books, 1978) and *Who's Hiring Who* by Richard Lathrop (Ten Speed Press, 1977).) Learners must be sure to include name, address, phone number, work experience, schooling and honors, and any references most applicable to the job in question. If they have none, they should simply use the statement "references available on request." We stress that the résumé must be brief (no more than a page) and it must look good.

Job manuals also provide tips for handling the interview. Basic requirements are to know something about the organization, dress neatly and conservatively, anticipate what will be asked and prepare answers, and have some intelligent questions to ask the interviewer.

Step three: Follow through

In order to improve the chances of obtaining an internship it is important to follow up the résumé and interview. Learners must find a way to reinforce the impression they have made and remind employers how well they fit the organization's intern needs. A useful strategy is to send a letter to the employer immediately after the interview. In it learners should thank the interviewer for having taken the time to meet them. They can use this letter to outline once again their strengths which could fulfill the organization's needs. Some students also send a further note several weeks after the interview has taken place or the application has been submitted to remind the employer that they are still interested and available.

Chapter References

Armstrong, S., Bieber, J., & Heitner, J. (1985). *Contact and Marketing Strategies for Internship Development.* Newsletter, National Society for Internships and Experiential Education.

Barbeau, J.E. & Stull, W.A. (1981). *Program manager's guide for learning from working: A guide for cooperative education/internship students.* Cincinnati, OH: SouthWestern.

Boeder Edward, in Polking, K., & Cannon, C. (1981). *1981 Internships.* Cincinnati, OH: Writer's Digest Books.

Directory of internships, work experience programs and on-the-job training opportunities (First Ed.). (1985). Thousand Oaks, CA: Ready Reference Press.

Fry, R. (Ed). (1991). *Volume 5: Internships: Radio and television broadcasting and production.* Hawthorne, NJ: Career Press.

Lowe, W., in Polking, K., & Cannon, C. (1981). *1981 Internships.* Cincinnati, OH: Writer's Digest Books.

Polking, K., & Cannon, C. (1981). *1981 Internships.* Cincinnati, OH: Writer's Digest Books.

Chapter 7

The Apprenticeship

Apprenticeship is an industry-based basic or initial training process. By definition:

> Apprenticeship is characterized by a contractual employment relationship in which the firm or sponsor promises to make available a broad and structured practical and theoretical training of an established length and/or scope in a recognized occupational skill category. Apprenticeship is a work-study training scheme in which part of the training occurs on the job and part occurs off the job in a classroom or workshop setting.

Glover, 1986

American apprenticeship typically has involved industry, organized labor, and state and Federal governments, as well as community colleges. Apprenticeship training is usually initiated by the employer. However, the goals and objectives of apprenticeship from the business training perspective are consistent with the goals and objectives of community/technical colleges. For instance, the general goals of apprenticeship are to:

- develop and ensure a supply of trained, skilled, and knowledgeable workers and supervisors for the operations;
- increase worker productivity and overall skills levels and versatility;
- lessen the need for supervision of employees by developing initiative, pride of craftsmanship, and speed and accuracy in work; and
- continue to attract a constant flow of capable workers into the craft or trade.

Martin, 1981

Apprenticeship, when it is coordinated with college classroom program study, provides a strong incentive for learners to stay in college and do well. A learner who combines apprenticeship and post-secondary college attendance gets multiple benefits. This learner avoids "either/or" kinds of choices, and begins building both skilled worker status and college credit towards a college degree. These goals are consistent with and complementary to the institutional goals of the community college (presented in Chapter 1) to offer programs in technical, occupational, and career areas, complemented with general study courses. Furthermore, as the workplace becomes more complex and technological, apprenticeship program operators recognize the need to introduce more advanced education and training into human resource training and development. As one apprenticeship coordinator stated, "...a decade ago it was hard to find a machinist with a knowledge of numerical control machines (*sic*), or an electrician with a knowledge of microprocessor or fiber optics..." (Tuholski, 1982).

Apprenticeship programs, an exemplary form of experiential learning, are discussed in this chapter and later in Chapter 9. These two chapters consider the role of the community college in joining forces with a firm or industry to support apprenticeship training by conducting related courses or providing administrative support for college credit and/or actually developing and operating these programs. Methods of conducting related training and education, complementary general studies, student personnel and counseling services, and of offering credit for the hands-on portions of the apprenticeship program are also described.

A History and Overview of Apprenticeship

In the Past

Apprenticeship is not new: it is one of the oldest forms of training through which skills and knowledge associated with skilled occupations are passed from an experienced worker to a novice learner. Evidence of apprenticeship training has been found in ancient Egyptian tombs. The Babylonian Code of Hammurabi provided a written account of a system of apprenticeship existing in 2100 B.C.

During the 13th and 14th centuries, expert craftsmen, such as silversmiths, weavers, coach makers, and blacksmiths, formed trade groups called guilds to maintain the highest possible standards of quality and workmanship in their individual trades. One of the main duties of the historical guild master was to train apprentices to carry on the skills of the trades. A youth, usually at the age of 16, was assigned to a master craftsman whose trade was to be learned. This apprentice not only worked for and learned from the master, but actually lived in the same home as part of the family during the apprenticeship, which lasted several years.

In the employer's shop, the apprentice was taught the skills of the trade, spending hours working under the careful supervision of the master. Work was checked every step of the way for skill and accuracy. In addition to learning the "secrets of the trade," the apprentice also learned to be industrious, reliable, and proud of good work. Such a skilled and honest craftsman was assured a position of honor and prosperity in the community.

The Tradition Continues Today

Historically, the system of apprenticeship proved to be an effective method for the transmission and acquisition of skills. It has survived through the ages and is still widely used today. Government, at both the state and federal levels, recognizes the importance of apprenticeship for developing an adequate supply of skilled craftsmen necessary for future economic growth and national defense. There are currently 300,000 registered apprentices—a number which has been relatively constant over the last decade—preparing for 800 skilled occupations (and many more non-traditional occupations). As practiced by modern industry, apprenticeship is a businesslike system designed to provide workers entering industry with comprehensive training by exposing them to both practical skills and the related technical and general education required in highly skilled occupations. Such laws as the Fitzgerald and Perkins Acts encourage the expansion of apprenticeship programs and regulate their operations. As modern industry requires even greater knowledge and skill on the part of today's craftsmen, apprenticeship program sponsors must provide more systematically planned training than did the guildsmen of the past.

Apprenticeship is now a unique planned training system through which learners acquire state-of-the art "high tech" trade and craft skills and knowledge. It combines on-the-job instruction with classroom theory and practice in those subjects related to the occupation or craft. The related theoretical information required to perform the job is learned in classes held either after work or during a part of the day set aside for classroom work. For instance, in related instruction classes, machinist apprentices learn the mathematics they must know, the quick checks, and the practical methods necessary for speed and accuracy. Blueprint read-

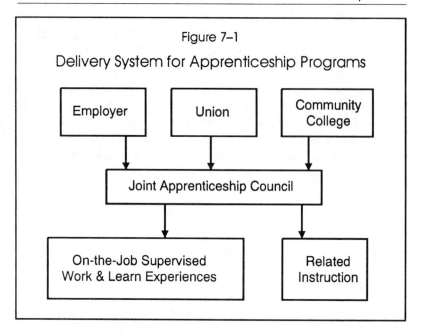

Figure 7–1

Delivery System for Apprenticeship Programs

ing, mechanical drawing, computer assisted design, safety, physics, and other sciences related to the work are studied. Apprentices also are exposed to aspects of the economic world, including industrial history, management practices, and labor relations. This training design provides for mastery of all of the practical and theoretical skills necessary for the chosen occupation.

During the apprenticeship, hands-on, practical aspects of the job are mastered as apprentices are rotated through all phases of the particular occupation, according to a written agreement which stipulates the period of apprenticeship and the objectives to be mastered (performance expectations). Related classroom instruction continues throughout the apprenticeship term and provides an opportunity to consider in depth the underlying principles of the job. Thus, apprentices have an opportunity to learn skills, perfect them over time, interrelate theory and skills, and learn to function within the work and organizational environment. Community colleges are appropriate institutions to provide this related instruction.

The typical combined arrangements are covered in the standard apprenticeship indenturing agreement drawn up between learners (apprentices) and employers—as well as state departments of labor, if an apprentice is formally registered. These arrangements ensure employability for learners and guarantee competent workers for the firm or industry.

Required duration of training ranges from one to six years, depending on the specific occupation. Since apprentices are full-time employees of the company in which they are apprenticed, the system includes a pay scale for them. Herein is one very significant benefit of apprenticeship as a form of cooperative education. Learners who cannot afford to be away from gainful employment while preparing for a new profession or career can "learn-and-earn" through cooperative apprenticeship. Usually the wage scale averages about half the journeyman rate in any particular trade or occupation. Wages increase progressively as the apprentices successfully master the training objectives and program segments.

Apprenticeship Program Design and Development

Once a decision has been made to initiate apprenticeship training, discussion between the firm or company and the education or training professions should begin. Apprenticeship programs are delivered in several ways.

Depending upon the company structure and size, and the state delivery system for apprenticeship, an apprenticeship program supported by a community college can be either:

- delivered in cooperation with a state joint apprenticeship council (JAC);
- delivered in cooperation with a labor union; or
- delivered internally within a firm or government agency.

However, all these configurations share some basic similarities. These follow in discussion (see Figure 7–1).

For which occupations or jobs is apprenticeship training appropriate?

The US Department of Labor lists approximately 700 occupations—trades or crafts—for which an apprenticeship training system exists (New York State Department of Labor, 1987). However, this does not preclude any particular industry or organization from adding to that list. Typically, such occupations as firefighter, automotive technician, X-ray technician, printer, police officer, and water treatment operator are included on the list. However, as new requirements emerge in an industry, new titles are added. For instance, in the fire and emergency services area, medical personnel are badly needed. The California Professional Firefighter Joint Apprenticeship Committee (CALJAC) has developed a program for emergency medical technicians, using apprenticeship as a training system (see Figure 7–2 below).

When is apprenticeship appropriate?

Apprenticeship is an appropriate method of training when a firm or industry wants to train new employees on the job to their specific standards and needs. When business and industry (or community college instructors or administrators) identify such a need they should explore the possibility of apprenticeship, given the following circumstances:

- A documented need exists in the community for workers with specific skills and knowledge in a defined occupation.
- Local firms need training support from the community college in the form of recruitment of trainees, classrooms, curriculum and course development, and, possibly, training funds.
- Learning objectives indicate that instruction should occur in both the classroom and the work environment or organization so as best to provide technical, organizational, and people skills.
- Learners need the opportunity to learn and earn.

The Organization of Apprenticeship Training

Faculty development

In a national apprenticeship program, employers provide the jobs—referred to as the learning stations or worksites. Journeymen are typically the on-the-job instructors. Therefore, community college faculty and administrators need to provide opportunities for those journeymen selected as instructors to develop instructional skills as adjunct faculty. States such as Wisconsin, California, and Maryland often provide funding for in-service faculty development for their instructors (Wisconsin, 1991). Certain professions also provide training assistance. For instance, in the firefighter profession, instructor development is recognized as essential. California has a series of instructor development courses which cover the basics of instructor training, leading to certification as a Firefighter Instructor. These courses also enable individuals to be certified as Community College Instructors—Fire Sciences in California (California, 1986). Opportunities for staff development can be funded through Perkins Vocational Education Amendments and other funding mechanisms, or through a state department of labor.

Apprenticeship committee structure

The Federal Committee on Apprenticeship (FCA) is one of the oldest permanent public advisory committees currently operating in the US Government. It was created by President Franklin D. Roosevelt in March of 1934, and continues under the National Apprenticeship Act of 1937 (29 USC 50). The committee is composed of 25 members, appointed by the Secretary of Labor. Ten represent employers, ten organized labor, and five, including the chair, are from the general public. The FCA advises the Secretary of Labor on apprenticeship and training policies, and labor standards affecting apprenticeship and research needs. It meets twice yearly, and the meetings are open to the public.

Twenty-nine states have state apprenticeship agencies or organizations. Many of these state organizations have staffs to assist employers and/or unions and educational organizations develop and administer apprenticeship training. These state organizations register apprentices for their programs and award a certificate upon successful completion of a program. The state apprenticeship office is also the channel for any funding available to help support the costs of apprentice training (Growbowski, 1989).

A local apprenticeship program is governed by a joint apprenticeship advisory committee, comprised much like the national or state joint apprenticeship council (JAC). The JAC includes representatives of business and industry, the union, if any, apprentices, and educational agencies, if involved in program delivery. The JAC often is involved in actual program operations or will appoint a standing committee for training. Either the JAC or the local committee will oversee recruitment, program operation, apprentice evaluation, funding, and outside vendors, such as the community college. As all decisions relating to curriculum, funding, staffing, and apprentice personnel matters are made by this committee, the community college should be sure to have representatives sit on it.

Apprenticeship program standards

If one were to identify the single most beneficial aspect of an apprenticeship training system, undoubtedly it would be its

Figure 7–2

The California Professional Firefighter Apprenticeship Program

California community colleges and the fire service enjoy a long-standing relationship which benefits the communities they serve. A firefighter's performance affects everyone's lives and property. California fire departments provide training through cooperatively sponsored apprenticeship with community colleges.

Fire service apprenticeship dates back to 1975 when the *National Apprenticeship and Training Standards for the Firefighter* was developed and adopted by the International Association of Fire Chiefs and the International Association of Firefighters, and subsequently certified by the U.S. Department of Labor's Bureau of Apprenticeship and Training.

The California Firefighter Joint Apprenticeship Committee (CALJAC) is a non-profit organization whose goal is to: (1) provide training support for California's firefighters, and (2) provide an avenue of entrée into the fire service for qualified, under-represented and targeted workforce populations.

Apprenticeship Ensures Quality Recruitment

To participate in CALJAC, each fire department must make apprenticeship training available to all trainees. To be recognized as a bona fide CALJAC apprenticeship program a fire department must describe in writing:

* how apprentices will be recruited and selected;
* what training the apprentice will receive;
* the length of the training period; and
* the wages to be paid the apprentice.

Responsibilities for the program are shared by the California State Fire Marshall (CFM) (representing management) and the California Professional Firefighters (representing labor).

CALJAC specifies standards to control and ensure training program quality. CALJAC apprenticeship programs encompass 17 different fire service occupations. As a three-year apprenticeship, the requirement for Firefighter I Certification is a total of 1000 hours. Other CALJAC job titles include Firefighter Medic, Fire Engineer, Fire Marshall and Fire Department Training Officer. To participate, each program must also provide all related and supplemental instruction; provide classrooms, instructors, drill grounds, A-V equipment, books and supplies; and assign an instructor of record who holds a designated California subjects teaching credential and who oversees the program's operation.

CALJAC also provides testing administration support services to each fire agency upon request. Upon completion of an apprenticeship program a transcript is produced for a trainee, listing hours and a grade for completion which can be presented to a local community college for credit consideration.

A typical fire service program receives CALJAC funding for approximately 10% of the total cost to support basic recruit training. Each participating fire department in California is eligible for reimbursement for apprentice training when its program is recognized as a CALJAC-approved apprenticeship training program. Apprenticeship enables fire departments to share training resources. It offsets training costs to the fire department without changes in staffing, resource allocations, or company manning. In fact, recruits go on-line earlier and learn departmental-specific techniques and procedures.

Some of the premier fire department programs operating are:

- *The Modesto City Fire Department* (MCFD) has a contractual relationship with Modesto Junior College (MJC) for its basic training academy. MCFD has apprentices registered with CALJAC and attending the community college fire academy. College credit is a plus for the MCFD trainee as an Associate degree is requisite to advancement in rank.

- *The Santa Ana Fire Department* (SAFD) uses apprenticeship for both reserve and firefighter basic training. SAFD uses the CALJAC program for firefighter journey-level training. Santa Ana Fire Department encourages a firefighter to attend Rancho Santiago College and earn a degree. Fire Dispatcher and Fire Prevention Officer are other job titles which are CALJAC-participating by SAFD.

- *Sacramento Fire Department* (SFD) operates training programs through a consortia agreement involving several fire departments and the Sacramento County Community College District. An advisory committee consisting of members of each of these parties meets monthly and governs the program's operation. The regional fire academy is staffed by the advisory board with fire department personnel assigned to various courses. Three community colleges participate in this consortium. The basic academy is paid for by the sponsoring agency; advanced work is paid for by the firefighter, although the community college provides financial aid and assistance as necessary.

Some of the participating California community college programs include:

- *Modesto Junior College* offers an Associate in Science degree in Fire Science. The fire service community served includes 23 agencies within the county, and 30 additional agencies in surrounding areas. MJC awards college credit for completion of fire academy basic training, which can represent up to one-quarter of the college degree. An advisory committee consisting of seven area fire department chiefs and training officers guides the MJC fire service program. All adjunct instructors in the program are fire service personnel.

- *Rancho Santiago College* serves as the fire service training center for sixteen Orange County, California, fire departments, including the Santa Ana Fire Department under the direction of the Orange County Fire Chiefs Association and the Orange County Firemen's Association. These departments have designated the college as the delivery system for the various fire protection instructional programs. Rancho Santiago College's fire curriculum was developed and is monitored by subject-matter experts representing the fire departments in the consortia. Adjunct instructors are drawn from the various fire departments. Fire service personnel who are certified as fire service instructors serve as adjunct faculty.

Part of the recruitment process in a fire department is the administration of various admissions and screening tests which are used for placement and counseling. The National Fire Protection Association (NFPA) Standard 1001 Physical Agility Tests are also administered. The college provides this as a service to the fire department as part of the cooperative relationship—a very desirable benefit to the fire department! Additionally, reserve firefighters are assigned to fire stations and companies for practical skills training as part of a mini-academy or pre-apprenticeship program.

establishment and maintenance of program standards. Each apprentice-ship program sets basic standards to make sure that the program provides uniform and effective training to develop the skills required of qualified workers. To be registered by a recognized state apprenticeship committee or council, or by the US Bureau of Apprenticeship and Training, a program must identify the standards that will be maintained in training. While these differ from trade to trade or occupation, each set of standards will deal with at least the following issues (New York State, 1987).

Specific tasks to be taught

The standards must outline the work processes (specific tasks) that the apprentice will be trained to perform through supervised on-the-job training and work experiences. The standards should also specify how much time will be spent in each major section or division of the trade. A community college instructor/program administrator can be invaluable in assisting a firm or industry to identify, through occupational and task analysis, these specific tasks. In doing so, the community college will be taking on and demonstrating one appropriate role it can play in the overall training. In addition, the community college can identify those parts of the program for which it can deliver instruction, and/or award credit towards a degree or certificate to the apprentice as a college student. (*Note:* See Figure 8–3 in the next chapter for an example of how these processes are stipulated in a written agreement.)

For example, Tidewater Community College and Thomas Nelson Community College in Virginia had a role in developing the Shipbuilding Trades Apprenticeship programs for the US Navy. The colleges worked with Navy instructional developers to plan the specific on-the-job train-ing and related trades theory classes which should comprise the pro-grams. Together the employer and college then delivered the programs.

Related instruction

The apprenticeship standards should also lay the basis for organized instruction in technical subjects related to the apprentice's trade. This instruction may include supervised correspondence or self-study courses as approved by applicable law or by policy of the state agency. At least 144 hours of instruction for each year of apprenticeship is recommended. The community college can provide this related instruction in different ways, for example, through the continuing education (non-credit) divi-sion in the form of customized non-credit classes or by offering actual credit courses toward college degrees, as negotiated by the firm, union, and college. The cost of such training and education will determine much of the decision making in this area. (Chapter 9 will discuss dual enroll-ments of apprentices towards college degrees.) The Port Authority of New York and New Jersey cooperates with vocational/technical institutes to provide such training; the International Union of Operating Engineers (IUOE) (Figure 7–3 below) collaborates with community colleges for both credit and non-credit course offerings. At some community colleges (e.g., Trident Technical College in South Carolina; Catonsville Commu-nity College, Maryland), full-time coordinators and off-site training centers provide related education and training and student personnel support. More about this in Chapter 9.

Program evaluation

As more and more community colleges begin to underwrite and guarantee the competence of their learners upon exiting from training, program evaluation standards assume greater importance. Included in these standards is the framework for how the program will be reviewed periodically and how the apprentice will be monitored and evaluated in both job performance and related instruction. Many apprenticeship pro-grams designate evaluation as one of the functions of the local JAC.

Standards must also specify how apprentice records and progress reports will be kept. A major task for community college program administrators is guaranteeing the confidentiality of records. The US Privacy of Information Act prohibits releasing information relating to apprentice progress to anyone inside or outside the educational institu-tion. Therefore, if the college is a training agency for an apprentice program, a release-of-information form must be devised and adminis-tered so that course grades and related information can be given to the JAC and/or firm as needed. College grades may not have to be included on this form if the courses in question are outside the scope of the apprentice program. Finally, a process for credentialing the training process and the individual's training accomplishments must be instituted. For example, the fire service uses competency-based examinations for this purpose.

Number of apprentices to be employed

Standards should specify what ratio of apprentices to journeymen is consistent with proper supervision of training and continuity of employ-ment. For instance, the US Navy's Apprenticeship Program, supporting the civilian technical trades workforces across the Navy, specifies that the apprentice workforce should equal ten percent of the total civilian workforce. This figure has remained constant for a long time and has

Figure 7–3

The International Union of Operating Engineers Apprenticeship Program

Community college apprentice dual-enrollment is not new to union-sponsored training. A concern of organized labor is to identify a more effective and appropriate means for attracting, training, and educating a 21st century workforce. Organized labor's interest in dual-enrollment processes for apprentice training in cooperation with community colleges dates back to the mid-1970s, with IUOE-developed programs. Apprenticeship traditionally involves partnerships of contractor-employers and unions, and sometimes the government.

The International Union of Operating Engineers (IUOE), representing heavy equipment operating engineers in the construction industries, supports Associate degree-earning apprenticeship programs across the nation. IUOE initiated dual-enrollment apprenticeship training in twenty states beginning in the late 1970s. By 1975, 53 programs in 20 states, based on an IUOE master curriculum plan, were operating nationally.

Each local has an apprenticeship coordinator who interfaces with a Joint Apprenticeship Training Committee (JATC).

IUOE leadership believes that a parallel exists between the technical knowledge and educational discipline required of an indentured apprentice in the operating engineer trades, and the knowledge required of an undergraduate student in the first two years of study. Like most high technology industries, rapid technological changes in equipment and building processes necessitate better trained personnel in the operating engineer trades. IUOE views these programs as a means to help operating engineers keep up with the rapid changes taking place in the trades by working cooperatively with management and public education. They also view the college degree as a means to produce better trained management personnel in the future.

IUOE's programs were designed and developed to be implemented regionally and locally through community/technical colleges. The operating engineer trades differ depending on a locality's construction procedures. Each local was encouraged to establish a dialogue with its community/technical college for dual-enrollment opportunities. A national model curriculum was drafted to serve as a baseline. A national program director provides direction and advice.

Contractor's payroll tax-levy for apprenticeship training varies from IUOE local to local.

IUOE college programs vary in the way in which they award credit for OJT. Catonsville Community College programs have an agreement for credits towards the degree program. The college has a full-time college apprentice program coordinator to interface with all unions in program delivery. Catonsville services IUOE union programs in an off-site faculty dedicated to these kinds of programs. Central Arizona College also has this kind of process for awarding 15 college credits. In each state a coordinating body oversees the programs, and discusses common problems and potential solutions. The IUOE locals use national standards to develop and implement their programs. Each local has curriculum autonomy.

worked successfully to maintain a constant supply of well-trained workers in all jobs for which apprenticeship is the training system (see Figure 7–4 below).

The initial steps to follow in determining the suitable ratio are: 1) define the present supply of skilled workers; 2) project the numbers of workers needed for the future; and 3) project the numbers which will be trained under the present program.

Equal opportunity in apprenticeship

Apprenticeship programs bring non-traditional workers into the workplace. As the national population becomes more culturally and ethnically diverse, mechanisms to ensure that this diversity is reflected in the workplace become necessary. The apprenticeship system can be such a mechanism. Standards should affirm that the program will provide equal opportunity in recruitment, selection, and all phases of employment and training in compliance with Title 29, Code of Federal Regulations, Part 30, as amended; and with state equal employment opportunity plans filed and approved pursuant to these regulations. All programs must be conducted and operated in a nondiscriminatory manner in all aspects of apprenticeship, without regard to race, religion, color, sex, handicap, or national origin.

Term of apprenticeship

Standards should set a term of apprenticeship that is adequate to meet training requirements as established by industry practice. Figure 7–5 below lists typical firefighter apprenticeable occupations and their training times for all aspects of the apprenticeship.

Probationary period

Standards should establish a probationary period that is reasonable in relation to the total term of apprenticeship. Apprentices should receive full credit toward completion of their apprenticeship for time served during this period. The college can make use of this period by offering additional training in areas related to the apprentice's specific occupation and current work assignments.

Safety and health training

Standards should state how the program will provide safety training in a healthful workplace for apprentices, both on the job and in related instruction.

Figure 7–4

The United States Navy Apprenticeship Programs

As a form of structured training, the U.S. Navy apprenticeship dates back to colonial days. U.S. Navy apprenticeship training is perhaps the oldest continually operating program in the United States. The Navy's first "apprentice boy" was hired in the Washington Navy Yard in 1810. The first formal U.S. Navy apprentice school opened at Mare Island Navy Yard in 1858, under the administration of David Farragut. Yet, it remains one of the most vital forms of training for today's civilian defense worker, especially in high-technology areas. Today all eight Naval shipyards (Portsmouth, NH, Philadelphia, PA, Norfolk, VA, Charleston, SC, Long Beach, CA, Mare Island, CA, Puget Sound, WA, and Pearl Harbor, HI) operate some form of apprentice training. Other Navy activities also use apprenticeship.

Each operates an apprenticeship training program for their new technical workers. These programs provide training in approximately 43 different trades, depending on the shipyard's needs. In total there are about 2500 apprentices across the eight yards, representing approximately 10% of the total worker population — a goal that the U.S. Navy strives to maintain in order to ensure a continual supply of trained manpower. Apprentice-trained journeymen comprise a majority of each of the shipyard workforces. The apprenticeship programs are important to these shipyards not only as a source of skilled workmen, but also because apprentice-trained journeymen provide the pool from which supervisors and managers are drawn. [Some 87% of the naval shipyard superintendents (heads of the major shop and trade groups) are former apprentices. This system of internal advancement provides shipyards with dedicated upper-level management skilled in the "nuts and bolts" of ship construction and repair.]

Despite recent modernization and automation in the shipbuilding industry, effective and safe ship repairs remain dependent upon the knowledge and abilities of large numbers of highly skilled craftspeople. There are no assembly lines in ship repair. Craftspeople work independently at non-repetitive tasks and must apply analytical abilities and initiative, as well as judgment, to accomplish their work.

The apprenticeship training in all trades is designed in a 4-year program. Each of the shipyards is unique in its organizational configuration, the availability of geographically local educational services, worker population characteristics, and potential pools of labor. Apprenticeship training program design is modified locally in order to ensure that each program meets the local shipyard's needs and requirements. Each of the yards' personnel department apprentice training coordinators matches their apprentice-related training requirements to the local community college program offerings. Hands-on training and related classroom instruction takes place in the shipyard. College instructors will work, on-site, in the yard. Some of the programs do use college facilities for portions of the shop instruction or for additional classroom space. Encouragement is given to the apprentice to complete an Associate degree in conjuction with the apprentice training. The Navy firmly believes that naval shipyard (NSY) trades workers should earn a college degree. Each of the NSYs has worked with their local college to make this as feasible as possible.

Most of the NSYs now "front-load" their regular apprentice programs, whereby the community college provides the apprentice with the required related trade and general education and training during the first year of the apprenticeship.

The NSY and other Navy programs constitute a large population of students for Trident Technical College in Charleston—half of all cooperative education students are Navy workers at Trident.

Trident awards credit for the apprenticeship. An Associate in Technology degree is offered to apprentices. Trident participates actively with the NSY employer, and has a full-time coordinator and a Shipyard Advisory Committee which provides guidance to the program. The program was initially developed under a Federal Title VIII Cooperative Education grant.

Community college assistance in recruiting students for cooperative apprenticeships in the NSYs is readily provided by all colleges operating cooperative programs. Trident Tech and Tidewater Community College report excellent results in such efforts. Most of the colleges also provide remedial and basic academic skills learning opportunities at the NSY for apprentices.

Most apprenticeship training costs are borne by the government. Award of college credit for apprenticeship training, and/or the related trades theory classroom work offered by the college varies from NSY to NSY; and the college costs also varies among the states in which the NSY and college are located. All of the colleges report counseling students about PELL, GSL, and other sources of funds for any portion of the training program that they must personally pay.

Other Federal Apprenticeship Programs

U.S. Navy-NAVAIR rework facilities operates a 4-year apprenticeship program in several trades in cooperation with Tidewater Community College. Students accepted into the cooperative program complete the first year as a full-time engineering student at the college. Summer is spent at a Navy facility working as an apprentice. The student is evaluated during the first year. Upon satisfactory completion of the first year of the program, and acceptance into the yard, the student becomes an apprentice and works under the supervision of a master technician for three more years. College work then continues on a part-time basis.

Curtis Bay Coast Guard facility sponsors a 4-year apprenticeship program. Anne Arundel Community College provides on-site related instruction to accompany this program. Some of the related instruction can be applied towards college credit.

Figure 7–5

CALJAC Apprenticeable Occupations

Occupation	Academy Hours	Related & Supplemental Hours	Total Hours	Total Dollars Per Apprentice
Firefighter	400	200 × 3 yrs = 600	1000	$2,750.00
Firefighter—Medic	480	200 × 3.5 yrs = 700	1180	3,245.00
Firefighter—Diver	480	200 × 3.5 yrs = 700	1180	3,245.00
Fire Supp. Tech	400	200 × 2 yrs = 400	800	2,200.00
Wildland Firefighter Spec.	100	200 × 1 yr = 200	300	825.00
Emerg. Medical Technician	113	200 × 1 yr = 200	313	860.75
Paramedic	812	200 × 2 yrs = 400	1212	3,333.00
Fire Engineer	160	200 × 1 yr = 200	360	990.00
Fire Apparatus Engineer	400	200 × 3 yrs = 600	1000	2,750.00
Fire Officer	320	200 × 3 yrs = 600	920	2,530.00
Fire Equip Spec.	300	200 × 4 yrs = 800	1100	3,025.00
Fire Inspector	240	200 × 2 yrs = 400	640	1,760.00
Fire Prev. Offcr	280	200 × 2 yrs = 400	680	1,870.00
Fire Marshall	280	200 × 2 yrs = 400	680	1,870.00
Hazardous Materials Tech.	320	288 × 2 yrs = 576	896	2,464.00
Training Officer	280	200 × 2 yrs = 400	680	1,870.00
Arson & Bomb Investigator	280	200 × 2 yrs = 400	680	1,870.00

Courtesy California Firefighter Joint Apprenticeship Committee, CALJAC, 1991.

Operating an Apprenticeship Program

Community colleges cooperate with employers to conduct apprenticeship training. For example, Northcentral Technical College in Wisconsin publishes this description of apprenticeship training opportunities in its catalog.

> An apprenticeship is a training program that combines paid on-the-job experience with classroom instruction. Apprenticeships are offered in four occupational areas: construction, industrial, service, and graphic arts. You must be 16 years or older and have a high school diploma or its equivalent before you can be accepted into most apprenticeship programs. You must also be physically fit and have aptitude for the trade or industry that you plan to enter.

1990–1992 Catalog; p. 73

In the Wisconsin Technical College System, the participating college works with employers to recruit apprentices (see Figure 7–6 below). The apprentice then signs an apprenticeship indenture (Figure 7–7 below). This is a written agreement between the learner-apprentice, employer, and state (e.g., state of Wisconsin, Division of Apprenticeship). The agreement states that the apprentice will work for the employer for a specified period of time and that the employer will pay a specified wage and provide the apprentice with specified skills and competencies.

The apprenticeship period usually lasts for four (4) years, but some are shorter (e.g., firefighter, 3 years; barber, 2 years). During this period the apprentice earns between 40 to 60 percent of a journeyman's wage for the occupation, increasing from base to maximum in 5 percent increments every six months.

The agreement specifies the on-the-job and related instruction to be received. The employer/supervisor provides the hands-on training, which is coordinated by a college-based supervisor of apprenticeships. Some colleges provide college credit for this on-the-job training. The college reviews the employer's apprenticeship training in order to determine what portions of the training can be accepted for college credit. The related trades training is provided by the college in the evening. At Northcentral Technical College, an apprentice attends classes on campus one or more times per week. Many colleges employ trades journeymen as adjunct instructors for the related trades classes.

Figure 7–6

Northcentral Technical College Apprenticeship Programs

Northcentral Technical College (NTC) in Wisconsin provides apprenticeship programs and program support for 14 different trade programs, ranging from Barber/Stylist to Machinist. The college acts as a representative for the Wisconsin Bureau of Apprenticeship Standards. NTC operates an Apprenticeship Office directed by the Associate Dean. The office provides a central place for information and coordination of apprenticeship programs.

Trainees desiring apprenticeship training may visit NTC's Apprentice Office to receive general information about the apprenticeship training process. The trainee is then referred to a list of potential employers who will consider sponsoring an apprentice. Alternatively, trainees may secure employer sponsorship first and then proceed to the college for formal registration. Once an apprentice and employer are matched, NTC provides the formal Indenturing Agreement for all parties to sign. This agreement establishes the framework for training. A Joint Apprenticeship Advisory Committee receives an apprentice's application and reviews it for acceptance into a program. The JAC monitors an apprentice's progress over the duration of the program.

NTC provides formal related courses for all of the programs. These classes are on-campus, and often in the evening. Journeyman craftspeople work as adjunct instructors for the courses.

A typical statement of the apprenticeship term might be:

The bricklayer apprenticeship program is three years in length. Four hundred hours of related instruction is required. This is based on a four-hour-per-week or the equivalent, and is paid for by the employer. The apprentice will attend evening school and take such courses as the committee requires. A total of one hundred ten hours of evening school are required. This will be on the apprentice's own time and at his own expense. Some of the courses required are as follows: First Aid and Personal Safety, Beginning Stick Electrode Arc Welding, OSHA (US Occupational Safety and Health Act), Builders Level Transit (Wisconsin Bricklayer).

At some colleges, such as American River College, in California, the related instruction is listed in the college catalog with equated college credit. For example, American River College provides the following:

American River College offers a number of apprenticeship-related training programs. Given below are the courses required for receiving the Certificate of Achievement in each of these programs. Completion of graduate requirements, in addition to the Certificate of Achievement requirements, will qualify you for an A.A. degree.

See Figure 7–8 for a typical course program at American River College.

Figure 7–7

A Sample Apprenticeship Indenture Agreement

Not Valid
Unless Approved
by DILHR

WISCONSIN DEPARTMENT OF
INDUSTRY, LABOR AND HUMAN RELATIONS
JOBS, EMPLOYMENT AND TRAINING SERVICES DIVISION
Bureau of Apprenticeship Standards
Box 7972 Madison, Wisconsin 53707

Ed _____
Appr Dist _____
Trade Code _____
Committee _____
School Dist _____

APPRENTICE INDENTURE

Emp No _____
Dist Rep _____
FEIN _____

This Indenture prepared by _____ Date_____

THIS INDENTURE, Made in quadruplicate between _____
                                                        (Name of Employer)

hereafter called the first party, and _____
hereafter called the second party,   (Name of Apprentice)

WITNESSETH, That the first party agrees to employ the second party as an apprentice
_____ upon the terms and conditions in this indenture.
          (Trade or Craft)

That the apprenticeship term begins on this date _____
                                                              (Month, Day, Year)

and terminates upon the completion by the apprentice of _____

_____
                    (Term of Apprenticeship)
of employment for said employer in said trade, craft or business.

That the said apprentice agrees to diligently and faithfully fulfill all the obligations of this apprenticeship.

Social Security No._____

Date of Birth_____

_____   _____
(Apprentice Legal Name - Print or Type)   (Firm or Corporation Name)

_____   _____
           (Street Address)   (Street Address)

_____   _____
(City)   (Zip Code)   (City)   (Zip Code)

The provisions binding on the parties hereto are contained in exhibit "A" which said exhibit is made a part hereof.
The Department of Industry, Labor and Human Relations may annul this indenture upon application of either party after a satisfactory showing of good cause.
The Department of Industry, Labor and Human Relations shall issue a certificate of apprenticeship to the apprentice who has satisfactorily completed the terms of this indenture.
The apprentice's signature authorizes the school to release progress, grades and attendance reports to the Department and the signatory to this agreement while the agreement is active.

IN WITNESS WHEREOF, The parties have caused this indenture to be signed as required by Chapter 106.01 of the laws of Wisconsin.

X_____   ✓_____
      (Apprentice Signature)   (Official Signature)

_____   _____
(Parent or Guardian Signature, if apprentice is a Minor)   (Official Name and Title – Print or Type)

JETA-4224 (R.05/92)

Figure 7-7 (contd.)

PAGE 2

The Text of the Law (Chapter 106) Under Which Apprentices Shall be Indentured

The Wisconsin Department of Industry, Labor and Human Relations hereafter called the Department

APPRENTICE DEFINED

Section 106.01. 1. The term "apprentice" shall mean any person, 16 years of age or over, who shall enter into any contract of service, expressed or implied, whereby he/she is to receive from or through the employer, in consideration for his/her services, in whole or in part, instruction in any trade, craft or business.

INDENTURE DEFINED

2. Every contract or agreement entered into by an apprentice with his/her employer shall be known as an indenture; such indenture shall be in writing and shall be executed in triplicate, one copy of which shall be delivered to the apprentice, one to be retained by the employer, and one to be filed with the Department of Wisconsin, at Madison.

WHO MAY BE INDENTURED

3. Any minor, 16 years of age or over, or any adult, may, by the execution of an indenture, bind him/herself as hereinafter provided, for a term of service not less than one year.

WHO MUST SIGN INDENTURE

4. Every indenture shall be signed:

(a) By the apprentice.

(b) If the apprentice has not reached age 18, also by the father or mother; and if both the father and mother are dead or legally incapable of giving consent, then

(c) by the guardian of the minor, if any.

(d) If there is not parent or guardian with authority to sign then by a deputy of the Department of Industry, Labor and Human Relations.

(e) By the employer.

CONTENTS OF INDENTURE

5. Every indenture shall contain:

(a) The names of the parties.

(b) The date of the birth of the person indentured.

(c) A statement of the trade, craft or business which the apprentice is to be taught, and the time at which the apprenticeship shall begin and end.

(d) An agreement stating the number of hours to be spent in work, and the number of hours to be spent in instruction. During the first two years of the apprenticeship, the period of instruction shall be not less than four hours per week or the equivalent. If the apprenticeship is for a longer period than two years, the total hours of instruction shall be not less than four hundred hours. The total number of hours of instruction and service shall not exceed fifty-five per week; provided that nothing in this paragraph shall be construed to forbid overtime work as provided in subsection 7. of this section.

(e) An agreement as to the processes, methods or plans to be taught, and the approximate time to be spent at each process, method or plan.

(f) A statement of the compensation to be paid the apprentice.

(g) An agreement that a certificate shall be given the apprentice at the conclusion of the indenture, stating the terms of indenture.

APPRENTICE MAY BE INDENTURED TO ASSOCIATIONS OF EMPLOYERS OR EMPLOYES

(5i) (a) The proper persons described in paragraphs (a), (b), (c), (d) and (e) of subsection 4, of this section may enter into such an indenture with any organization of employes, association of employers or other similar responsible agency in this state. Such organization, association or other agency shall thereupon, with the written consent of the other parties to the indenture, and the written acceptance thereof by the proposed employer, assign the indenture to the employer, the employer and the apprentice named in the indenture shall be bound by the terms thereof. Such consent and acceptance shall be executed in triplicate and one copy of each shall be delivered, respectively to the Department, to the employer and to the apprentice and in each case shall be attached to the proper indenture. The approval of the Department shall first be had in each transaction. Such organization, association, or other agency shall have the exclusive right to assign the indenture, and the apprentice shall not be permitted to enter into any

other indenture. The period transpiring before assignment to any employer shall not be credited toward the period of apprenticeship.

TRANSFER OF APPRENTICE FROM PRIVATE EMPLOYER TO ASSOCIATION OR VICE VERSA

(b) Any employer may assign the indenture, with the approval of the Department, and the written consent of the other parties thereto, to any association of employers, organization of employes or any other similar responsible agency in this state. The period of time in which such association, organization, or other agency shall be such assignee, shall not be credited as time served by the apprentice. After such assignment, the association, organization, or other agency shall, with the approval of the Department, and the written consent of the apprentice, assign the indenture to an employer, but the apprentice shall not be bound by the assignment, unless the employer accepts, by the signed instruments, the terms of the indenture and that he/she will complete the employer's unperformed obligations thereunder; each such consent, and acceptance, shall be executed in triplicate, and one of each, respectively, shall be delivered to the Department, to the assignee employer, and to the apprentice, and in each case, shall be attached to the proper indenture. Upon acceptance, the employer shall, for all purposes, be deemed a party to the indenture.

TRANSFER OF APPRENTICE FROM ONE EMPLOYER TO ANOTHER

(c) Any employer, with the written consent, executed in triplicate of the other parties to the indenture and the approval of the Department may assign such indenture to another employer whose written acceptance shall be upon the instrument of consent. One copy of such consent and acceptance shall be delivered, respectively, to the apprentice, to the assignee employer, and to the Department, and shall, in each case, be attached to the indenture in their respective possessions. After assignment, the new employer shall perform the unperformed obligations of the indenture. The Department shall continue to have jurisdiction over the indenture assigned, pursuant to the provisions of this subsection, and the parties bound after such assignment.

AUTHORITY OF DEPARTMENT TO CANCEL INDENTURE ON ITS OWN MOTION

(5j) The Department may, and it shall have power on its own motion, or on the complaint of any person, after due notice and a hearing had, make findings and issue orders declaring any indenture contract or agreement, at an end, if it shall be proved at such hearing that any apprentice, employer or such organization, associations, or other agency is unable to continue with the obligations under the contract or has breached the same. Upon the termination of the indenture, the apprentice released therefrom shall be free to enter into a new indenture under such conditions and terms as the Department may approve, and which are not inconsistent with the provisions of this section.

(5k) The Department shall, upon request, furnish a copy of any instrument required to be filed with it under the provisions of this section, to any party whose name appears on such instrument.

PROVISION FOR SCHOOLING

(6) The employer shall pay for the time the apprentice is receiving related instruction for no fewer hours than specified in sub. 5 (d) at the same rate per hours as for services. Nothing herein shall prohibit a agreement between the parties requiring the apprentice to take additional instruction on their own time in excess of the number of hours required by statutes. Attendance at school shall be certified by the teacher in charge.

OVERTIME

7. An apprentice may be allowed to work overtime. All time in excess of the hours of labor as limited to the particular craft, industry or business and as to the particular employer, shall be considered overtime. For overtime the apprentice's rate of pay shall be increased by the same percentage as the journeyman's rate for overtime is increased in the same industry of establishment.

(Text of law continued on page 3)

Figure 7–7 (contd.)

PAGE 3
EXHIBIT A

NOTICE: No apprentice indenture will be legal which does not have this exhibit filled out as indicated below. (Chapter 106, Wisconsin Statutes)

EXTENT OF PERIOD OF APPRENTICESHIP — (Here must be stated the length of time to be served, wherever the trade can determine, the exact length of each apprenticeship year.)

See attached (Exhibit "A")

SCHOOL ATTENDANCE — (Here specify the number of hours of school attendance required to complete the contract.)

See attached (Exhibit "A")

SCHEDULE OF PROCESSES TO BE WORKED — (Here must be stated the processes, methods or plans to be taught and the approximate time to be spent at each process, method, or plan — to conform to the character of the individual trade. If additional space is needed, use additional sheet.)

See attached (Exhibit "A")

COMPENSATION TO BE PAID — The apprentice shall receive in wages:

See attached (Exhibit "A")

SPECIAL PROVISIONS — These to be stated here.

See attached (Exhibit "A")

(Continued from page 2)

PENALTY FOR VIOLATION OF CONTRACT

8. If either party to an indenture shall fail to perform any of the stipulations thereof, they shall forfeit not less than one dollar or more than one hundred dollars, such forfeiture to be collected on complaint of the Department of Wisconsin, and paid into the state treasury. Any indenture may be annulled by the Department of Wisconsin upon application of either party and good cause shown.

9. It shall be the duty of the Department, and it shall have power, jurisdiction and authority, to investigate, ascertain, determine and fix such reasonable classifications and to issue rules and regulations, and general or special orders and to hold hearings and make findings, and render orders thereon as shall be necessary to carry out the intent and purposes of section 106.01.1. Such hearings, investigations, classifications, findings and orders shall be made pursuant to the proceeding in sections 101.01 to 101.28, which are hereby made a part hereof,

so far as not inconsistent with the provisions of section 106.01; an every order of the said Department shall have the same force and effec as the orders issued pursuant to said sections 101.01 to 101.28, and th penalties therein shall apply to and be imposed for any violations c section 106.01, excepting as to the penal ties provided in sectio 106.01 (8). Said orders shall be subject to review in the mann provided in Chapter 227.*

DETERMINATION OF INSTRUCTION

10. It shall be the duty of all school officers and public scho teachers to cooperate with the Department of Wisconsin and employ ers of apprentice to furnish, in a public school or any school supporte in whole or in part by public monies, such instruction as may b required to be given apprentices.

* Department Law.

APPRENTICESHIP RULES

Ind 95.001 Definitions. In this Chapter.

(1) "Apprentice" has the meaning specified in s. 106.01, Stats.

(2) "Department" means the department of industry, labor and human relations.

(3) "Division" means the division of employment and training policy, bureau of apprenticeship standards, of the department.

(4) "Indenture" has the meaning specified in s. 106.01, Stats.

Ind 95.01 Standards. (1) The Department may adopt statewide or area apprenticeship standards covering minimum training requirements, procedure in processing indentures, qualification of applicant employe and apprentices, functions of joint apprenticeship committees, and such other matters as constitute an apprenticeship program in a particular trac

(2) The Department may recognize but will not be a party to agreements as to apprenticeship standards or similar understandings when su standards in their entirety are part of a bargaining agreement between the management and its employes.

(3) In trades for which no uniform apprenticeship courses or schedules of training have been adopted by the Department, the employer m execute a special agreement with the apprentice, subject to the approval of the Department.

Ind 95.02 Area Joint Committees. (1) The function of joint apprenticeship committees is to act in an advisory capacity to the Department a to be parties to indentures as provided in s. 106.01 (5i) (a), Stats. Equal employer-employe representation is a requirement. Candidates f membership are nominated by the organizations which the members are to represent. To be recognized as a joint apprenticeship committee, ea individual member shall be officially so designated by the Department. The geographical jurisdictional area of each such joint apprenticesh committee shall be determined by the Department.

(2) This rule does not apply to shop or plant sponsored apprenticeship programs or to joint apprenticeship committees created under the ter of a bargaining agreement between the management and its employes.

Ind 95.03 Application forms. Where the Department requires application forms to be filled out by applicant employers and apprentices, the for shall be approved by the Department.

Ind 95.04 Apprentice Wages. (1) An apprentice indenture wage scale is deemed adequate when, during the term of training, it averages 60 of the current journeyman rate. The indenture should provide for a graduated scale progressing in periods as approved by the Department.

(2) In determining the journeyman or skilled wage rate, the following formula governs: In trades in which it is common practice to barga collectively on a community-wide or area-wide basis, the journeyman wage is that rate received by a greater number of journeymen in the sar trade and community than any other rate. The Department will not normally approve a skilled rate for apprenticeship purposes more than 20% belc the journeyman rate in the area. In controversial cases, growing out of the fact that the committee's jurisdictional area is so great as to extend ir communities in which application of this policy proves impracticable, the department reserves the right to make exceptions.

(3) In other trades or trade groups in which collective bargaining is on the basis of an individual plant or establishment, the skilled rate is tl rate specified in the bargaining agreement. In establishments not covered by bargaining agreement, the skilled rate is that rate paid the great number of competent journeyman mechanics in like establishments in the community, or such other rate deemed adequate by the Departmen

Ind 95.05 Procedure in Processing Indentures Where There are Area Joint Apprenticeship Committees. In trades and communities having acti area joint apprenticeship committees recognized by the Department, a copy of the application for approval of indentures will be referred to su committees by the Department for recommendation. The Department will expect applicants to appear personally before committees if and wh requested to do so by the committee. If no recommendation is received by the Department from the committee within 40 days after receipt

(Text of law continued on page 4).

Figure 7-7 (contd.)

by the Department on showing of good cause. Joint apprenticeship committee recommendations on individual appli cations shall by subject to review and revision by the Department in the event applicants are dissatisfied with committee action.

Ind 95.06 Effect of Bargaining Agreements. Where conditions of employment of apprentices are stipulated by collective bargaining agreement, the Department will be guided by the terms of such agreement provided such terms are not in conflict with state statutes or ch. Ind 95 or 96.

Ind 95.07 The Indenture. (1) All apprenticeship indentures shall be made upon the blank forms provided by the Department.

(2) No indenture shall be considered in force unless it has had the approval of the Department.

(3) Proof of age must be furnished the Department in all cases involving minors between the ages of 16 and 18 years before approval of indenture will be given.

(4) The indenture shall state the extent of the probationary period in hours if possible but in no case shall it exceed 6 calendar months. The probationary period shall constitute part of the apprenticeship period. During the probationary period apprenticeship agreements are voidable by either party upon written notice to the Department.

(5) The Department may give such time credit on the term of apprenticeship as the character of previous practical experience may warrant, which time credit shall b e stated in the indenture or an amendment thereto.

(6) Upon the completion, interruption or proposed termination of any apprenticeship indenture, the employer shall notify the Department immediately stating the reasons therefore.

(7) Minors indentured under provisions of ch. 106, Stats., shall not be subject to the law relating to prohibited employments for minors, insofar as such minors at the time of injury, are performing service within the provisions of contracts of apprentice indenture approved by the Department.

(8) The terms of an existing indenture may be modified subject to approval of the Department.

Ind 95.08 Manual. The division shall keep on record and make available to all interested persons the apprenticeship manual as approved by the Department on July 17, 1956, or as thereafter amended.

Ind 95.09 Forms. The following form is listed in accordance with s. 227.013, Wis. Stats., and may be obtained by writing the Bureau of Apprenticeship Standards, P.O. Box 7972, Madison, Wisconsin 53707.

ETPA-4224 Apprentice Indenture.

Ind 95.10 Apprenticeship in family owned business.

Ind 95.15 Criteria for apprenticable occupations.

Ind 95.20 Enforcement of indenture agreements.

Ind 96.01 - 96.17 The Wisconsin equal opportunity plan for apprenticeship.

Complete copies or updates on above rules are available at Department of Administration, Document Sales, 202 S. Thornton Avenue, Madison, WI 53703.

Once the decision has been made to organize and develop a program, certain key issues and areas must be addressed to successfully operate the program.

Recruitment Techniques

One of the prime reasons for using apprenticeship as a form of structured work-based education and training is to facilitate the creation of a qualified workforce. Community colleges provide much of the assistance in recruiting, testing, and placing learners into cooperative worksites. Therefore, an employer receives very definite benefits by participating with the community college in apprenticeship training.

How can apprentices be identified and recruited into a program? This can be accomplished through placing advertisements in local newspapers. Recruitment can also be coordinated with the community college. For example, learners seeking work-and-learn opportunities can be matched to available apprenticeship and other cooperative education opportunities made available by employers in cooperation with community colleges.

Other recruitment avenues include local and state departments of labor and their offices of apprenticeship and training. Some states have

Figure 7–8

A Typical Course Program Listing

American River College

Sheet Metal Service Technician

150A First Course in Apprenticeship (2.5)
Introduction of Sheet Metal Service Technician Apprenticeship — orientation, tools and components, basic electricity, and basic electricity heat controls, air filters, blowers and fans.

150B Second Course in Apprenticeship (2.5)
Covers basic controls, heat-cool combination, electrical theory and motor design, construction and operation. Diagnosis and repair of refrigeration lines.

151A Third Course in Apprenticeship (2.5)
Reviews electrical theory; practical electrical review; air distribution system, residential and commercial; pneumatic controls.

151B Fourth Course in Apprenticeship (2.5)
Basic piping, and heat pump circuitry and controls, expansion value systems, capillary tubes, chimneys, vents and flues.

152A Fifth Course in Apprenticeship (2.5)
Service person time management, residential oil-fired warm air furnace, industrial and commercial refrigeration systems.

152B Sixth Course in Apprenticeship (2.5)
Covers trouble shooting of electrical furnaces, electronic filters, gas and oil furnaces, cooling systems and heat pumps.

153A Seventh Course in Apprenticeship (2.5)
Covers boilers, chilled water systems, chiller-boiler nations systems, air distribution and air balance.

153B Eighth Course in Apprenticeship (2.5)
Pneumatic and electrical control systems, hydronic and control. Energy load management systems.

1992–1993 Catalog; p. 87

state joint apprenticeship committees, representing certain industries, who can offer assistance. For instance, the California Firefighter Joint Apprenticeship Committee provides information on positions available within participating fire departments and communities. They maintain a candidate data base and lists of special interest groups and interested parties. Published materials, including orientation booklets describing the firefighter's responsibilities, working conditions, physical and job training requirements, and entrance and testing requirements, are also published and distributed by the California Joint Apprenticeship Committee (CALJAC).

Recruitment screening

Apprentice applicants apply to the apprenticeship program JAC committee. Much like any other college program, the applicant will present high school transcripts, or General Equivalency Diploma (GED) equivalent, and evidence of any other college work or training completed. Many trades require an entrance test, which is developed and administered by JAC committee members. Some trades use standardized tests. For instance, the International Brotherhood of Electrical Workers (IBEW) electricians give the General Aptitude Test Battery (GATBE). Many of the maritime firms in the Tidewater Virginia area rely on their neighboring community colleges for assistance in apprentice candidate recruitment and screening. The process often involves local manpower agencies, the state department of labor, and regular community college intake and screening avenues. The colleges then provide testing services to determine the basic skills of the candidates. Often, the testing includes:

- Armed Services Vocational Aptitude Battery (ASVAB) testing for vocational ability;
- California Achievement Test for basic skills abilities; and
- other academic and vocational placement tests developed by the college.

Once these basic entrance requirements are met, applicants are interviewed by the JAC committee. Those meeting entrance requirements are issued a letter of acceptance. With the letter of acceptance, the apprentice candidate may search for a sponsoring employer.

Many colleges, such as Northcentral Technical College (WI), Catonsville Community College (MD), Fresno City College (CA), and American River College (CA), work closely with employers in the community to refer acceptable candidates for apprenticeship. In many of these states, many trades and occupations other than the usual skilled trades are apprenticeable (e.g., police officer, secretary, emergency medical technician).

Once an employer accepts an apprentice, the indenture is completed and filed with the state and college. The JAC committee reviews apprentice progress every six months.

Earning College Credit for Apprenticeship

Many community colleges now also award degree credit for hands-on portions of apprenticeship training. Under the sponsorship of the Joint Industry Board of the Electrical Industry, apprentices of International Brotherhood of Electrical Workers (IBEW) Local 3 can earn an entire Associate of Science degree while studying technical subjects in electrical theory and completing their on-the-job apprenticeship training (Electrical Industry, 1989). The electrical theory course work, taught by IBEW union journeymen through the New York City Public Schools, has been evaluated by Empire State College and is accepted as the equivalent of approximately 40 college level credits.

Empire State College grants approximately 32 credits towards the Associate degree to every matriculated apprentice who has completed the electrical theory courses and has passed the "M" test, the final mastery test in the apprenticeship program, devised jointly by the union, the joint industry board, and the college. The Associate degree requires the completion of 64 credits of which at least 32 credits must be in liberal arts and taken at the college. The remaining 8 electrical course credits are applicable towards a bachelors degree at Empire State College (College Catalog, 1989–1991).

In Chapter 9 the processes for integrating apprenticeship instructional methods into associate degree programs are discussed. This practice is now making it possible for many learners in non-traditional high-tech occupations to participate in higher education. It also makes the community college a more accessible training resource for business and industry.

Chapter References

American Association of Community and Junior Colleges (AACJC). (1991, December 3). Colleges moving to guarantee their graduates. *Community Technical and Junior College Times*, III(22), 1.

California Firefighter Joint Apprenticeship Committee. (Author). (1989). *Descriptive Brochure.* Sacramento, CA.

Electrical Joint Apprenticeship and Training Committee. (1989). *Local apprenticeship and training standards for the electrical contracting industry.* New York: Author.

Empire State College (Author) (Undated). *Apprentice Handbook.* New York City, NY.

Glover, R.W. (1986). *Apprenticeship Lessons from Abroad. Information Series No. 305.* The National Center for Research in Vocational Education, Ohio State University. Columbus, Ohio.

Grabowski, Donald J. *Testimony of Donald J. Grabowski, President, National Association of State & Territorial Apprenticeship Directors before the Commission on Workforce Quality & Labor Market Efficiency.* National Association of State and Territorial Apprenticeship Directors, Northlake Community College, May, 1989.

Martin, Sharon T. (October, 1981). *Apprenticeship - School Linkage Implementation Manual.* CSR, Inc., Washington, DC.

New York State Department of Labor, Apprenticeship and Training Council. (1987). *An overview of apprentice training.* Albany, NY: Author.

Tuholski, R.J. (1982, October). Today's Apprentices - Tomorrow's Leaders. *VocED*, 37-38.

Wisconsin, Bureau of Apprenticeship Standards. (1991). *A guide to apprenticeship in Wisconsin.* Madison, WI: Author.

Chapter 8

Clinicals

The purpose of this chapter is to describe the clinical practicum and internship. These experiential learning activities are offered as part of health careers programs at many community colleges. Although obvious benefits are offered, the clinical practicum poses special concerns and problems for colleges and health care operators alike, including the necessity to adhere to the requirements of external accrediting bodies, to address the issue of liability, and to secure insurance coverage. This chapter will discuss these concerns, as well as provide guidelines for planning the clinical practicum.

Programs in nursing, dental hygiene, speech pathology and audiology, and other allied fields require that clinical cooperative education experiences be part of the curriculum in order to acquire a degree or certificate. Such on-the-job practica are most often prescribed by an accrediting board which sets professional standards and is external to the college. The amount of time to be spent and areas of experience are also generally stipulated.

For example, New York City Technical College offers several health technology programs. Each has a specified clinical requirement (see Figure 8–1). This college's practicum courses prescribed as part of the Dental Lab Technology Program include:

DL 411 Complete Denture Practicum

This course is designed to provide a practical application of the techniques and procedures learned in the basic or specialized courses previously studied. The student will be provided with models or impressions of previously fabricated restorations together with copies of the original work authorizations and/or instructions furnished by the dentist. Included in this course will be externship in local veterans' hospitals, dental college laboratories and selected local laboratories.

Prerequisite: Completion of all 3rd semester courses, 6 lab hours, 1 lecture hour, 3 credits.

DL 412 Fixed Prosthodontics Practicum

The student will be provided with models or impressions of previously fabricated restorations together with copies of the original work authorizations and/or instruc-

Figure 8–1

Sample Course of Study

The College will grant an Associate in Applied Science degree (A.A.S.) with a major in Dental Laboratory Technology upon satisfactory completion of the required 70 credits listed below.

COURSE NUMBER AND TITLE   CREDITS

FIRST SEMESTER

DL 106	Science Dental Materials	3
DL 110	Tooth Morphology	3
DL 111	Complete Dentures	3
DL 112	Fixed Prosthodontics I	2
BY 500	Elements of Human Biology	4
WS 101	English Composition I	3
	Total	18

SECOND SEMESTER

DL 210	Principles of Occlusion	3
DL 211	Complete Dentures II	3
DL 212	Fixed Prosthodontics II	3
DL 213	Removable Partial Dentures I	2
MA	Mathematics Elective	3
	Elective	3
	Total	17

THIRD SEMESTER

DL 306	Science Dental Metallurgy	3
DL 311	Complete Dentures III	3
DL 313	Removable Partial Dentures II	3
DL 314	Ceramics	3
	Electives	6
	Total	18

FOURTH SEMESTER   *Specialization I

DL 408	Lab Operation, Ethics & Jurisprudence	3
DL 411	Complete Dentures Practicum	3
DL 413	Removable Partial Dentures Practicum	3
DL 415	Orthodontics	2
	Electives	6
	Total	17

OR

FOURTH SEMESTER   *Specialization II

DL 408	Lab Operation, Ethics & Jurisprudence	3
DL 412	Fixed Prosthodontics Practicum	3
DL 414	Ceramic Practicum	3
DL 415	Orthodontics	2
	Electives	6
	Total	17

*Students may elect Specialization I or Specialization II. In order for a student to elect Specialization II, the student must have passed DL 212 and DL 314 with a minimum grade of "B," or permission of the Chairperson.

New York City Technical College, 1985-1986 Catalog

tions furnished by the dentist. Included in this course will be externship in local veterans hospitals, dental college laboratories and selected local laboratories.

Prerequisite: Completion of all 3rd semester courses, 6 lab hours, 1 lecture hour, 3 credits.

DL 413 Removable Partial Denture Practicum
   The student will be provided with models or impressions of previously fabricated restorations together with copies of the original work authorizations and/or instructions furnished by the dentist. Included in this course will be externship in local veterans hospitals, dental college laboratories and selected local laboratories.

   Prerequisite: Completion of all 3rd semester courses; 6 lab hours, 1 lecture hour, 3 credits.

DL 414 Ceramic Practicum
   The student will be provided with models or impressions of previously fabricated restorations together with copies of the original work authorizations and/or instructions furnished by the dentist. Included in this course will be externship in local veterans hospitals, dental college laboratories and selected local laboratories.

   Prerequisite: Completion of all 3rd semester courses, 6 lab hours, 1 lecture hour, 3 credits.

1985–1986 Catalog; p. 38

As seen in this course display, the clinical practicum amounts to no less than 6 credits of the total program.

Planning the Clinical Experience

   Clinical practica require very careful planning and administration. Because both the employing organization (e.g., hospital, medical practitioner) and the college are liable for learner mistakes or misactions, insurance coverage for organizations and learners must be secured. Carefully constructed letters of agreement stipulating roles and responsibilities of all parties are essential to ensure program success. Thus, preliminary planning must be thorough, and supervision of learners by both college and employer must be close, planned, and continual.

Determining Standards and Requirements

   During initial planning, obtain detailed information on the standards and requirements of the health program involved. For instance, for audiology technology, the American Speech-Language-Hearing Association stipulates the minimum numbers of clock hours in clinical observation and clinical practicum required of a learner in order to sit for a certification examination after completing a degree or certificate pro-

Figure 8–2

New York City Technical College Health Programs and Clinicals

Program	Clinical Requirements	Standards
Dental Lab Technology	6 credits	National Board of Certification
Medical Lab Technology	2 credits/1000 hours	New York City Health Department American Society of Clinical Pathologists
Histology	5 credits	ASCP-HT Examination (Clinical Pathology)
Nursing	35 credits, integrated with classwork	National League of Nursing ADN Accreditation Examination by National Licensure Council
Ophthalmic Dispensing	24 credits, integrated with classwork	New York State Examination
Dental Hygiene	16 credits	National Board of Dental Examiners
Radiological Technology	14.5 credits	New York State Bureau of Radiological Technology; American Registry of Radiological Technologists Examination

gram (see Figure 8–2 above for examples of standards and accrediting agencies). This kind of information is essential in order to ensure that the educational activity complies with established standards.

Establishing Clinical Sites

Clinical sites are identified in the same way and manner as are other internships (see Chapter 6). The advisory committee for the health program includes for consideration all major employers in that area and maintains contact with other employers if possible. The committee and the program coordinator draw up appropriate agreements with the employer. A sample agreement form is shown in Figure 8–3 below. A sample college letter of learner introduction is presented in Figure 8–4 below.

It is important for all parties (college and health care agency) to understand that the college must control the content of the program, thus ensuring maintenance of the health care accrediting standards underwriting the curriculum. The role of the employer is to provide experiential learning opportunities and supervise the learner's work effort. The employer must adhere to the college's curricular goals and objectives.

The employer also must recognize the college's role in selecting instructors/coordinators for the clinical experience, and must provide an opportunity for these coordinators to communicate with an employer-designated contact for the duration of the clinical internship activity.

The employer's staff needs to be fully familiar with what will occur during the clinical experience and understand its relationship to the overall health career program. To achieve this, the employer must visit the college to become familiar with the clinical experience requirements, courses of study, and faculty and staff.

While employers certainly have a right to control the learners who work at or visit their facility, assignment of learners to a clinical experience must be controlled by the college. The employer and college should decide together how learners are to be selected for the clinical phase of the program.

The college should also assume responsibility for establishing and maintaining a process for learner discipline. The college should communicate with the employer and remove learners from the clinical experience if they engage in actions detrimental to the participating facility and/or to the learning experience.

Figure 8–3

Sample Agreement Form

Letter of Understanding, dated _____, between the Department of Speech and Theatre of Herbert H. Lehman College of The City University of New York (hereinafter the "College") and _____ (hereinafter the "Facility").

It is the intent of the College and the Facility to cooperate in providing educational experiences for Master's students in the Speech Pathology/Audiology Program of Lehman College at the Facility. It is, therefore, mutually agreed as follows:

1. The College will assume full responsibility for planning, administering, and implementing the curriculum for the educational program.

2. The College will provide instructors for the coordination and guidance of students assigned to the Facility, as well as for consultation with Facility staff as needed.

3. The College will provide orientation to the educational program for the Facility staff.

4. The College will have the responsibility for assigning students to the Facility according to a schedule developed in consultation with the Facility. Students will adhere to the College calendar as regards attendance.

5. The College will withdraw any studnet from the Facility if the Facility determines, upon a reasonable basis, that the student is unacceptable to it for reasons of health or unacceptable practices or performance, or if, in the academic judgment of the College, the practicum experience becomes unsuited to the student's educational program.

6. The Facility will retain full responsibility for the care of patients and will maintain administrative and professional supervision of the College's students insofar as their presence affects the operation of the Facility and the direct or indirect care of patients.

7. The student will be evaluated jointly by faculty members and Facility staff. The College will provide an evaluation guide. The College will keep all records and reports on the student's experience.

8. A periodic review of program and policies will be conducted by the College.

This Letter of Understanding will become effective _____, and will continue in full force and effect unless terminated as hereinafter provided. The Letter of Understanding may be modified at any time by the written consent of both parties. It may be terminated by one party upon written notice to the other at least three months in advance of the beginning of a training experience.

By: _____   By: _____
    For the Facility   Department of Speech and Theatre
                                          Herbert H. Lehman College of
                                          The City University of New York

Reprinted with permission of Professor Robert Goldfarb, Lehman College.

Figure 8–4

Letter of Introduction

Julie Adam
Speech-Language Pathology
New York Medical Center
1600 Jerome Avenue
Bronx, New York

Dear Ms. Adam:

This will serve to introduce Ronnie Wolfe, who has been assigned to your facility for a clinical internship in speech-language pathology, concurrent with her registration in SPE 229 (Clinical Practicum in Speech-Language Pathology) for the summer 1993 semester here at Lehman College.

Ms. Wolfe has completed most of the academic and clinical practicum requirements for the degree of Associate in Arts in Speech-Language Pathology and Audiology. However, there are undoubtedly areas of specialized training, particularly involving diagnostic evaluations and report writing, where additional instruction will be necessary to familiarize her with the specific requirements of your facility.

It is mutually understood that, according to the requirements of the American Speech-Language-Hearing Association, Ms. Wolfe will be supervised no less than 25% of the time when involved in speech-language therapy, and no less than 50% of the time when involved in diagnostic evaluations. I plan on one visit to your facility during the summer, which will be supplemented by regular contact with you and the student via telephone and letter. Upon completion of the internship, I will ask that you complete a supervisor's evaluation form.

Please contact me if there are any questions or comments. Best personal regards.

Cordially,

Most health care organizations require the agreement to include specific wording which protects their right to control the ultimate delivery of services to their clients or patients.

Obtaining Insurance

All clinical experiences present serious potential problems because the learner is exposed to real situations and procedures, and real people in need of care. Thus, the learner, employer, and college must act to protect all these parties in the event of litigation resulting from unforseen accidents.

Learner insurance

Colleges can secure group insurance policies to cover participating learners at clinical sites. These policies are offered by a number of insurance companies. The premiums are based upon the number of participating learners each year. Colleges then prorate the premiums to the learner, based on the total numbers of participants. Recommended levels of coverage are $1,000,000 per occurrence with a total amount of $3,000,000.

Instructor insurance

Professional insurance is invaluable and recommended for faculty and staff. These policies are available through professional associations, such as the American Vocational Association.

Evaluating Clinical Skills

In a typical evaluation process the employer's clinical supervisor observes learner performance and records the results. A rating form should include general instructions for the supervisor.

Grading and evaluation of the learner's work and progress should be a joint responsibility of college staff and the participating employer. An evaluation method must be developed, and the process for recording this information should be discussed and mutually understood. The college will then assume responsibility for administering the grade. Procedures for this are covered in Chapter 14. A specific form for a clinical evaluation used at Lehman College is presented in Figure 8–5.

Figure 8–5

Clinical Skills Evaluation

Preceptor Instructions:

Please rate this clinical student on each of the following items pertaining to the clinical assignment.

	Exceptional 5	Very Good 4	Satis-factory 3	Minimal 2	Poor 1
Attitude					
1. Works well with other staff.					
2. Is confident when working with patients.					
3. Puts patients at ease.					
4. Respects patient confidentiality.					
5. Is punctual and attends regularly.					
Clinical/Diagnostic Skills					
6. Interviews patient appropriately.					
7. Listens & records data accurately.					
8. Is competent in on-task behaviors associated with profession.					
9. Counsels patients carefully, accurately and appropriately.					
10. Communicates information to seniors and peers.					

Additional Comments:

_____   _____
Dated   Signed

Finally, provisions for overall program review of the clinical practicum should be developed and agreed upon (see Chapter 14).

Chapter 9

Cooperative Training: Apprenticeships and Technical Education

Partnerships with business and industry continue to grow in importance to community colleges for a variety of reasons: the training is needed, the community colleges have the expertise to provide that training efficiently and well, and the colleges often receive lucrative benefits for these linkages. So far this book has discussed cooperative education programs that are either initiated or directed from the community college base. However, many more businesses and industries have become more involved in developing training programs for their employees. Some have created their own technical education programs and entered into cooperative relationships with community colleges to provide educational opportunities for their learners. Community colleges should understand how these programs operate and how to take advantage of the valuable program resources they offer. The purpose of this chapter is to describe how to extend learning through apprenticeship into an accepted method of college instruction leading towards the Associate degree.

Benefits of Cooperative Apprenticeship

The increasing focus on worker training is an outgrowth of the changes occurring in all sectors of American industry where it is difficult to obtain workers sufficiently well prepared technically to meet the evolving needs of the labor market. To qualify for a well-paying job a worker today needs a higher level of skill than was required in previous years. For example, more and more occupations will require the equivalent of two years of post-secondary education and training.

These circumstances indicate a need and an opportunity for our community colleges to join forces with business and industry to maximize resources for job training and proactive community economic development.

Figure 9–1

Industry-Developed Cooperative Education and Apprenticeship Programs

Organization	Associate Degree
US Office of Personnel Management	Office Administration
US Navy	Shipyard Technician
National Machine Tool Association	Toolmaker/Machinist
National Automobile Dealers Association	Automotive Technician Automotive Management
Toyota Motor Corporation	Automotive Technician
International Brotherhood of Electrical Workers	Electrical Technician
International Union of Operating Engineers	Heavy Equipment Technician

Figure 9–1 lists some of the prominent firms and organizations that have developed cooperative education and apprenticeship programs to address their need for trained workers.

As an example, the goals and objectives of the Toyota Motor Corporation cooperative education/apprenticeship programs are to:

• establish a program that the community will embrace and support because it produces direct benefits for everyone involved;

• establish post-secondary training capable of providing the level of training necessary to accommodate the demands of industries or firms throughout the nation for entry-level technicians and workers;

- create training courses and methods for entry-level technicians and workers that emphasize creative problem-solving skills or diagnosis and the philosophy of "Get it Right the First Time";

- establish a work study (cooperative education and/or apprenticeship) program that enables learners to work side-by-side with experienced master craftsmen and technicians;

- provide a learning environment that stresses professionalism and integrity, leading to increased learner and customer satisfaction;

- motivate school performance by providing an award/donation support system based on the completion of specific program objectives;

- establish a path for learners to continue the kind of education at the college/university level that can lead to management positions with the company; and

- enable college instructors to learn corporate technologies from corporate training instructors. This includes regularly scheduled update training as new technology is introduced.

Gains for business and industry from this kind of program development and sponsorship include:

- development of mutually beneficial relationships between the educational community and the industry, firm, or organization sponsoring the program;

- more and better trained entry-level workers and technicians to meet the demands generated by increased business, sales, and/or demand for services;

- education and training of tomorrow's corporate management; and

- improved community image of the participating organization.

For instance, the automotive industry was one of the earliest industries to adopt cooperative education and apprenticeship program development. Toyota Motor Corporation offers the following points as rationale for their program development and implementation:

- There is increasing difficulty finding technicians who can diagnose and successfully repair sophisticated "hi-tech" vehicles. Learners enrolled in traditional community college technical education programs lack exposure to late model vehicles and current automotive technology. Their skills are inadequate for success in the rapidly changing, highly technical new car dealership environment.

* The cost of state-of-the-art training aids is too high and current levels of instruction are falling short of meeting industry's educational standards.

* Current methods of implementing cooperative work experience programs are not designed to provide opportunities for learners to learn from experienced technicians.

* Training programs are not placing enough emphasis on diagnosis, which results in increased comebacks and customer dissatisfaction.

* A negative perception exists in many communities about the career of an automotive technician.

* With the growth in the number of dealerships and in vehicle sales, Toyota needs to find qualified entry-level management candidates to meet demands.

Toyota Motor Corp., T–TEN *Literature, 1994*

How Cooperative Apprenticeship Programs are Developed

Course and Program Development

To understand how colleges can participate with business and industry, let's look at how automotive manufacturers independently developed networks of colleges and dealers.

Each manufacturer developed course materials and instructor training to enable post-secondary schools to teach learners advanced state-of-the-art technology and prepare them for employment. They worked with colleges to recognize and overcome the diverse state mandates, rules, regulations, and curricula that presented obstacles to changing and improving teaching methods.

Each manufacturer produced program guides to provide specific direction on how to accomplish program objectives, yet allow for:

* flexibility to integrate corporate-specific programs into existing generic programs;

- creativity to design a program that best meets the needs of individual demographic regions;
- incentives to promote completion of program objectives; and
- encouragement to colleges to integrate corporate technology into existing generic automotive curriculums.

Figure 9–2 is a typical manufacturer-suggested curriculum. It is strongly recommended that colleges provide Associate in Arts (AA) or Associate in Applied Science (AAS) degrees for automotive learners in corporate programs. Each college establishes a work-study (co-op) situation with local stores or dealerships. The colleges appoint a faculty member to follow up on learner co-op employment at the stores or dealerships. Corporate programs provide extensive company product

Figure 9–2
Typical Manufacturer-Suggested Curriculum

AREA OF CERTIFICATION	TOYOTA MASTER TRAINING COURSES
Engine Repair	One Engine with Stand
Automatic Transmission/Transaxle	Electronic Control Transmission Assembly, Automatic Transmission Transmission/Transaxle Course #262
Manual Transmission/ Transaxle	Manual Transmission/Transaxle Course #301
Suspension/Steering	Suspension/Steering Course #450, Alignment Simulator and Animated Transparencies
Brakes	Brake Course #550 and Animated Transparency
Electrical Systems	Electrical Course #622 Electrical Course #652
Heating and Air Conditioning	Heating and Air Conditioning Course #750
Engine Performance	Electronic Fuel Injection (EFI) Course #850

Reprinted with permission of Toyota Motor Sales, U.S.A., Inc.

knowledge, which separates the corporate-specific student from other entry-level technicians.

Each program has a name that is created to represent the program's purpose and that can be easily associated with it (e.g., Toyota Technical Education Network or T–TEN).

Toyota uses a system of mutually beneficial awards/donations granted for accomplishment of pre-assigned corporate objectives. Awards/donations were selected that would enhance college automotive programs and their ability to attract the best learners. This, in turn, became a motivator for college acceptance of the program. Objectives were developed to ensure that colleges would be capable of teaching the latest technology. Together with the colleges, the corporation helps to:

- recruit qualified learners;
- involve dealers;
- upgrade curriculum and facilities;
- upgrade college instructors' competencies; and
- improve college placement procedures.

Figure 9–3 displays an articulation agreement used for learner recruitment and placement by community colleges. Figure 9–4 below is a dealer sponsorship agreement.

Corporations encourage interaction between all participants in the business partnership. This is done through an advisory committee representing all parties.

The US Navy has a process for articulation of their programs with local community colleges (See Figure 9–5 below).

Public Service Training Academies

Public service training academies provide basic and advanced training for police, correctional, and allied law enforcement officers, firefighters, and emergency medical service personnel. These training programs are developed by the agency or agencies for which the training is intended and often are operated through community/technical colleges. In many states and localities (Florida and California, for example), it is now the general practice to use community colleges for the basic and advanced training of police and fire personnel.

Figure 9–3

Sample Articulation Agreement

Based upon the mutual concern for the needs of students pursuing a program of study in automotive service technology skills, and in an effort to provide a continuing articulated program that builds on past learning experiences and eliminates unnecessary duplication of instruction, the following are agreements to which we subscribe:

- The high school technology instructor will maintain a competency record that identifies the task achievement of the student in the automotive technology skills areas identified below.

- _____ will accept the record of task achievement in these areas as
  College Name

  documented by the high shcool automotive technology instructor.

- The student will be given advanced standing upon successful completion of the following tests:

  _____

  _____

  _____

- Designated representatives from each instutution will meet as necessary to review the tasks and competency levels required for the automotive technology areas identified below.

- The student will not be required to repeat the below units for one year after completion.

  _____ courses:
  College Name

  _____ Introduction to Automotive Technology _____

  _____

  _____

  _____

- This agreement will be automatically renewed on an annual basis unless cancelled by either party.

Signatures:

_____
Date

_____   _____
Superintendent   President

_____   _____
School District   College Name

Reprinted with permission of Toyota Motor Sales, U.S.A., Inc.

Figure 9–4

Sample Dealer Sponsorship Agreement

NAME OF T-TEN SCHOOL		T-TEN COORDINATOR		TODAY'S DATE
STUDENT'S LAST NAME	FIRST	MIDDLE NAME		STUDENT WORK SHIRT SIZE MED ☐ LRG ☐ XL ☐ XXL ☐
HOME PHONE ( )	SOCIAL SECURITY #	DATE ENTERED T-TEN		T-TEN SCHOOL CODE
DO YOU HAVE A VALID DRIVERS LICENSE? YES ☐ NO ☐	NAME OF HIGH SCHOOL			DATE GRADUATED

ADDITIONAL EDUCATION (COLLEGE, MILITARY, SEMINARS, ETC.)

THE FOLLOWING SECTION TO BE COMPLETED BY THE SPONSORING DEALERSHIP

As a T-TEN student sponsor we agree to appoint a dealership coordinator to maintain close communication with the school T-TEN Coordinator, provide Cooperative Education Work Experience and dealership uniform in accordance with the program, pay a competitive wage that reflects trainee's progress, and provide student with the same considerations shown all dealership employees.

DEALERSHIP _____ DEALER CODE _____ PHONE (___) _____

ADDRESS _____ CITY _____ STATE _____ ZIP _____

AUTHORIZED SIGNATURE _____ DATE _____

PRINT / TYPE NAME _____ TITLE _____

DATE OF STUDENT'S FIRST CO-OP _____ STARTING WAGE _____

Reprinted with permission of Toyota Motor Sales, U.S.A., Inc.

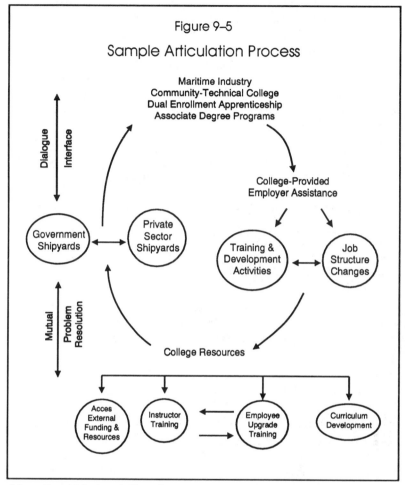

Figure 9-5

Sample Articulation Process

Meeting Mutual Goals

In this way, by sponsoring and operating training academies for current and/or future employees, community colleges support the community's public service agencies. These academies provide basic entry-level training, as well as advanced training, in many technical areas. The public service agency, which requires a constant supply of trained entry-level workers, turns to the community college for help and support with training, thus ensuring a high-quality state-of-the-art worker.

Community colleges usually offer credit towards college degree programs while training academy learners in their occupational areas. For instance:

- At Hillsborough Community College in Tampa, Florida, the Southwest Florida Justice Administration Institute provides basic academy training for seven sheriff's departments in the surrounding counties. The college as a training academy provides initial training in basic police, correctional, and advanced sheriff's techniques, and also serves as an entry-point for advanced coursework in the Associate of Science degree program in Justice Administration.

- The California community colleges provide fine academy training for their local fire and emergency medical service agencies. For example, Modesto City Fire and Rescue cooperates with Modesto Junior College, as do the Santa Ana Fire Department and Rancho SantiagoCollege, to run programs.

Setting Uniform Standards

A unique benefit of the collaboration between the community/technical college and the public agency is the creation of uniform and consistent standards to which the academy—and thus the Associate degree program itself—adheres. Much like corporate programs, all public service training academies are required to meet industry-specific standards. At the state level these standards prescribe the programs offered, culminating in certification. For instance, in the fire service, basic and advanced training standards are stipulated by the International Association of Firefighters and National Fire Protection Association Standards 1001. Similar standards are promulgated for allied fire service fields, such as paramedic, dispatcher, and engineer. (See Figure 9–6 for a sample program standard.) In corrections, the American Correctional Association sets similar standards. In law enforcement, each state has uniform standards for officer training. These standards are developed according to International Association of Chiefs of Police and other national law enforcement guidelines.

Establishing the Program Advisory Committee Structure

Training academies are governed by an advisory committee comprised of the participating public service agencies, the community college, and other state or local representatives having an interest in the training of public service officers. For instance, the Hillsborough Community College Public Academy is often represented by:

Figure 9–6

Orange County Fire Services
Fire Academy 060 - Basic Fire Academy

Orange County Firemen's   Orange County Fire Chiefs'
Association   Association
Managed and Administered by: Rancho Santiago College

FIRE ACADEMY 060
(Offered in 2 different schedules)

Schedule 1: *Intensive*	Schedule 2: *Part-time*
12 weeks (485 hours)	28 weeks (485 hours)
Monday through Friday weekdays, 40 hours per week	Two 4-hour evening sessions on Tuesdays and Thursdays and 8-hour sessions on Saturday and/or Sundays
Concurrent enrollment in F/AC 007A	Concurrent enrollment in F/AC 007A

There are 15 subjects:

Physical Training - 61   Wildland Fire Control - 12 hours
EMT-1-FS-112 hours   Ventilation - 24 hours
Fire Control - 24 hours   Heavy Rescue/Extrication - 32 hours
Fire Prevention/Investigation   Breathing Apparatus/Search
  - 8 hours   & Rescue - 24 hours
Hose - 56 hours   Hazardous Materials - 4 hours
Ladders - 48 hours   Forcible Entry - 8 hours
Rope/Knots - 24 hours   Facilities Maintenance - 8 hours
Salvage - 24 hours

Fire Academy 060, Basic Fire Academy has strict grooming standards. The candidate should possess a high degree of self-discipline, maintain a healthy mental attitude to handle stress, and be able to adjust easily to a structured organization. Fire Academy 060 emphasizes attitude, teamwork, self-confidence, self-discipline, quick thinking, and the ability to follow exact instructions and orders.

Successful completion of Fire Academy 060, Basic Fire Academy with a grade of "C" or better qualifies a candidate for placement on the Orange County Firefighter 1 Trained List for one year. To remain on the list for more than one year, students must attend and pass a minimum of 8 hours in Fire Academy N61, Advanced Fire Academy. Additional hours of retraining may be required. Orange County Firefighter 1 Trained List indicates to the potential employer that candidates meet and maintain Orange County Fire Service Entry Level Firefighter 1 Qualifications (i.e. medical, physical, academic and manipulative skills.)

Reprinted with permission of Rancho Santiago Community College District.

- the community college director of public service training;
- training officers of the several participating local sheriff's departments;
- the sheriff of each county;
- chief instructors (adjuncts from the sheriff's departments in the major training subjects);
- the state's attorney of the county;
- the Florida Department of Corrections training officer;
- the Florida Highway Patrol training officer; and
- sometimes the Tampa Police Department.

This Committee meets prior to the commencement of each academy class to plan the delivery of the academy instruction. The chair of the committee is the community college director of public service training. The committee plans the following activities:

- The numbers of recruits to be accepted from each agency.
- The instructors (adjuncts to the college faculty) to be assigned to each block of instruction. Instructors are chosen from the participating agencies. They work either on their own time or on the "sheriff's clock" depending on their work schedule. The committee must agree on the choice of instructor(s).
- The location of instruction. Typically, instruction occurs at either the municipal police academy facility or the community college (classrooms). However, when a gym is needed, other campuses are identified.
- The order of blocks of instruction. A block of instruction at Hillsborough's academy is a 4-hour sequence of instruction. Typically, a block of instruction would be "Courtroom Demeanor" or "Patrol Practices."
- The committee also meets as needed during the year to resolve problems that arise or to plan the graduation ceremonies and choose guest speakers.

This committee has made significant decisions over the years, such as including conversational Spanish in the training program when it became necessary for officers to have a functional knowledge of that language.

Public service advisory committees should also overlap (i.e., have members from) the credit programs operating at the college, which correspond to training offered by the public service academy (e.g., Justice Administration AS degree—Police Academy). In this way, a closer relationship is developed between the academy and the Associate degree personnel. This connection leads to better program coordination and a better chance that trainees will continue and enter the degree program upon completion of the academy courses.

In some instances, such as in California, a statewide advisory committee also exists to give advice and support to the public service academy. The California Firefighter Joint Apprenticeship Committee (CALJAC) (see Chapter 7) provides support to the local advisory committee on standards, curriculum, and fire department coordination.

Screening and Recruiting Trainees

The training academy provides a cooperative educational experience for the training of public service personnel. It also provides a structure for recruitment, screening, and placement of students, thus supporting the agency/employer. For instance, Rancho Santiago College (CA) runs a fire academy program for the Orange County Fire Chief's Association. Rancho Santiago College also carries out testing and screening for firefighter candidates.

Entry-level testing

Basic testing and screening of public service workers is necessary. Typically, as at Rancho Santiago College, a standardized screening test is given (e.g., the College Board Assessment and Placement Test). The college offers remedial courses to assist candidates who do not meet the basic requirements in reading, mathematics, and English. For instance, the following courses are provided at Rancho Santiago College:

> *Reading:* Applicants not able to pass the basic (CBAPT) reading test, take Reading 090A and must pass the reading proficiency exam at the 12th grade level.

> *Math:* Applicants not able to pass the Math Diagnostic Testing Project Exam take Math 050 and must achieve a grade of "C" or pass math proficiency exam at the 10th grade level.

> *English:* Applicants not able to pass the basic (CBAPT) English test enroll in English 061 or English 101 for 3 units and must achieve a grade of "C" or better. (Rancho Santiago College, 1991)

Police and corrections candidates also must meet entrance requirements. At Fresno City College, for instance, the following course is
offered:

> Basic Academy (Police): Students must possess either a high school
> diploma or a G.E.D. certificate. Check description of courses for
> specific requirements. (Requires special counseling)

Fresno City College Catalog 1992-1994

Physical fitness requirements

College public service academies also assist recruits in obtaining
medical exams and meeting physical agility tests.

In the case of the fire service, the medical and physical fitness
requirements are stipulated in an industry standard, The National Fire
Protection Association (NFPA 1001). Fire service candidates are required
to have a physical exam every two years. To meet the physical agility
test, Rancho Santiago College offers the following course:

> Fire Technology 121: Fire Technology 121, Physical Fitness for
> Public Safety Personnel, is a course designed to provide students
> with training necessary to achieve and maintain physical condition-
> ing and agility. Students who have completed (within one year) Fire
> Technology 121 with a passing grade and complete the fitness
> assessment, demonstrating no contraindications to exercise, may
> participate in Fire Academy NO8, Physical Agility, without the
> required medical examination.

Figure 9–7 below describes a physical agility requirement for a
firefighter. The community college is in a position to offer a full program
of physical education to meet public service agency needs. Most public
services require continual physical fitness improvement, agility development, and the upgrading of qualifications. Meeting this need provides
a source of continual enrollment for the college.

Selecting Instructors

Training academies rely heavily on adjunct instructors, often sup-
plied by the participating public service agencies. The community college uses adjunct instructors for the purpose of teaching in the academy
and often provides training in instructional methodology to them.

Compensation for the adjunct's services typically may come from a
number of sources. In many cases, the adjunct works in the academy
while on the agency's "time clock." In these cases the community college

will work out an in-kind (quid pro quo) agreement for instructional services, waiving tuition for the candidates (trainees). It is important to ensure that the adjunct is recognized as an instructor at the college for insurance and liability purposes. In California, the firefighter academy is often sponsored by CALJAC, in which case the instructors are compensated by CALJAC.

Adjunct instructors in the public service academies also provide vital services to the college credit programs. By bringing some very specialized and up-to-date talents and skills to the college, these adjuncts strengthen the Associate degree programs through the relationship of the academy to the community college.

Sharing Facilities

A major benefit to both the community college and the public service agency is the possibility for sharing of facilities for academy training. At Hillsborough Community College, in the early years of the program (1980s), the fire and police programs were conducted at both the community college and the Tampa Training Academy, a facility owned and operated by the City of Tampa, Florida. The facility is outfitted and equipped to provide much of the hands-on training necessary for both police and fire operations.

To complement the academy training, the community college is able to offer classrooms and laboratories, physical education facilities, learning resource centers, and libraries. Such sharing offers the public service candidate the optimum training environment.

Many public service programs have benefitted also from allotments of monies from such vocational training sources as the Perkins Technology Education Act. These funds often permit hiring additional faculty and acquiring equipment.

Other benefits derived from the sharing of facilities include access to the apparatus and equipment necessary for a community college to offer and operate a program, such as fire science technology, weapons ranges for police programs, and corrections facilities for corrections programs.

Figure 9–7

A Physical Agility Requirement for a Firefighter

Rancho Santiago College
Orange County Fire Academy

Continuous Physical Agility

Description

The Physical Agility will begin with a 1.5 mile run which has a 12 minute time standard (Six laps around the grinder). Candidates must call out their last name and their lap as they pass the proctor. At the end of the run the candidate's time will be recorded. A minimum of 5 minutes will be allowed for cooling down and stretching.

After running and cooling down, all candidates will meet in front of the large tower for a demonstration of all seven remaining agility events. A proctor will demonstrate the events in order, and in a continuous manner. Questions may be asked at any time during the demonstration.

The candidate will put on a turnout coat, breathing apparatus, gloves, knee pads, and a Pompier belt. The proctor will start the stopwatch when candidate is fully equipped. Candidate begins at the starting line in front of the tower. Once the proctor says "GO", candidate will advance forward, pick up a 75 pound hose bundle and begin running up the stairs to the fourth floor. Candidate must hit each step, failure to do so will result in disqualification. It is recommended that the hose bundle be carried on the left shoulder to allow the candidate to use the right arm to hold the railing while running up the stairs. Once the candidate reaches the threshold of the fourth floor he turns around and returns to the third floor where he will drop the bundle and be given the next event.

The candidate returns to the third floor where a proctor will help hook candidate's Pompier belt onto the railing to insure safety for the next event. A rope, with 50 pound hose bundle suspended from it, is tied off on the third floor railing. Candidate must raise the hose bundle from the ground to the third floor, pull it over the railing and ground it on the floor. Upon completion of this event candidate will walk down to the first floor and out of the tower to a marked spot where a proctor will help candidate out of breathing apparatus and Pompier belt. Candidate will *walk* not run to the next event. (The definition of running is when both feet are off ground at same time.)

After completion of the tower events, candidate will walk to the wet hose load event starting line. In this event, candidate must pick up five hose rolls (one at a time) and place them on top of each other on the rear step of a pumper. After completing stacking process, candidate must re-cross the starting line and walk to next event.

In joist walk event, candidate must pick up a 55-pound hose bundle, (the bundle may be carried on the shoulder or horseshoe around the shoulders) and carry it up and back walking on the joists. Candidate walks up the joists (not using the center wood supports) turns around, and walks back crossing the original starting line. If candidate falls off joist en route or during turn, the candidate must return to the beginning of the joist and begin again. If candidate falls off joist while returning he/she must return to the opposite end and begin again. Upon completing this event, candidate must walk to starting line and drop the hose bundle before walking to next event which is the Climb, Crawl, Drag.

Candidate will begin at starting line placed in front of the six foot wall, go over the wall, pick up a charged inch and a half hose line, drag it under 3 barriers (29" high), place it on the line provided, pick up a different hose bundle, also on the line, and drag it back the other way under the same three barriers. The hose bundle and candidate must cross finish line. After completion, candidate then walks to Halyard pull event.

Candidate positions himself/herself behind the 35-foot wooden extension ladder. One foot must be placed on the outside brace of the ladder. Candidate must raise the extension section of the ladder twice controlling the halyard and not letting it slip through the hands on the way up or down. The candidate will be told to stop when the ladder has been raised fully each time. The upper body only should be used to raise the ladder, if the lower body is used the candidate will be disqualified. Upon completion of the two pulls, the candidate moves on to the last event which is the hose extension.

The candidate places the hose harness on his/her shoulder and holds on to the ends of a charged two and a half inch hose. Three sections of hose are connected to the hydrant. The candidate must extend the hose 25 feet forward at which point a right turn is made and the candidate follows the arc indicated on the ground until reaching the finish line. The course is marked and the candidate must stay within the marked lines. If the candidate steps out of bounds he/she must reenter in bounds where they went out and continue to finish line.

This concludes the Physical Agility!! A candidate must complete the agility in 5 minutes 30 seconds or less to pass.

It is recommended that each candidate cool down and stretch after the test. It is also highly recommended that you be in your best physical condition before attempting this agility.

*Reprinted with permission of Rancho Santiago
Community College District.*

Granting Degree Credit for Academy Learning

Community colleges recognize the educational value of academy training. Many colleges offering academy training grant academic credit towards an Associate degree upon successful completion of the academy training.

To accomplish this, a trainee will dual-enroll in credit courses that parallel the academy areas of study. For instance, at Rancho Santiago College, a fire academy trainee would enroll in the following courses:

Courses Required for Entrance to the Academy

Fire Tech 101 Introduction to Fire Technology. 3 units
Fire Tech 102 Physical Science. 4 units
Fire Tech 121 Physical Fitness for Public Safety Personnel. 5 units
Fire Tech 103 Fundamentals of Personal Fire Safety. 3 units
Fire Tech 104 Fundamentals of Fire Prevention. 3 units
Fire Tech 105 Building Construction for Fire Protection. 3 units
Fire Tech 106 Fire Protection Equipment and Systems. 3 units
Fire Academy N08 Firefighter 1 Physical Agility. 0.2 units

Note: Fire Tech 104, 105, and 106 may not be taken without first taking and passing Fire Technology 101 and 102.

At Victor Valley College (CA), two fire academy levels are offered on a part-time or full-time basis, with two corresponding courses for which credit is granted. Additionally, fire inspection academy and skills maintenance courses are offered:

FT 90 PAID CALL FIRE FIGHTER ACADEMY, 2.0 units. The paid Call Fire Fighter Academy will provide basic training for individuals interested in becoming a Paid Call Fire Fighter. Two lecture hours, six laboratory hours per week for eight weeks.

FT 95 BASIC FIRE ACADEMY, 10.0 units. Introduction to basic fire fighting theory and skills; study of the characteristics and behavior of fire; practice in fundamental fire suppression activities, with special attention on safety, first aid and rescue procedures. Fourteen lecture hours, 27 laboratory hours per week for eight weeks.

FT 96 FIRE INSPECTION ACADEMY, 9.0 units. A course designed to prepare an entry level Fire Inspector for conducting fire inspections on new and existing buildings; use of effective written and verbal communications and use of effective public relations methods. Nine lecture hours per week, plus an additional 3 hours per semester.

FT 101 FIRE FIGHTER SKILLS MAINTENANCE, 4.0 units. (Prerequisite: FT 30 and FT 90 or FT 95 or equivalent. Employment as career firefighter or paid call firefighter recommended.) A series of lectures and manipulative drills designed to provide maintenance of skills learned, including updates in technology relating to fire department organization, hose, ladders, tools and equipment, salvage, fire chemistry, extinguisher and agents, fire control, prevention, arson, crowd and traffic control, mutual aid, communications, fire safety and emergency rescue techniques. Two lectures, six laboratory hours per week. This course will not apply to the Associate Degree.

FT 102 SKILLS MAINTENANCE FOR PAID CALL FIREFIGHTER, 1.5 units. (Prerequisite: FT 30 or FT 90. Employment as a Paid Call Firefighter recommended.) A Series of lectures and manipulative drills designed to provide maintenance of skills learned, including updates in technology relating to fire department organization, hose, ladders, tools and equipment, salvage, fire chemistry, extinguisher and agents, fire control, prevention, arson, crowd and traffic control, mutual aid, communications, fire safety and emergency rescue techniques. One lecture, two hours laboratory per week. This course will not apply to the Associate Degree.

1991–1992 Catalog; p. 88.

Fresno City College offers police and corrections academies at various levels:

ADVANCED OFFICER ACADEMY. Students must have either satisfactorily completed the Basic Police or Basic Correctional Academy or be employed and/or affiliated with a Criminal Justice Agency with the experience equivalent to a Basic Police or Basic Correctional Academy.

SUPERVISORY ACADEMY. Students must satisfactorily substantiate that they are currently serving in a supervisory capacity within a Criminal Justice Agency (or will be within a one year period), or have completed six specified Administration of Justice courses.

PEACE OFFICER ORIENTATION. All qualified students as specified in the Fresno City College catalog may be admitted.

BASIC CORRECTIONAL ACADEMY. Students must possess either a high school diploma or G.E.D. certificate

1992–1994 Catalog; p. 123.

Community/technical colleges have found that when learners complete the courses of public service academies, they often go on to enroll and complete degree programs. This increased enrollment demonstrates the educational value of credit award for academy training. See Figure 9–8 for a sample (Rancho Santiago) community college degree program structure.

Drawing Up Agreements

The inter-agency agreement is an essential component of the relationship of an academy and a community college. This agreement details the roles and responsibilities of each partner, resources to be provided,

Figure 9–8

Sample Degree Program Structure

Fire Technology
Suggested AA/AS Degree Program for Part-time Students

Students should *take transfer level general education courses. For guidance make an appointment with a Fire Technology Counselor.* Although general education courses may be taken concurrently, general education courses taken prior to the Fire Technology Program could substantially improve performance and therefore improve opportunity for success. Students are encouraged to complete a transferable general education program before enrolling in Fire Technology courses. Students are encouraged to speed the educational process through the use of appropriate RSC programs such as advanced placement with credit, career advanced placement and credit by examination. These programs are explained in the RSC catalog. All students must make sure that reading and math requirements are met for A.A./A.S. degrees.

First Semester	Second Semester
Fire Technology 101 (3 units) Fire Technology 102 (3 units)	Fire Technology 121 (5 units) English 061 or 101 (3 units)
Third Semester	Fourth Semester
Fire Technology 103 (3 units) U.S. History or Political Science 101 (3 units)	Fire Technology 104 (3 units) Humanities course (3 units)
Fifth Semester	Sixth Semester
Fire Technology 105 (3 units) Social Science elective (3 units)	Fire Technology 106 (3 units) Cultural Breadth Course (3 units) Fire Academy N08 (0.2 unit)
Seventh Semester	Eighth Semester
Communications and Analytical Thinking (3 units) Oral Communications (3 units)	Fire Academy 060 (12 units)

Advanced Fire Academy/Skills Maintenance

After you graduate from the Basic Fire Academy you will want to get a job, and it is important that you keep your knowledge fresh and skills sharp. The competition is keen; Rancho Santiago College offers the following classes to help maintain your skill level:

Fire Academy N61, Basic Fire Academy Validation

Fire Academy N61A, Skills Assessment for Employed Firefighter 1

Fire Academy N61B, Skills Assessment for Non-Employed Firefighter 1

Fire Academy N61C, Basic Fire Academy 060 Criteria Assessment

Fire Academy N61D, Skills Maintenance

Reprinted with permission of Rancho Santiago Community College District.

Figure 9–9

A Release of Information Form

COMPLIANCE FORM CSFS 80-1 REV 7/83	STATE OF CONNECTICUT **COMMISSION ON FIRE PREVENTION AND CONTROL** 294 Colony Street, Meriden, Connecticut 06450

Date: _____

RELEASE FROM LIABILITY

I,_____,hereby acknowledge and agree that the State of Connecticut Commission on Fire Prevention and Control, its Commissioners, officers, agents or employees shall not be liable for any injuries sustained by me during the course of, or as the result of my attendance and participation in the Connecticut State Fire School training program.

_____
(Signature of Applicant)

COMPLIANCE INFORMATION

(This information is needed to comply with governmental requirements and reports and will not be used for any other purpose.)

COURSE APPLIED FOR

SEX	FIREFIGHTER STATUS	HANDICAPPED
☐ MALE ☐ FEMALE	☐ PAID ☐ VOLUNTEER	☐ YES ☐ NO

Describe yourself in terms of one of the following groups:

A. ☐ AMERICAN INDIAN   B. ☐ BLACK/AFRO   C. ☐ WHITE/CAUCASIAN

D. ☐ HISPANIC/SPANISH   E. ☐ ORIENTAL/ASIAN

F. ☐ OTHER (Specify)

funds provided or charged, insurance requirements, and other local or jurisdiction stipulations. A well-devised agreement is essential to long-term, mutually satisfactory relationships.

Some factors which must be included in each agreement:

- *Limits of liability:* How will the inter-agency relationship handle the question of liability for the academy operation? This is of particular importance when potentially dangerous grounds or equipment, such as fire vehicles, pistol ranges, and practice grounds, are used for cross-agency training. The agreement should indicate exactly how the agencies and the college share liability.

- *Instructor accountability:* Who is the instructor's primary employer when working in the academy? When instructors are involved in training, it is customary to employ them as college adjunct faculty. If this is not the case, how the chain of command is to operate must be determined. This organizational structure must take into account the question of liability as well.

- *Use and maintenance of facilities:* Who will use what facilities, and how will they be maintained? If the academy uses the training center of a participating municipality will compensation be provided for upkeep and maintenance? How will these costs be shared?

- *Academy contact:* Will the agency or the college assume the spokesperson role for outside reporting?

- *Release of information:* The collection, use, and reporting of information relating to trainee records must be addressed. A format for releasing this information must be drawn up which takes into account the Privacy of Information Statutes prohibiting release of data outside of the training agency. A format for this release is presented in Figure 9–9 above.

Testing and Certification

Finally, the community college must ensure that a procedure is developed to test and certify those who complete the academy program. The very same standards developed for the operation of the academy should become the baseline for exit testing and certification. The testing program should be implemented and administered by the academy advisory committee in cooperation with the college. These evaluation procedures should also include mechanisms for recordkeeping and reporting to participating agencies outside the academy.

Chapter References

Burgess, M. (1980). Technology apprenticeship programs. *American Technical Education Association Journal,* (8)3, 13–15.

Johnston, W.B., & Packer A.E. (1987). *Workforce 2000: Work and workers for the 21st century.* Indianapolis, IN: Hudson Institute.

National Alliance of Business. (1989). *Time: The disappearing quality of the U.S. workforce: What can we do to save it?* Washington, DC: Author.

US Department of Labor. (1989). *Work-based learning: Training America's workers.* Washington, DC: Author.

US Department of Labor, Education and Commerce. (1988, July). *Building a quality workforce.* Washington, DC: Author.

Westbrook, R.C., & Butler, R.L. (1981, Fall). Apprenticeship-vocational education linkage: A course of action. *Viewpoints in Teaching and Learning,* 57(4), 65–70.

Chapter 10

Mentoring and Volunteerism: Service Learning

The subject of this chapter is service learning in the form of mentoring and volunteerism, activities which are becoming much more common at community colleges and increasingly popular with their learners.

The word *mentor* comes from Homer: Odysseus asked his friend, Mentor, to teach the virtues of life and of being Greek to his son Telemachus. Thus, a mentor is one who instructs, tutors, or guides. In cooperative education, as a result of the mentoring relationship, an adult protégé develops self-confidence, gains access to networks previously unattainable, and masters job-related skills. And a youthful protégé profits from having as an advocate and role model an adult who encourages academic and personal achievement, and who acquaints him or her with different cultural norms and values concomitant with community college goals. But the mentoring relationship is not just a one-way street; it is mutually advantageous as mentors also benefit from the activity. Adults who mentor gain personal satisfaction; they have "made it" and are able to help others succeed. As well as being motivated by altruistic feelings and rewarded by a sense of pride, the mentor also gains practical career benefits: if the protégé is successful, the mentor's own career and reputation are enhanced.

For the college and community as a whole, mentoring offers many benefits. The college increases productivity by using learners to offer remediation to other learners. As a result, attrition is often reduced—thus the community benefits from having fewer learners drop out of college. In addition, participating in mentoring and volunteer activities enables learners to develop cognitive and problem-solving skills, academic knowledge, and leadership abilities, as well as civic and social skills (NAISSE, 1988).

Mentoring (and volunteerism, to be discussed shortly) supports and promotes many of the goals of community college education, including the development of:

- a sense of personal responsibility to the larger community;
- an understanding of self;
- analytic and critical-thinking skills; and
- life-long learning skills.

In both business and education, mentoring is recognized as an effective method of training workers and/or learners by providing them with a behavior model. This practice enables business to provide cost-effective, on-the-job training and new employee indoctrination, as well as supervision for new workers on the job. In the community college, it offers a way to counsel, coach, remediate, and tutor learners who are otherwise in danger of falling behind and leaving the academic mainstream. Because of these benefits, the community-at-large recognizes that the mentoring process offers real value.

Volunteerism is yet another kind of experiential learning. Abundant opportunities exist for learners who want to contribute to their community, help others, and work on problems that are important to them. These experiences are particularly beneficial for learners seeking to enter careers in the social sciences, medical fields, and humanities.

Volunteer opportunities include direct service positions, such as working in shelters for the homeless, hospitals, food centers, and clinics. Political science students often find openings in lobbying organizations or political leaders' offices. Organizations such as *Volunteers in Service to America* can provide leads for volunteer work. A learner's own imagination need be the only limitation to opportunity.

Literacy education is also an appropriate and common area in which a learner can volunteer time and effort. Community colleges offer literacy education as a routine service. For instance, Northampton Community College (PA) offers the following kinds of services:

> Adult Literacy: Funded primarily through federal state grants, the Adult Literacy program at the College serves the basic needs of our local community. Education covers basic communications, mathematics at all levels, beginning ESL classes for non-native adults progressing through ABE (Adult Basic Education) to the General Equivalency Diploma (GED) diploma. They are generally daytime and in community locations. Recently the College expanded its efforts to the local community and business/company employees, improving basic skills/attaining GED/customizing training in job-site basic skills. In general, programs have both classroom and tutorial components.

College Catalog, 1989–1990

The Student Literacy Corps provides this kind of program. The US Department of Education spent $5.2 billion in grants during 1993 to develop student literacy corps and mentoring programs in community colleges.

Mentoring Opportunities

Mentoring at Community Colleges

Several examples of opportunities for training in mentoring offered by community colleges are described below.

At Chesapeake College:

> Tutoring advisement and instruction are provided to eligible students under the federally funded Student Support Services grant through the US Department of Education.
>
> The free tutoring is available for eligible students taking courses in English, the Natural Sciences, Mathematics, Computer Programming and Logic, Business, Accounting, the Social Sciences, Office Education and Technology, and in the many other technology programs offered at the College. Instruction is offered in note-taking, test-taking, and study skills.
>
> Special accommodations will be made for physically handicapped and learning disabled students.
>
> *1990–1991 Catalog; p. 20*

At Dundalk Community College:

> Tutor Service: Dundalk Community College provides tutoring for students enrolled in most credit classes. Students who need tutoring should contact the Tutor Coordinator. An application must be completed before tutoring begins.
>
> The Tutor Service trains qualified students to act as tutors in a wide variety of courses. Tutors must be recommended to the Tutor Service Coordinator by faculty before training begins. Tutors are paid by the college.
>
> *1989–1991 Catalog; p. 20*

To train student tutors the following kinds of courses are offered:

At Fresno City College:

> Tutor Training, 2 units, 1 hour lecture, 3 lab hours. Combines the study of methods and materials for tutoring with supervised practice in applying the concepts, principles and methods in the process of

Figure 10–1

Citrus Women in Higher Education

Women and minority community college learners face a multitude of problems and barriers. Oftentimes, their backgrounds exacerbate academic problems. Nontraditional women college students, those returning to gain a higher education after a number of years' absence, face barriers to academic success and lowered career aspirations for several reasons, among which are the overwhelming practical difficulty of finding affordable, dependable child care (if applicable), and, due to the culture in which they have been reared, the lack of confidence, assertiveness, and competitiveness needed to succeed.

To address these concerns, the staff and faculty at Citrus Community College (in California) established a support group, *Citrus Women in Higher Education.* A key feature of this support group was a mentoring program.

Potential protégés go through a rigorous selection process. If accepted into the program, they are matched to their mentors according to the mentors' professional experience, students' choice, mentors' choice, and interview committee suggestions. Once paired, the protégés work alongside their mentors for fifteen hours per week for two semesters. The protégés also receive a stipend for their contributions.

The goals of the program are enhanced self-esteem and professional development by exposing learners to crisis management, decision-making, and problem-solving situations. These goals are met by having the student/protégés shadow their mentors, who are college administrators or individuals from the business community, during leadership situations. Activities include involvement in such campus projects as workshops and conferences, introductions to on- and off-campus professionals, participation in professional conferences, and ongoing analyses of the students' involvement in the program.

Participants demonstrate much professional development and career growth. The women selected appear to have benefitted from being able to formulate clear educational and career goals as a result of their participation.

conducting individual and small group tutorials. Designed for peer tutors working in college tutorial, math and English learning centers and for adult students employed or desiring future employment as educational or instructional aides or teachers.

1992–1994 Catalog; p. 151

At Consumes River College:

Beginning Peer Assistant Training, Prerequisite: Eligibility for English 57 or as determined by the assessment process. Acceptable for Credit: CSU

Three hours lecture

Fosters the student's understanding of CRC regulations and procedures, campus resources, study skills, and career planning; trains students in basic communication and counseling skills, including goal setting, problem solving, time management, and decision making; encourages students to develop a sense of responsibility and commitment to help others; prepares students to participate as Peer Advisors in a college setting.

1992–1993 Catalog; p. 129

Mohegan Community College offers a program in Peer Counseling Training. Their program is described in the college catalog as follows:

Peer Counseling Training

Peer counselor training is offered by the Student Development Center at Mohegan Community College in conjunction with the Women's Center of Southeastern Connecticut. The Peer Counseling training course, Counseling 211, carries three (3) semester hours of college elective credits and is offered during the fall and spring semesters. The course is designed to help prepare and develop skilled empathetic Peer Counselors for field placement in Mohegan's Student Development Center and Tutoring Center, the Women's Center of Southeastern Connecticut in New London and Norwich, and other approved community agencies.

All Peer Counselor trainees who successfully complete Counseling 211 may apply for a Peer Counselor position the following semester. Accepted applicants will enroll in Counseling 212: Peer Counseling Practicum and serve as a Peer Counselor under the supervision of a professional staff member at the placement site.

1990–1991 Catalog; p. 126

This service requires the completion of these Mohegan Community College courses:

COUN 211 Peer Counseling, 3 semester hours

This course is designed to help prepare and develop skilled empathic Peer Counselors for placement in positions at the College and

Figure 10–2

CUNY/BOE Student Mentor Program

Also concerned with America's future workers, and as part of the history of collaboration between the New York City Board of Education (BOE) and the City University of New York (CUNY), the *CUNY/BOE Student Mentor Program* was established in 1985. Supported by the CUNY central office, the goals of the program are threefold: (1) to create favorable learning experiences for area high school students (ninth and tenth graders at risk of dropping out) so that they are motivated to finish high school; (2) to help these students set realistic educational and career goals; and (3) to enhance the professional development of college learners who serve as their mentors.

The mentor program, which runs for 15 weeks (one semester) at a time, operates at approximately 19 CUNY campuses. Each campus is linked with one or two local high schools. The mentors gain college credit for their participation (the program is either the field work component or the main thrust of a college course). During weeks 1 through 5, mentors and protégés receive training and orientation, meet together as a group for icebreaker activities, and are paired according to similar abilities and interests. During the rest of the semester (weeks 6 through 15), each pair (there are currently 300 such pairs) agree to meet for two hours per week. Each group of protégés and mentors also meet separately as groups with their respective coordinators, and there are occasional special activities scheduled for all protégés, mentors, and coordinators.

The college learners' main responsibilities as mentors are to serve as role models and listeners. By encouraging participation in career and school activities, they help their protégés get better grades and finish high school. Suggested activities include touring college campuses, visiting museums or galleries, tutoring, discussing career options, and attending classes together. (This list is, by no means, exhaustive.) The mentors are also encouraged to help their protégés select and achieve one realistic goal for the semester.

The strength of the program depends on the relationships between the high school and college coordinators, and the support of the central office staff. The program has been very successful despite the complicated logistics required to administer it. Furthermore, the program has not only benefitted the learners in terms of increased self-esteem, but has benefitted the mentors as well. They have gained professionally by their participation and have improved problem solving, research, and communication skills.

Since its inception, the program has expanded (number of participants and sites), and there are plans for further expansion, training, and support. The underlying purpose of the mentor program is dropout prevention. For those relationships that seem to be working well, the program is currently developing a second semester mentor program—a model that would capitalize on these relationships.

in the community. The techniques, methods, and functions of peer counseling will be explored and integrated with theoretical concepts to be applied in a variety of settings. Prerequisites: Completion of at least one semester at Mohegan with a minimum of 6 credits and a 2.5 GPA. Successful completion of PSY 111 or equivalent course, training or experience, or consent of instructor.

COUN 212 Peer Counseling Practicum, 1–3 semester hours

Students who have successfully completed COUN 211 will apply peer counseling skills and methods through supervised placement in a College or community setting. Prerequisites: COUN 211 and consent of instructor.

1990–1991 Catalog; p. 126

Mentoring in Business

Community colleges prepare learners for careers and for life. Many learners, as eventual business leaders, will be faced with certain challenges. Entrepreneurs now and in the future will need to manage their businesses or organizations in spite of the decline in the skills of basic entry-level workers, the growing labor shortage, the changing composition of the workforce, the increasing numbers of multicultural workers, and the loss of managerial talents and skills resulting from mergers and acquisitions. Mentoring can serve as a tool for the professional development of employees at all levels of an organization and thus becomes a necessary skill for managers to acquire and employ. By improving skills, corporate productivity and creativity is decreased, turnover is reduced, and communication is enhanced. According to Davis (1991), when a protégé is guided by a more powerful advocate (familiar with company politics and willing to lobby on his or her behalf), that protégé becomes better integrated into the organization and gains a sense of belonging. This is especially true for women and members of minorities who might not have easy access to information available through the "old-boy network." Mentoring also provides opportunities for managers to acquire cross-cultural training.

Developing Mentoring Programs

Principles for Success

Mentoring opportunities should be made available across all college programs and campuses. Mentoring programs succeed when they are guided by fundamental principles. Carefully consider the following factors.

Full support and commitment

Successful programs usually include one key individual who strongly believes in, advocates, instigates, and participates in their formation. In addition, successful programs are solidly supported by all participants. For example, sponsors show their commitment to the goals of mentoring programs by concrete action, such as providing mentors with orientation and training.

Clear and specific goals

All successful mentoring programs have clearly defined goals dedicated to ensuring that all learners have the best opportunity for college success and will recognize the value of education. At a minimum, learners who are being coached are expected to advance in college work, as well as improve study attitudes and aptitudes. These results fulfill the institutional goals of enabling learners to make a successful transition from college to work and/or further higher education.

Active recruitment of mentors and careful matching with learners

Voluntary participation of college learners as mentors is now an intrinsic part of many college programs. For these programs recruitment should be conducted through the college student activities office and the career services center, as well as through individual departments and courses. Faculty and administrators should take care to match participants according to geographic proximity, college schedules, and similar occupational and educational interests.

Sufficient time

Time plays a most important role in these programs. To be successful, relationships between mentors and protégés require enough time to allow for the development of trust and respect, and to impart knowledge and skills. Successful sponsors will commit to multi-year relationships.

Figure10–3

Sponsor-A-Scholar

Founded two years ago by Dr. Marciene Mattleman (former Temple University professor and Director of the Mayor's Committee on Literacy), Philadelphia Futures is a non-profit organization dedicated to helping children stay in school, attend college, and pursue careers. Its *Sponsor-A-Scholar* (SAS) pilot program is a natural outgrowth of the organization's other mentoring efforts and interventions.

Philadelphia Futures received a grant from the Commonwealth Fund to develop and launch the SAS pilot program, a creative long-term initiative. Philadelphia Futures recruits sponsors from the business community. These sponsors, individuals or corporate employees, commit to mentor students who range from ninth grade through the first year of college. These high school students must show academic promise, desire to attend college, and financial need. The money to be set aside serves as "last dollar" monies to fill the gaps between their financial aid packages and college expenses.

The sponsors meet with their learners once a month and are in touch, either by note or telephone, at least one more time during any given month. The relationships are somewhat casual; mentors are "big brothers/big sisters." For example, the mentor/protégé pairs might go to movies, museums, or out to eat. Depending on the relationship, the mentor might also offer academic advice and support.

Mentors: Making Contributions

Mentors are people who possess special talents and are motivated to share these talents with others. Mentors can make contributions in the following areas:

- technical or specific knowledge;
- leadership skills;
- citizenship education;
- mental and physical fitness;
- social skills;
- personal values; and
- character development.

Some programs and activities which have worked successfully are:

- In Rutgers University "Soup-Kitchen Classroom" learners work in the soup kitchen of a homeless shelter in Newark, New Jersey. A Rutgers learner generally volunteers 4–5 hours per week in a team with other learners and earns regular course credit in political science plus extra credit for service. The learners discuss the issues involved and implications of their service with team leaders. This program began as a part of a Rockefeller Foundation grant.

- The Stamford "Women's Project" in Stamford, Connecticut, is one in which learners from Norwalk Community College work with welfare recipients to assist them to prepare for employment. Single mothers are paired with a mentor who is in a successful career and who can act as an advisor and role model.

- City University of New York Community College learners serve as mentors to New York City public school students. College learners are paired geographically with youth to assist with school studies and serve as role models. College learners also work along side their pupil's classroom teachers. The program has prevented student dropout from public school and helped college learners make choices about teaching as a career (Figure 10–2).

- Coopers & Lybrand (C&L) works with community-based organizations, such as SEO, an organization that identifies bright and motivated minority high school students who have the potential and ability to go to college but might otherwise not be able to because of their background. C&L provides staff to serve as mentors to these students. C&L and SEO recruit community/technical college learners to work as mentors also.

- Butte College (CA) fire science learners serve as volunteer firefighters in the community. They receive college credit in the fire science program for their service.

Mentors: Making Choices

What should college learners consider when choosing to participate in mentor/volunteer experiential learning?

Goals

First, potential mentors/volunteers must take into account their own personal, long-range career goals. They should focus on gaining the kinds of experiences that can be helpful in making career choices, and/or can

Figure 10–4

The Puente Project

Community colleges in California recognized a need in the early 1980s to help their Mexican American and Latino students reach their academic goals. A statewide academic program, the *Puente Project*, initiated in 1982 at one community college, had two broad goals that addressed those needs: to reduce the dropout rate of Latino and Mexican American community college learners, and to increase the numbers of these learners who transfer to four-year colleges and universities. Co-sponsored by the California Community Colleges and the University of California, the program operated at 19 California community colleges and served approximately 1,800 learners.

The Puente project focused on three problems that stand in the way of academic success for Mexican American and Latino community college learners: lack of: (1) writing skills, (2) knowledge of the educational system, and (3) role models. To address those concerns, the project trained English teachers and Hispanic counselors to work together in teams. These teams instituted year-long English writing courses and conducted culturally based academic counseling geared specifically to these college learners. They also linked their students with mentors from the Hispanic communities. These mentors were successful professionals (for example, judges, lawyers, accountants, university administrators, doctors) who donated over 15,000 hours of their time. Over 600 people served as role models and demonstrated to Puente students that it is possible to succeed without abandoning cultural identity. These mentors also provided their learners with internships and scholarships.

The Puente project was deemed successful in achieving its stated goals; more Hispanic students were transferring to four-year colleges. It appears that all three elements of the program—special English writing classes, academic counseling, and mentoring—played an important role in the program's success. A continual concern was obtaining adequate funding.

---

provide the practical experiences that will be useful when job hunting. Usually an offer of volunteer service is easier to "sell" to a firm or agency than a job—as no compensation is involved.

Interests

Next, learners should consider what they like to do as a hobby. This may suggest a direction in which to look for volunteer opportunities. It is not unusual for community college learners to volunteer for reasons other than direct career advancement. Sometimes, personal interest, social value, or civic concern are prime motivators. For example, a learner who is an amateur radio enthusiast may act as a mentor to a person seeking to qualify for a ham radio license. Student clubs are prime grounds for hobby or special interest mentor recruiting.

Education and/or experience

A learner's past education and experience is another good basis on which to choose where to mentor and volunteer. Some colleges encourage students to tutor weaker learners in shared subjects in which they have specialized or done well. Physics, mathematics, technical subjects, literacy education (reading, writing, basic math) are all areas in which learners can provide leadership and assistance to others on a volunteer basis.

Special skills

Using special skills and knowledge in volunteer activity is also valuable. Learners gain useful practice and experience both vocationally and avocationally when they possess and share special skills and knowledge, such as firefighting, electronics, computer programming, stress management, technical writing, to name just a few.

Special interests

Finally, learners should consider what they are "passionate" about. Perhaps their special interest, politics, community issues, working with children, etc., would lend itself well to mentoring or volunteerism. The activity might not necessarily earn any college credit, but rather would be of civic or social value.

Mentors: Preparation

Community colleges with successful mentoring programs establish a mechanism (e.g., a preparatory course) in order to prepare and orient learners for mentoring and volunteer assignments. Included in these courses are some of the following topics (Shea, 1992).

Setting goals and expectations

A learner must know what to expect from a mentor/protégé or volunteer relationship. Therefore, goal-setting is a necessary skill. "Up-front" communication with and understanding of the protégé and supervisor is critical to ultimate success and self-satisfaction. Expectations of the protégé and the volunteer agency must be clearly determined and understood at the commencement of the assignment.

Acquiring teaching skills

A basic knowledge of the teaching and learning process is also necessary, as a mentor will share critical knowledge and provide educational experiences. Assistance with career development is a primary objective of the volunteer/client relationship. Mentors must establish an agenda of challenging ideas and goals for a protégé. Therefore, an understanding of adult learning or child/adolescent psychology is helpful.

Building learner confidence

Mentors or volunteers will find that a large part of their task will involve building their clients' self-confidence and confronting negative behaviors and attitudes. Therefore, a preparatory course should contain information and activities to help volunteers in this process. It will be important for them to understand how to:

- develop learner self-esteem to overcome acquired helplessness;
- get close to a protégé;
- give praise contingent upon a response; and
- catch them being good (Cantor, 1992).

Serving as a model

Mentors must clearly understand that when serving in a mentor/volunteer capacity they are professionals and must act the part. Scheduling, organizational policy and procedure, maintaining a professional relationship and decorum, dress, etc., are all topics which should be discussed. Setting an example through appropriate behavior, thus inspiring the client, is a perfect way to serve.

In the role of counselor a mentor will find it necessary to develop other skills, including: knowing how to listen and how to coach; keeping a confidence; offering wise counsel; providing encouragement; offering friendship; and encouraging winning behavior.

The mentoring/volunteer experience will provide learners with life-long memories, in addition to valuable learning, complementary to a degree program.

Chapter References

Cantor, J.A. (1992). *Delivering instruction to adult learners.* Toronto: Wall & Emerson.

Davis, R.L. (1991). *Mentoring: The strategy of the master.* Cambridge, Ontario: Thomas Nelson.

Fitzpatrick, J. (1991, March 17). Mentors help women travel from welfare to independence. *New York Times, 12,* 1.

Goldberg, V. (1992, September 22). The soup-kitchen classroom. *New York Times,* 49-50, 72.

Haugsby, T.R. (1991, Winter). Service learning and cooperative education: Serving God or Mammon. *Journal of Cooperative Education, 27*(2), 99-106.

Kendall, J.C. and Associates. (1990). *Combining service and learning* (Vols. I & II). Raleigh, NC.: National Society for Internships and Experiential Learning.

National Society for Internship and Experiential Learning. (1988). *Combining service and learning* (Vol. III). Raleigh, NC: (Author).

Shea, G.F. (1992). *Mentoring: A practical guide.* Los Altos, CA: Crisp Publications.

Chapter 11

Learning from Life Experience

Community colleges now often incorporate a learner's accumulated life experiences into formal degree programs for credit. These experiences often include: (1) past employment; (2) training from business and industry; (3) military training; and/or (4) general life experiences. The methods by which community colleges administer a life experience program are discussed in this chapter.

As well as accumulating extensive and significant learning experiences outside the college classroom on the job, during military training, and through involvement in community activities, many adult learners have also participated in valuable self-initiated learning activities in such areas as art, education, photography, auto mechanics, computer programming, music, theater, electronics, management, typing, and many others. These personal skills and competencies now may be used to meet some degree program requirements.

Most adult learners want to complete a certificate or degree program as quickly as possible for obvious personal and/or career reasons. They do not wish to be required to enroll in courses for which they already have developed equivalent skills or competencies. Thus, they wish, if possible, to obtain college credit for what they have already learned.

Through several processes of assessment of prior learning (e.g., portfolio assessment, challenge exam, etc.), community colleges can evaluate and recognize such experiences for credit towards a degree.

Recognizing General Life Experience

Portfolio Development

The process of evaluating the relevance of a learner's accomplishments to a particular program of study often begins with the development of a portfolio. Many community colleges offer a specific course to help learners assess their prior experience and prepare a personal portfolio of achievement for presentation. The objectives of such a course include:

- helping learners consider and analyze their overall life and educational goals;

- providing classroom-based activities in which learners can explore their own backgrounds and determine how best to achieve life experience credit (e.g., portfolio assessment; challenge exams; military experience credit);

- offering assistance in gathering and preparing documentation or other evidence to support learning claims;

- encouraging learners to consider the life experience credit within a framework of broader educational goals.

Specifically the following questions need to be considered in order to clarify learner needs and determine the content and direction of the portfolio presentation.

- Does the learner need to learn more about a particular field?

- Does the learner want to qualify for a new line of work?

- Does the learner need to prepare for a license or occupational certificate?

- Does the learner need to complete a degree?

- Does the learner want to gain admittance to graduate school?

Simosko, 1985

An example of a successfully implemented formal procedure for enabling students to present past achievements for credit is Dundalk Community College's *Life Experience Portfolio Development* course. The course description reads:

APL 101 Portfolio Development (3) (Three hours of lecture a week, one semester) Prerequisite: Consent of Coordinator of Assessment of Prior Learning.

This course is designed to assist students to examine their past experiences to identify and clarify college-level learning in a format that can be evaluated by a faculty assessor for possible credit awards for existing courses.

1989–1991 Catalog; p. 92

The benefits of such a process are as follows:

- All learners can receive the same directions for the assembly of a portfolio.
- Guidance is given the learner in a disciplined college environment.
- A fair, administratively approved process exists for compensating faculty for the portfolio evaluation workload.

Through courses such as these, learners are shown how to review and analyze their prior experiences and how to present this experience effectively when constructing a life experience portfolio.

A learner generally must meet certain prerequisites to participate in life experience programs. At Lehman College, as well as at many other colleges, these requirements include:

- matriculation in a degree program;
- a minimum of 15 credits completed;
- a minimum grade point average of 2.5;
- being at least 25 years of age;
- having a reasonable amount of paid work experience.

Credit for life experience is based solely on the learner's ability to demonstrate learning of an academic nature acquired through life experience. This acquired knowledge often must fall within one or more academic disciplines offered by the college (e.g., art, speech, engineering technology). A learner's application will be reviewed for credit by faculty members of the department representing the academic discipline(s) cited by the application for credit. A typical portfolio coversheet is presented in Figure 11–1 below.

The learner specifies for which acquired skills he/she is requesting credit within a given discipline and writes a brief statement about each area of experience. For instance, a group worker in a teen center may have acquired knowledge that falls within the academic discipline of sociology. The specific skill learned might be "how to deal with the identity struggle during adolescence." The actual experience might include "guiding groups to deal with feelings of rebellion against parents and other authorities," or "organizing activities which give the teens themselves a chance to be in positions of responsibility," and so on. Skills gained through leisure activities also may relate to certain technical areas.

Figure 11-1

An Application for Life Experience Credits

NAME: _____   DATE: _____

ADDRESS: _____   SOC. SEC.# _____
_____   TEL. (Home) _____
_____   TEL. (Work) _____

I. Name the academic discipline within which you are seeking credit:

_____

II. List the actual experiences (either paid or volunteer jobs) which provided you with the skills of the academic discipline cited above:

    1. Place of Employment: _____

       Your position/title: _____

       Date engaged in this experience: From __/ /__ to __/ /__

    2. Place of Employment: _____

       Your position/title: _____

       Date engaged in this experience: From __/ /__ to __/ /__

    3. Place of Employment: _____

       Your position/title: _____

       Date engaged in this experience: From __/ /__ to __/ /__

III. Please attach to this application a full and comprehensive description of the specific skills which you have mastered through the experiences listed above. For each skill you should describe the actual duties and activities performed. List and number these skills—e.g., Skill #1, Skill #2, etc.

For instance, a ham radio enthusiast will have acquired extensive electronics expertise which should be noted.

To find out which skills may be appropriate to include in a life experience portfolio, guide learners to ask the following questions:

- Have I performed specific duties at my job?
- Do I have specific technical skills?
- Have I done volunteer work in a special area such as counseling?
- Do I read extensively in a particular field?
- Have I held elected office?
- How do I spend my leisure time?

Simosko, 1985, p. 37

To organize this information the learner can apply the following strategies:

- Write down a chronological list of jobs held, both full time and part time.
- Record all non-credit and business-related training completed, including military training.
- Draw up a list of people, places, and things from the past.
- Record key events or milestones, successes (or failures) from life.
- Develop an interest or hobby list, including procedures, skills, projects done or developed.
- List books read, concerts attended, or museums visited.

Simosko, 1985, p. 36

In addition, the learner can list specific skills acquired, with a brief statement about each, giving examples from actual experience to illustrate what was learned.

For instance, be sure to list:

- skills performed on the job;
- outstanding areas of performance on the job;
- oral presentations made at the workplace;

Figure 11-2

Worksheet: Identifying What You Know

Year & Activity	What I Did	What I Had to Know	What I Learned
1977-1980 Held Administrative Assistant position in Union/ Community Services Agency	Maintained inventory control of publications	Organizational procedures	How to develop inventory control system
	Corresponded with clients	How to solve problems	How to write more effectively
	Wrote copy for press	How to write buisness letters and memos	Public relations
		How to prepare news copy	How to deal with media personel
	Prepared budget reports	How to set up account books	How to monitor accounts receivable and payable
	Supervised clerical staff	How to get along with others	Personnel policies and procedures
		How to deal with difficult personnel issues	Group dynamics
1978 Elected SchoolBoard Treasurer	Prepared budget proposals for Board's consideration	Throrough knowledge of state and local budgets	Budgeting on a big scale
	Reviewed expenditures	How to be careful	Fiscal management
	Worked with state auditors	How to explain budget and provide information	Professional writing procedures
	Prepared budget statements	How to write	How to be persuasive
	Gave public presentations of Annual Budget Report	How to speak	How to improve my public speaking

From Simosko, 1985, p. 38. Reprinted with permission of
The Council for Adult and Experiential Learning.

- leadership roles (e.g., union representative, chamber of commerce liaison);
- other languages spoken, computer program language expertise, special skills (e.g., Cardio-Pulmonary Resuscitation).

Simosko, 1985, p. 36

Figure 11–2 is a typical example of a planning worksheet from this kind of activity.

Using college catalogs

When preparing their portfolios, learners should carefully analyze the college catalog. One process often used by community colleges when evaluating portfolios is to determine if the experiences and knowledge presented can be matched to specific college courses. Again, some colleges offer an alternate method of evaluation—"challenge by exam"— which allows learners to write an examination to get credit for specific courses. By analyzing specific course descriptions, learners can determine what relationship, if any, their work experiences bear to the course content and which method of evaluation might be most appropriate. It is usually easier for a learner to carry out these kinds of analytical tasks after reviewing the course descriptions in the college catalog. In doing so, the learner should ask the following questions.

Do I know:
- the terminology of the field?
- specific facts in the field? (I can relate, list, name, recall, define, record...)
- conventions and practices? (I can propose, categorize, set up, formulate...)
- classifications and categories? (I can design, arrange...)
- criteria? (I can debate, examine...)
- principles? (I can express, discuss...)
- theories? (I can manage, construct...)

Simosko, 1985, p. 45

Documenting life experiences

It is important for learners to provide sufficient documentation to support the assertion that they were engaged in the experiences outlined. Documentation of life experiences generally comes from a number of sources, including, for example:

- letters written on a learner's behalf (see below);
- manuals, articles, books, brochures written or co-written;
- patents obtained;
- computer programs written;
- music created or art composed;
- audio/visual tapes of work performed;
- photographs taken; and
- commendations received.

Letters written on a learner's behalf

Letters may be written by:

- previous or present employers;
- co-workers or partners;
- teachers;
- community or government leaders; and
- personal acquaintances or long-time friends for hobby or avocational purposes.

Simosko, 1985, p. 63

A typical letter documenting employment is presented in Figure 11–3.

Portfolio Evaluation

Learners prepare comprehensive packages which are submitted for formal assessment to determine whether or not their experiences can earn credit. Typically, community colleges have in place specific parameters for credit award.

Some colleges use a *college course model* whereby competencies are clustered into components for credit award in a discipline area. This college course model method requires the learner to provide documen-

Figure 11–3

A Letter Documenting Employment

Confectionery Importers
14 West 8th Street
New York, NY 10001

TO WHOM IT MAY CONCERN:

Mr. James Thorpe has worked for this firm from July 2, 1987 through June of 1990. During these years Mr. Thorpe was an account technician. His duties included monitoring our accounts receivable, and posting invoices. He performed his duties diligently, and was a trusted employee. For your information, a detailed job description of an account technician is attached.

Please call upon me if further information is necessary.

Sincerely,

Joseph Crutch,
President

tation demonstrating proficiency in each major performance objective cited in the syllabus. The documentation may include, for example, writing samples provided by the learner in the case of a course such as technical writing, or professional certificates, e.g., "Master Electrical Systems Technician," earned by the learner in a course in automotive electrical systems. In some instances, outside evaluation organizations, such as the National Occupational Competency Testing Institute (NOCTI), can be useful for documenting such learning.

Figure 11-4

Sample Learner's Statement of Relevant Life Experiences

Olden and Allied Temps

During the period from March 1982 to February 1985, my work experience came from employment at various companies. Some of these assignments (through Olden and Allied Temps) were performed at Mobil Steel, Bay Bank, and Legal Services. At each of these firms, I worked as a word processing operator utilizing all of the Wang systems—Wang PC, Wang VS, and the Wang OIS. My duties and responsibilities at these firms were word processing, filing and answering the telephone.

- Skill #1: Word processing was done on the Wang and the IBM PC. I improved both my ability to use these systems and my typing skills. My typing speed increased from 40 words per minute to 60 wpm. I typed the documents on which I worked in a timely and accurate manner. Sometimes I was given handwritten documents of about 25 pages to type. My supervisor frequently complimented me on how quickly I was able to return an accurate finished product.
- Skill #2: Part of my job was to answer the telephone. Due to the large volume of calls received by these firms, my telephone techinques improved. For example, I learned to juggle 3 or 4 incoming telephone calls, take messages if any, and transfer the calls to the appropriate person.
- Skill #3: Putting executed or pending documents away required a knowledge of filing. I sharpened my organizational skills. Arranging paperwork in an orderly way allowed for easy access to documents when they were needed.

Bay Bank

My experience at Bay Bank in 1985 (through Olden and Allied Temps) exposed me to clerical work, the Wang PC, and the IBM PC. I became proficient at installing different software packages and monitoring a telephone support hot-line at Bay's "Computer Store," a service provided to thousands of Bay Employees. I also handled maintenance contracts for each department within Bay.

- Skill #1: When I started working at Bay Bank, I was a clerical worker and a wordprocessing operator for one of the Vice Presidents. My duties included typing documents, filing, and answering the telephone for a group of 10 people. Documents were typed on the Wang PC, and I became proficient with this System. I also improved my communications skills as a result of the constant telephone contacts with clients and arranging meetings for my boss. I filed important documents so that they could be easily retrieved and referred to when needed.
- Skill #2: After a few months, my boss was very impressed with my knowledge of the inner workings of the PC, mainly DOS, and trans-

ferred me from secretarial duties to the Computer Store. I was trained to install and test software that we received from companies anxious to sell their products to the bank. Everyone around me was amazed at how easily I was able to retain information about computers. I soon became the primary person to whom questions were directed regarding PC problems. It was interesting and exciting to work with so many people within the Bay community. Every day my knowledge increased as a result of solving someone else's problem.

• Skill #3: My department within Bay was called "The Computer Store." The department was responsible for the installation of software on the IBM PCs in Bay Plaza and other branches of the Bank. In addition to the installation of software, I was required to test software packages that were presently on the market. When Bay hired new secretaries, I was one of the people to install the appropriate software for the hiring department. If no disk space was available on the hard drive, I would delete the unused programs so that the software I was installing would run without memory conflict.

• Skill #4: I also provided telephone support to the PC user working at Bay Plaza and other Bay branches. Most of the questions I answered came from new PC users who were not familiar with the software or who were recently trained. Typical questions that I answered include: (1) how to set up a merge for mass mailing; (2) how to format a diskette and copy a document onto it; (3) how to remove a document from the print queue after it has started. I must confess that I handled some of the questions by telling the person I would call them back with the answer and would thereafter set out to resolve the problem. This part of my job was very satisfying because I was helping an individual and improving my knowledge of the system as well.

Working in the Computer Store at Chase Manhattan Bank and monitoring the Chase hot-line improved my communication skills immensely because of the need to direct PC users and explain various concepts to them over the telephone. I also became knowledgeable in the area of computer software, because I had to be familiar with the major software products available on the market in order to provide support to the end users.

The *learning components model* method requires a subjective judgment on the part of the evaluator of the portfolio. In this case, a faculty member assesses the learner's written statements and the evidence provided. Consider the example in Figure 11–4 in which the learner is requesting credit award consideration for previous employment as an office administrative assistant. The life experiences consist of wordprocessing and clerical skills gained during a five-year period. The learner has presented the skills in a numbered sequence, citing increasingly responsible levels of proficiency.

In the example contained in Figure 11–4, the faculty evaluator must group the skills into discrete components such as:

- wordprocessing;
- office administration (e.g., filing, telephone); and
- bookkeeping and basic accounting.

And then a level of proficiency must be assigned to each component. For example:

- wordprocessing—60 words-per-minute;
- office administration—advanced—helped to organize systems and train others;
- bookkeeping and basic accounting—intermediate—performed skills with little supervision necessary.

The next task is to assign a credit value to the findings of the portfolio assessment. Many colleges use the *"Carnegie Formula."*

> A standard three (3) credit-hour course requires learners to spend 45 hours of class time and 90 hours of out-of-class work in order to receive credit.

The wordprocessing skills outlined in Figure 11–4 were acquired from March 1982 to Febraury 1985 in the course of assignments through Olden and Allied Temps. By analyzing earnings statements, presented as part of the portfolio to document a minimum of 90 clock hours of actual work experience, the learner could earn 3 credits in *Wordprocessing Practice,* which would be posted on the college transcript. This experience then can be equated with the college course requirement of 60 WPM proficiency. Similarly, the other learning components can be equated in order to award credit.

Typically, a learner would describe skills gained more fully as in the example in Figure 11–5.

General Guidelines for Evaluating Life Experience Applications

Some colleges permit only mature adults to be accepted into a life experience course, and specify a minimum age requirement. For example, learners may have to be at least 25 years old. This ensures that, as a result, learners applying for credit for life experience generally have had a fair amount of work or volunteer experience.

Figure 11–5

Learner's Statement of Relevant Life Experiences with Fuller Description of Skills Learned

Hanover Trust Company

During the period of April 1981 to March 1982, I was placed by Office Temporaries at The Hanover Trust Company. My major duties and responsibilities included checking detailed listings of bonds and coupons for accuracy in their maturity dates, payment rates, numbers, series, and denominations. I also worked on the daily activity reports on these same bonds and coupons, making corrections and adjustments where necessary. I reconciled various accounts and analyzed cash statement data that covered money transfers, overdrafts, and account descriptions. I also arranged, sorted, and filed invoices, correspondence, and other miscellaneous material. I retrieved and refiled items as requested from the vault.

- Skill #1: By working with so many figures, I improved my mathematical ability. I was able to check the series and denominations on the bonds and coupons. I was able to organize the figures, some of which added up to thousands of dollars, in the proper columns so that they could be totalled correctly.
- Skill #2: I developed a very strong proof reading ability by constantly checking and examining the maturity dates of bonds and coupons for errors.
- Skill #3: I improved my filing skills. I retrieved files from the bank vault. These were usually organized according to the names on the accounts. Organization was therefore an important part of my work. When my work was done for the day, I correctly refiled those files which were all arranged in alphabetical order.
- Skill #4: Report writing was also part of my job. I was required to write an analysis of accounts that were not balanced. I had to give a detailed description of the problem and possible resolutions. As a result of this work, my abilities to write clearly and accurately were sharpened.

In completing the application, the learner's aim is to demonstrate learning of an academic nature that has taken place through direct experience. The learner is instructed to express this in terms of skills, giving explicit examples of on-the-job tasks through which skills and knowledge have been acquired. In addition, the learner also lists relevant readings and/or work-related training programs and/or civic or volunteer work.

In evaluating the learner's experience, faculty should keep certain guidelines in mind. First, remember that this is *not* an application for specific course credit. Learners who consider themselves to have the specific knowledge offered by a particular course should be encouraged to apply directly to the department concerned for course credit by challenge exam. The life experience portfolio is used to document more non-specific learning experiences. The learner may possess knowledge that will include some aspects of the content of several courses, but that will not be adequate to enable the learner to pass the course exams. For example, a learner may have had a great deal of experience in running his or her own business, during which time knowledge has been acquired that may cover some of the material of several business courses, but not fully cover any one specific course. Another learner may possess knowledge which clearly falls within a particular academic discipline, but for which the department offers no equivalent courses.

Recognizing Business and Industry Life Experience

Credit Received in Business and Industry

Many community colleges grant life experience credit for training received as an employee in business and industry or in government agencies. Often colleges use the *National Guide to Credit Recommendations for Non-Collegiate Courses* (American Council on Education) as a guide for appropriate credit award. Another resource for making decisions about which experiences are appropriate for college credit is the *Cooperative Assessment of Experiential Learning* (CAEL) literature and guidelines. The *Program on Non-Standardized Instruction* (PONSI) system also offers guidance in these areas. Some industry-sponsored training programs award continuing education units (CEUs). The continuing education unit or CEU is designed as a uniform unit of measurement to facilitate the accumulation and exchange of standardized information about individual participation in non-credit continuing education courses. One continuing education unit is defined as ten clock hours of participation experience under responsible sponsorship, capable direction, and qualified instruction.

Amount of credit

More often than not, faculty consensus is reached on the principle of granting credit for competence achieved outside of the classroom, but achieving agreement on exactly how much to award is difficult. Without specific documentation of competence it is extremely difficult to assign a definite number of credits when the usual time frame of the classroom is lacking. While it seems to be a relatively simple task to decide that a learner has learned something, the quantification of that learning into credit units poses a major problem.

Regardless of the methods employed, faculty are often unhappy with what they consider to be a "numbers game" in a process that bears no relation to the usual means of accumulating credits. Therefore, demonstration that performance objectives have been met is necessary. And, sometimes, the only readily available guide is the class itself (course equivalent). If learning can be categorized and measured in terms of one or a combination of course equivalents, or grouped in disciplinary areas according to beginning, intermediate, and advanced levels, then the amount of credit to be granted is based on existing and understood standards.

The direct translation of past work experience into credit is handled in much the same way. In some programs the number of years employed becomes the number of credits to be awarded. Thus, a person who has worked successfully for three years as an accountant, and has a letter from an employer verifying this, automatically receives 12 semester hours of accounting (4 semester hours for every year worked). Whether this experience will be considered as beginning, intermediate, or advanced depends on the third-party evaluation and the description of duties. Obviously, each program puts a limit on the number of credits to be granted in this manner. A person who has worked for twenty-five years as an accountant cannot receive 100 semester hours of credit in accounting!

Meyer, 1975, p. 171

Life/work experience (a typical formula)

- Each year of full-time work in area of concentration = 6 semester hours. Proof will be drawn from learner's employment records.

- Each year of full-time work outside area of concentration = 2 semester hours.

- Not more than one-half of the total degree will be credited for work experience.

Meyer, 1975, p. 22

A standard amount of credit to be awarded for prior learning across all programs is not realisitc. We have not yet instituted a system of competency-based education, or a system of established and documented standards for which learners must demonstrate competence. The predominant method of assigning credit for college courses is based on hours of scheduled time in the classroom, rather than on the knowledge and skills gained. Faculty often have difficulty equating what learners have achieved on their own with what they supposedly are learning within the framework of clock hours spent in a classroom, laboratory, or supervised field experience. Time spent on the job in an accepted work context is more easily understood by faculty, administrators, employers, and learners.

At some colleges, the faculty evaluator can award up to a maximum of 15 credits, based on such factors as the types of experiences, the learner's understanding and mastery of these, the level of achievement, and the length of time spent. These credits are then recorded as *general* credits towards a degree and may not be applied towards fulfillment of area of concentration requirements at most colleges.

All faculty should know how credit will be awarded. If crediting is to be done by course equivalences, then the formula should be agreed on by all involved.

Recognizing Military Education and Training

Many community college learners have successfully completed military education and training. Many of these programs have been evaluated and recommended for college-level credit by the American Council on Education and by the National Program on Non-Sponsored Instruction. The guide used for award of credit is the *Guide to the Evaluation of Educational References* in the Armed Services from the American Council on Education. Often a grade percentile of twenty or above is required of the learner. Appropriate documents and transcripts verifying basic military training, in-service training, or credit earned at a participating serviceperson's opportunity college need to be presented by the learner for such evaluation. This supporting material may include a copy of separation papers for each primary military occupational specialty. Additionally, the learner may have to obtain a minimum number of credits in residence at the college with a minimum grade point average. To be counted, military training may also have to be in an area related to the intended major.

For instance, Fresno City College grants credit for military service training according to their catalog statement as follows:

> "...any person who has completed basic military training can re-
> ceive 6 semester units of credit towards graduation; 2 of which may
> be used to fulfill the health education requirement; and/or, of which
> 2 meet P.E. requirements."

College Catalog 1992–1994

Credit can also be granted for courses taken by correspondence through the Defense Activity Non-Traditional Evaluation Support (DANTES).

Faculty Compensation

There are several methods employed by colleges to compensate faculty for carrying out assessment of prior learning. However, at those colleges where experiential learning is an integral part of the overall college program, assessment of learners' prior experiences is simply part of faculty counseling and advisement duties. Thus, no additional compensation is expected.

Some methods of compensation include granting release time and providing overload pay. Where significant numbers of learners are assigned to a faculty member, release time from other assigned courses is generally offered. Alternatively, overload pay is used where only a limited number of faculty are available to carry out assessment in a given technical program.

It should be recognized by the college administration that the assessment of prior learning is an important component of the college program, and faculty contributions in such assessment should be duly recognized in promotion and tenure decision making.

Chapter References

American Council on Education. (1946). *A guide to the evaluation of educational services in the armed services* (G.P. Tuttle Editor [Registrar U of IL]). Washington, DC: Author.

American Council on Education. *National guide to credit recommendations for non collegiate courses.* Washington, DC: Author.

Meyer, P. (1975). *Awarding college credit for non-college learning.* San Francisco: Jossey Bass.

Simosko, S. (1985). *Earn college credit for what you know.* Washington, DC: ACROPOLIS Books.

Chapter 12

Articulated Programs

An articulated or joint program is a partnership between several educational institutions—the secondary school, the community college, and/or senior colleges—that involves the coordination of curricula across two or more of these institutions and is formalized by "articulated" agreements. (These partnerships also are referred to as Tech Prep and/or 2+2 programs.) This chapter will review the development of these programs.

Why Articulated Secondary/ Postsecondary Cooperative Education?

The recent movement towards linkages of secondary and postsecondary technical education programs reveals the growing interest in the sharing of resources for workplace education and training, and a greater recognition of the advantages conferred by cooperation between educational institutions at several levels. The articulated or Tech Prep program is one model that has been developed to help learners prepare more directly for careers in today's society by ensuring that they possess the knowledge, skills, and technical expertise necessary for successful employment.

Articulated cooperative education programs, such as Tech Prep, have a single overriding goal—to provide learners with effective preparation for life and work. These programs are based on a philosophical belief that there should be a structured plan for technical education, beginning as early as possible.

Tech Prep is an "advanced-skills" articulation model, because it enables learners to use the instructional time saved through secondary/college coordinated coursework to acquire more advanced occupational knowledge and skill (Robertson-Smith, 1990). The Carl Perkins Act Amendments make funds available to the states for Tech Prep programs (Mensel, 1991).

However, not all linkages of secondary school and community college programs are Tech Prep sponsored. "Work-Based 2+2" models, linking the final two years of high school with a two-year community college program, have existed for many years in states such as Florida. Some of these programs include structured worksite experiences which progressively increase in time over the period of schooling to provide a graduated transition for the learner from part-time to full-time work.

In these programs, instructors and worksite preceptors jointly create curriculum and instruct learners, and discuss, guide, and monitor learner progress in the classroom and at the worksite. Learners receive a high school diploma upon completion of the high school portion of the program and an Associate degree and certification in their respective fields upon completion of the community college program. They are usually paid by their employers for time spent in worksite learning.

Figure 12–1 is the Tech Prep model proposed by the Center for Occupational Research and Development.

Benefits of articulated programs to the learner

These programs help learners by:

- increasing motivation;
- ensuring that learning is relevant to ultimate career goals;
- maximizing the use of learning time from high school through higher education; and
- facilitating admission to college for the high school student.

Benefits of articulated programs to the high school

Articulated programs also benefit the secondary school by:

- improving the overall behavioral environment of the school through providing stronger motivation to learners and thus reducing problems;
- facilitating student transition to postsecondary education by coordinating the high school curriculum with college curriculum; and
- promoting professional development through interaction with other faculty.

Figure 12–1

A Model for Tech Prep

TECH PREP/ASSOCIATE DEGREE (TPAD)
The K-12...14...16 Connection

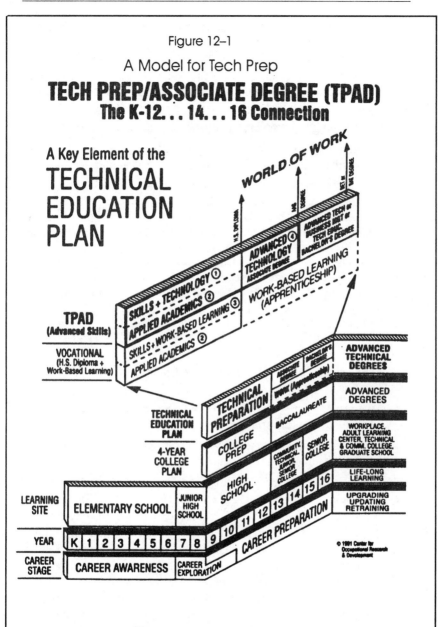

A Key Element of the

TECHNICAL EDUCATION PLAN

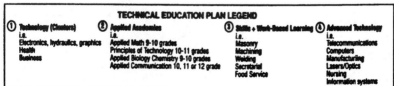

Reprinted with permission of The Center for Occupational Research and Development.

Benefits of articulated programs to the community college

Advantages of articulated programs to the community college include:

- ensuring that learners are well prepared to pursue their chosen curricula and careers;
- eliminating unnecessary duplication of courses; and
- motivating business and industry to participate in education through structured work experiences such as apprenticeships and internships.

Articulated Program Structure

The primary objective of articulated program development is to modify, combine, or create curriculum in order to prevent duplication of coursework and shorten the time required for high school learners to complete a postsecondary program.

Articulated programs vary in structure. Basic approaches include the following:

- the articulation or coordination of currently existing individual courses;
- the articulation of modified courses and course sequences in part of a technical program area; and
- the articulation of completely new courses and course sequences in a program area.

These approaches can be instituted in some combination between two institutions or among a larger number. For example, in the State Center Community College District (Fresno, California), Fresno City College staff participated in a 2+2 Tech Prep program with twenty-three high schools and two regional occupational programs. Given the high number of participating institutions, the District and its partner schools began developing Tech Prep programs by articulating several existing courses. Initial course selection for articulation was based on enrollment levels, denoting demand and popularity, and on how simple coordination of curriculum would be. The courses with consistently high learner enrollments and relatively similar content at the two institutional levels were chosen first. These were drafting, electronics, welding, accounting I, and child care worker.

Once the process of articulation gets underway, most college staff and partner schools usually become more comfortable with the concept, and, if necessary or desirable, the programs then can be expanded to form 2+2+2 programs. In the case of the State Center Community College District, the initial articulation process eventually led to the establishment of further articulated courses with California State University at Fresno.

The general curriculum for articulated programs, such as 2+2 partnerships and Tech Prep, offers academic as well as technical courses. Secondary school educators recognize and acknowledge the importance of including appropriate regular academic courses (e.g., math, science, and English) in articulated programs so that learners receive some general education, as well as occupational training. Many schools and colleges strongly recommend, or even require, that this occur. Other schools encourage or require their learners to take a sequence of "applied" academic courses, such as applied math, applied communications, and principles of technology, if these courses, of a more practical nature, are more appropriate for their learner population.

In many locations, schools and colleges offer articulated programs structured to offer a sequence of technical and academic courses in a stepping stone approach in order to provide their learners with "career ladders." For example, in the health occupations program in the Bronx, New York City, learners in articulated Tech Prep programs in nursing can enter work after high school as Nurses' Aides; after one year of the community college program with a Certificate in Licensed Practical Nursing; or after two years of a community college program as an Associate in Science and a registered nurse.

Articulating Currently Existing Courses

Articulating currently existing classes clearly is easier to accomplish than any other option. With this approach, high school and community college instructors, who must decide how to coordinate their curricula, find the task much simpler as the course objectives, content, materials, and evaluation instruments already exist at both levels. Familiarity with the courses allows the process of articulation to move more smoothly and speedily. As a result of initiating this option, as was the case at Hillsborough Community College and Hillsborough County Schools in the data processing program, staff usually find that collaboration with colleagues is promoted and duplication of coursework at the postsecondary level is avoided. In situations where resources are limited or where obtaining release time is a major obstacle or where instructors find it difficult to collaborate, this approach is recommended.

Articulating Modified Courses

Another curriculum articulation approach is to modify the content of current courses and then articulate these altered courses in a logical planned sequence in one or several technical program areas. In most secondary schools and community colleges, modifications consist of adding and integrating new information and skills into already existing courses (Dornsife, 1992).

In practical terms these kinds of modifications usually take the form of introducing and using new materials, equipment, or technologies. For example, some high school courses frequently need to be reorganized as new textbooks or computer-aided instruction, which offer new approaches or information, are adopted. Also, the introduction of new equipment and machinery (e.g., computerized milling machines) into the workplace often must be recognized and dealt with in courses involved in those areas. Or, as was the case at Lehman College, when keyboarding, wordprocessing, and office technologies classes are articulated, typewriters must be replaced by computers and software packages. Even these straightforward kinds of course modifications are sometimes very difficult to achieve, especially if the two or more institutions involved have very different resources to spend or dissimilar procedures that must be followed when changes are instituted.

In addition to these relatively simple course changes, the most common form of curriculum modification for articulated programs is the adoption of performance objectives as the basis for their courses. (In fact, in some states, such as Florida and Oregon, there is a legislative mandate to this effect.) Performance-based education identifies and focuses on the skills necessary to participate in a particular field and, thus, is a system of instruction and evaluation that is directed toward measurable results. A performance-based curriculum can offer courses that provide specific and relevant information and skills for actual occupations. In most cases, each course in the sequence is articulated with a postsecondary institution, and the learner can earn either advanced placement or advanced skill competence credit. With this system of education, learners can see the direct relationship between school and work, and can better appreciate the importance of both. They recognize that this approach sets them directly upon a tangible career path toward achievable goals.

There are many advantages to modifying curriculum for articulation in these ways. First, the high school benefits through collaboration to rethink and reorganize its courses as it now can provide better preparation to learners for entry to community college. The college benefits from having learners who can better cope with community college level education, having received instruction specifically designed to lead to and prepare for these courses. Instructors benefit from discussing their courses with other colleagues who may have fresh ideas and approaches. They also gain by having access to new and flexible curriculum materials. In those states such as Florida, where state-wide curriculum projects have been initiated, many instructors welcome the changes and enjoy teaching the modified courses, partly because already developed materials are provided, including student learning activities, lab materials, problem sets, group exercises, and tests. And, of course, in turn, learners benefit from the improved curriculum and the new or modified instructional materials, because they are provided with up-to-date, practical information and training for careers in current occupations.

Articulating Newly Developed Courses

The third approach to the process of articulating curriculum is to link together newly developed courses and new course sequences, and develop technical and academic curriculum specifically designed to provide training along a career path. For example, Lehman College added new courses in health career areas to complement feeder community college programs, thus providing a new career path for its students.

In all three examples of articulated program development presented here, the articulated curriculum is designed as a coherent sequence of linked technical and academic courses. This sequencing provides learners with a clear educational plan, and, in many technical programs, presents them with the possiblity of "multiple exits" from which they may leave the program to enter the world of work. For example, the health careers program of Lehman Collge is so designed that a learner can exit after high school as a medical records clerk or continue into the community college to obtain a certificate in medical records technology. Accounting course sequences are often structured to provide learners with the entry-level skills necessary for immediate employment, or the skills required for continuing in an accounting program at a community college. And advanced technology programs provide learners with mid-level skills needed for employment, or for continuing in a similar program at a four-year college. (For a more detailed discussion of "career ladder" Tech Prep programs, see Hull & Parnell, 1991, p. 52; and Lovelace, 1990.)

Developing New Courses and Curriculum with Business and Industry

In many cases, articulated or Tech Prep curriculum is developed after direct input from and collaborative efforts with business and industry representatives. This interaction often results from changes that have taken place in occupations as new discoveries, inventions, and developments occur, or in order to reflect the routine upgrading that has taken place in local jobs (e.g., integrating widely used computer packages into the curriculum of business, administrative, and drafting courses). In any event, revisions to existing curriculum become necessary.

In some cases, however, input from business and industry leads to the development of entirely new courses to provide training for new or changing employment needs in the community. For example, in response to significant changes in local employment trends, the Eastern Iowa Community College District (Davenport, Iowa) developed Tech Prep programs in hazardous waste materials technology. Specific courses were developed with the assistance of the Hazardous Materials Training and Research Institute in Davenport, Iowa. Similarly, the Community College of Rhode Island (CCRI) developed Tech Prep programs in advanced technology, because traditional employment in local manufacturing industries had been replaced with opportunities in such high-tech industries as robotics, lasers, biomedical instrumentation, and telecommunications. The CCRI programs were developed with the assistance of local business and industry representatives, who serve on an advisory board for Tech Prep programs (Dornsife, 1992).

The most effective Tech Prep programs offer learners a sequence of technical courses linked with a sequence of academic courses. Although the specific courses may vary from program to program, some form of linkage is created in order to offer learners a program designed to provide the skills and training needed for employment or for community college education.

Articulated Program Development

As noted, many articulated programs actually begin by expanding or redesigning existing seconday/postsecondary articulation agreements, many of which predate Tech Prep. A program articulation agreement is drawn up which specifies the terms under which a learner can receive college credit for work completed while enrolled in a particular high school course or program.

To initiate an articulated program agreement, faculty and administrators of both the community college and high school institutions should initiate a series of actions which are discussed below (Dornsife, 1992; Robertson-Smith, 1990).

Establish the rationale for program participation

An articulated agreement is intended to streamline programs and eliminate duplication of course content, thus providing benefits to the learner, the secondary school, and the community college. The college credit earned for even one high school course provides a strong incentive for most learners to continue their education. Research indicates that many learners not planning to pursue a community college education actually do attempt to complete a two-year college degree after receiving college credit for a course provided by a high school. Often space is made available on the college campus for instruction, even if only for part of a course. The high school learner usually finds going onto the college campus for a course an exciting and motivating experience. In addition, both institutions benefit from faculty interaction through the sharing of ideas about the course/program or sharing resources (e.g., laboratory facilities).

Plan formal articulation meetings

Establish a schedule for planning and implementing articulation, and draw up a specific calendar of meetings. Faculty and administrators of both (or all) participating institutions should meet with a pre-planned agenda to decide how a linkage can be accomplished. Counselors, members of program advisory committees, college admissions representatives, registrars, and any other appropriate staff should also be present. Issues which must be addressed through collaboration at these meetings are discussed below.

Identify the course(s)/program(s) under consideration

Generally, course/program articulation occurs when a particular instructor, administrator, or program chair at either the high school or college level identifies a program or specific courses for which this kind of inter-school linkage makes sense. So, to begin the process, select an appropriate course(s) at both high school and community college levels and make available to all participants all materials relating to and supporting the course(s) (e.g., syllabi, lesson plans, books, packaged materials, tests).

Compare courses at both levels/institutions

On a one-for-one basis, look at:

- course objectives and competencies to be mastered;
- levels of performance required of learners; and
- course tests and their compatability.

This process often creates great difficulty for the faculty involved. In order to ascertain and analyze the specific competencies to be mastered and the levels of performance required, courses at both institutions must be supported by clear, detailed performance objectives. If these are not already in place, they must be identified. Tests are also necessary; these must be available and must actually evaluate the courses in question. (Look at Chapter 2 once again for additional information on course and program decision making.)

Determine which competencies and topics are common to the courses of both institutions

The faculty of each institution reviews all course documentation provided and draws up a detailed list of content/concepts/skills found in both. This becomes the blueprint for the articulated agreement.

Decide the format for program implementation

The body of knowledge and skills decided upon as appropriate for admission to advanced study at the college level, once completed successfully by the learner, must be equated to a recognized course at the college. Most often this is a first-level course in a program at the college (e.g., History 101; Computer Science 100). When learners complete the high school program, they will gain credit at the post-secondary institution for that particular body of knowledge.

In addition, a learner often will be required to complete a residency requirement prior to acceptance of these externally earned credits. If this is the case, both institutions must notify the learner.

Select evaluation techniques

College faculty also must decide on a method of ensuring the competence of the learner and his or her mastery of the course material, prior to accepting that body of knowledge as completed for credit purposes. Methods of evaluation worth considering include the following:

• a joint (high school/college) competency exam developed by the faculty and administered by the college;

• an externally developed and administered exam (e.g., College Board); and

• a written agreement between the involved institutions stipulating the terms under which credit will be granted.

Develop written articulation agreements

Lastly, those secondary and postsecondary institutions which decide to undertake the process of curriculum articulation must establish written agreements. Be sure to include:

• how the program will be administered to learners;

• how the courses will be presented;

• how grading will be accomplished;

• how successful learners will be guided to the college for admission;

• how the college will award credit; and

• how future communications will take place.

In addition, these agreements may cover such aspects as faculty exchange, equivalency exams, tuition arrangments, and dual enrollment. Agreements are drawn up to serve both local populations (e.g., one high school district and one community college) and regional populations (e.g., several high school districts and community colleges, and, in some cases, four-year colleges as well).

Figure 12–2

Advertisement for a 2+2+2+1 Program

GET STARTED ON YOUR CAREER RIGHT NOW!

WITH 2+2+2+1, YOU CAN GET A HEAD START ON EARNING THE COLLEGE DEGREE AND TEACHING CREDENTIAL YOU WILL NEED TO BECOME AN INDUSTRIAL ARTS OR TECHNICAL EDUCATION TEACHER. WHEN YOU COMPLETE THE 2+2+2+1 PROGRAM, YOU'LL ENTER ONE OF THE FASTEST GROWING CAREER FIELDS TODAY, AND, YOU WILL BE QUALIFIED TO EARN A STARTING SALARY OF $24,000 OR MORE! SO WHAT ARE YOU WAITING FOR?

WITH 2+2+2+1, YOU CAN BEGIN YOUR CAREER IN THESE FIELDS:

ARCHITECTURE I, II	METALS I, II
AUTO TECH I, II	POLICE SCIENCE
ADVANCED AUTO	VOCATIONAL
CABINETMAKING	WOODWORKING
DRAFTING I, II	WELDING
ELECTRONICS	WOODS I, II
GRAPHICS/PRINTING I, II	

HERE'S HOW 2+2+2+1 ADDS UP:

2 YEARS AT YOUR AREA HIGH SCHOOL EARNS YOU A HIGH SCHOOL DIPLOMA

+2 YEARS AT FRESNO CITY COLLEGE OR KINGS RIVER COMMUNITY COLLEGE EARNS YOU AN ASSOCIATE DEGREE

+2 YEARS AT FRESNO STATE EARNS YOU A BACHELOR'S DEGREE

+1 YEAR AT FRESNO STATE EARNS YOU A TEACHING CREDENTIAL

=A WELL-PAID CAREER AS A TEACHER!

Reprinted by permission of State Center Community College District, Fresno, California

Figure 12–2 is an example of a 2+2 (plus 2+1) program initiated by the State Center Community College District. This program is articulated with both their feeder high schools and the California State University system in order to assist students to transfer into a four-year institution upon completion of an Associate degree. These 2+2+2 programs are becoming particularly popular in many high technology areas. The process for articulation with the four-year institutions operates in exactly the same manner as with the high school. In states where there is a common course numbering system for college courses (e.g., Florida, California, etc.), transfer of credit by learners is simplified.

Forms of articulation agreements

Although there are many kinds of articulation arrangements, most community colleges draw up and use written agreements to establish standards for advanced academic standing. The objective of these agreements is to establish curriculum guidelines that offer the benefits of either (1) shortening the time for high school learners to complete community college courses, or (2) providing the learner with exit-level competencies needed to enter either the work force or another postsecondary institution. Other articulation agreements are written to cover a specific course in a selected technical area (e.g., public services, business, health occupations, trades and industry), or for an entire program. Figure 12–3 below is a typical articulation agreement.

Awarding college credit

The process by which community college credit is awarded for articulated courses varies from college to college. However, most institutions follow a process similar to that of the City University of New York Community Colleges. To receive college credit for articulated courses taken at high school, this community college uses a testing model whereby a learner must pass a written test administered by the college. In order to receive the credits and have them apply at the community college, junior and senior high school students must earn either an "A" or "B" on this test, and then enroll in at least a three-credit course within one year of graduation.

For advanced skill competency courses, a different procedure is followed: a learner receives college credit after he or she has completed a competency checklist administered by an instructor. This checklist includes tasks that have been identified as essential for entry-level in occupations offered at the college. As a learner demonstrates competency in each specific task, an instructor records this fact and sends the

Figure 12-3

A Typical Articulation Agreement

2 + 2 + 2

#1 in Steps to Articulation
(District Initiated)

REQUEST FOR ARTICULATION
WITH STATE CENTER COMMUNITY COLLEGE DISTRICT

Date Submitted: _____, 19___   Campus: FCC _____ KRCC_____

High School District: _____

High School Site(s): _____

Regional Occupational Center/Program: Fresno Metro. ROC/P _____ Valley ROP_____

Contact Person: _____

    Address: _____

      Phone: _____   Contact Time: _____

Course No. and Title (or related courses) to be considered from District:

Materials from District attached: _____ Course outline(s)
                              _____ List of competencies/objectives
Information:
  Length of course: _____
  Name of textbook(s) :

  Equipment used:

Name of teacher(s):

Name	Telephone No.	Contact Hours
_____	_____	_____
_____	_____	_____
_____	_____	_____

(To be completed by appropriate College Division Dean)
College course(s) to be considered:

Course No(s).	Course Name(s)

Dean: _____   Date: _____, 19___

College Department Head assigned: _____

Contact Date: _____(must be made within 30 days)

AP-1

Reprinted by permission of State Center Community College District, Fresno, CA.

completed checklist to the community college. The college verifies the checklist, sends out a letter of recognition, and records the credits on the learner's transcript. There is no need for an exam, because a successfully completed competency checklist is evidence that a learner received an "A" or "B" in the class. In most cases, a learner completes all the competencies after he or she takes three courses in a program area (e.g., health careers, medical laboratory technology, etc.).

Chapter References

Dornsife, C. (1992, February.). *Beyond articulation: The development of tech prep programs.* Berkeley, CA: National Center for Research in Vocational Education, University of California, Berkeley.

ERIC Clearinghouse on Adult, Career, and Vocational Education (1991). *Tech Prep Digest No. 108.* Columbus, OH: Center on Education and Training for Employment, Ohio State University.

Hull, Dan and Dale Parnell (1991). *Tech Prep/Associate Degree.* Fort Worth, TX: Center for Occupational Research and Development

Mensel, F. (1991, July 1). Tech Prep funding: The Ford to Harkin to Hatfield to Natches and Conte miracle. *Community, Technical and Junior College Times, 3*(1), 9.

Robertson-Smith, M. (1990). *Articulation models for vocational education information* (Series No. 343). Columbus, OH: Center on Education and Training for Employment, The Ohio State University.

State Center Community College District, CA. Descriptive brochures and materials.

Watkins, B.T. (1989, November 1). 2-Year institutions under pressure to ease transfers. *Chronicle of Higher Education,* A-35, A-38.

Chapter 13

Worksite Visitation

Once a worksite has been selected, a written training agreement signed, and a learner placed on the job, faculty coordinators must plan, set up, and carry out a series of worksite visits. Undertaken to monitor, evaluate, and counsel learners, and to check on fulfillment of worksite agreements, these visits are a major responsibility of the participating college and constitute an important component of administering an experiential learning program. In addition, they provide the basic continuing means of communication between college faculty and cooperating employers. The subject of this chapter is how to plan and conduct successful visitations.

The Purpose of Worksite Visits

There is a difference between purposeful visiting and just visiting. Employers are busy people and for the most part ordinarily do not have time to spend with visitors during work hours. Thus, each visit must have a clear and important purpose to justify the time required of the employer, as well as of you, the instructor/coordinator.

A number of legitimate reasons for instructor/coordinator visits to training worksites are discussed below. You should visit in order to:

- ensure that learners are benefitting educationally from their experiential learning situations;

- ensure that the employers/supervisors are familiar with college procedures and requirements for cooperative education, especially the necessary documentation of learners' progress and work schedules;

- counsel and advise learners about any potential or actual problems they may or do encounter in their work environment;

- meet with the management of the firm and the job supervisors in order to inform them about the college program;

- coordinate the on-the-job experiences at the firm with the courses or programs of the college;
- market the college and its program; and
- provide corporate training.

Ensuring Educational Benefit for Learners

A primary reason for undertaking regularly scheduled visits to each learner's worksite is to carry out course or program evelution in order to understand how to improve group and individual instruction. It is important to evaluate an individual learner's progress on the job—to determine how well he or she is meeting the stipulated performance objectives of the course or program and to determine how well the experiences provided by the firm contribute to meeting these objectives. In an on-going activity, such as experiential learning, evaluation should be formative in nature. It should have as its purpose making the current worksite experience more meaningful and useful for each learner.

As learner and job evaluation requires employer input, the instructor or coordinator and employer must work together. This process actually begins with the formalization of the worksite agreement betwen the firm and the college. This cooperative education agreement must specify learning objectives to be met by learners on the job. It must clearly list and define the expected experiential outcomes and activities. As faculty coordinator of the college, you have already discussed with the management and supervisor of the firm how this was to happen. Now, in the evaluation process, you will look to see how it is being carried out. If you are dissatisfied with what is occuring on the worksite, you must intervene quickly to correct the situation.

Be sure that you already have explained and clarified your responsibility for evaluating learners' performances with the management and supervisor of the firm. As faculty member, and therefore the representative of the college, it is your responsibility to award a grade to learners for their cooperative education program. Although the supervisor becomes an extension of the college staff in most college programs, the final determination of learner progress rests with you, as faculty member of record. This requires you to establish a close and cooperative relationship with the worksite staff and supervisor in order to receive the kind of detailed feedback about learners' overall progress that is necessary to enable you to make careful and reasonable judgments. A form that I use for that purpose is presented in Figure 13–1 below.

You also need to inform learners of their responsibilities for record-keeping. Some colleges and faculty require their learners to maintain a diary of daily events and work performed. This is an excellent system to reinforce learning experiences as they occur and allow for further reflection and insight. In addition, it provides instructors with evidence of learning and/or problems to enable them to help and evaluate learners more effectively. For my learners I use a simple log form, which is presented in Figure 13–2 below. On this form learners record the date, hours worked, activity performed, and signature of supervisor.

Familiarizing the Supervisor with Program Procedures

It is important to ensure that employers and supervisors are completely familiar with college procedures for cooperative education, particularly the required documentation of learners' progress and work schedules. In most cases, new worksite supervisors are not experienced in evaluating learners. Therefore, as soon as possible, you will need to spend some time with each new supervisor in the program in order to present the criteria to be used in evalution (e.g., as in Figure 13–1) and explain how these are to be applied in actual situations. It is helpful to prepare a written set of instructions to be used by new supervisors when evaluating learner progress. Learners are not workers-on-the-job. They must be judged for what they are—learners. This is often a completely new concept and experience for supervisors and requires some adjustment on their part.

In addition, be sure, in these initial discussions on evaluation, to alert supervisors to the need to keep progress reports about learners' academic achievement confidential. The US Privacy of Information Act (sometimes referred to as the "Buckley Amendment") makes evaluation of learners protected information. Therefore, as an extension of the college staff, supervisors must not discuss or show evaluation findings to anyone other than you. If a learner will be on the staff of the employer, a release form should also be completed by that learner. An example of such a form was presented earlier in Figure 9–9.

If other forms are required by the college as evidence of learner attendance, etc., make sure that the firm has a supply and understands how to fill them out, where to send them, and who to send them to.

Figure 13–1

A Form for Evaluating a Student at the Worksite

Name of Student _____

To: Worksite Supervisor of Internship

Please complege this form indicating your estimate of the student's work abilities. Please use the folowing rating scale by checking in the appropriate column.

The Student:	4 Superior	3 Very Good	2 Satisfactory	1 Unsatisfactory
1. Demonstrates command of the specific work-related tasks.				
2. Demonstrates a positive attitude and interest in training.				
3. Shows a wide range of intellectual interests.				
4. Demonstrates ability to work with people.				
5. Demonstrates understanding of psychological principles of training and adult learning.				
6. Maintains ethical standards in personal and professional relationships.				
7. Is punctual and dependable.				
8. Demonstrates ability to accept criticism				
9. Demonstrates ability to maintain an orderly training room.				
10. Shows increasing interest in professional responsibilities and opportunities.				

Comments: (Specific strengths or shortcomings)_____

_____

_____

Signature _____   Employer _____

Figure 13–2

Student Time Sheet for Fieldwork Experience

Name of Student_____Name of Instructor_____
Term Ending _____
Name of School where Fieldwork is being conducted
_____

Name of Supervising Teacher _____
Note: Fieldwork is rendered over a period of one semester to cover a minimum of 30 hours.

Month	Day	Hours	Type of Activity	School Personnel Signature

Total hours: _____

The evaluation form

Your institution may have its own evaluation form or you may need to create one to suit your particular circumstances. However, for purposes of this book the form presented in Figure 13–1 will be used as a basis for discussion. This form includes 10 fundamental criteria, to be ranked on a scale ranging from "Superior" to "Very Good" to "Satisfactory" to "Unsatisfactory." Supervisors should understand that learners generally will perform in the "Satisfactory" to "Very Good" range on most tasks. Occasionally learners will so excell at a task that they will fall into the "Superior" range. And, also, a few learners will earn only an "Unsatisfactory" grade. When this happens, make sure supervisors understand that you must be advised immediately so that you and the supervisor together can intervene and provide guidance and assistance. A discussion of the various criteria on the form now follows.

Demonstrates command of specific work-related tasks

In this section of the form, supervisors are asked to judge the competence of learners to perform the assigned job tasks. Again, caution supervisors that, for purposes of evaluation, they should judge learners as students, not as incumbent or actual workers. And learners must be judged on the tasks (performance objectives) spelled out in the training agreement for which learners are to be responsible.

Demonstrates a positive attitude to and interest in training

Here, in this section, supervisors are asked to make a judgment as to learners' attitudes on and towards the job. Characteristics such as enthusiasm, excitement, and commitment, or alternatively, boredom, disinterest, and apathy are key to making these kinds of judgments. With your supervisors, discuss these revealing behaviors and how learners may demonstrate them in actual work situations.

Shows a wide range of intellectual interests

While this is a harder judgment to make, it is important that learners demonstrate some degree of intellectual ability and interest. After all, experiential learning is a college level activity, and learners will be expected to show leadership qualities, including the ability to think clearly, make informed decisions, solve problems, etc., upon graduation. Supervisors, therefore, must make judgments about learners' intellectual capacity.

Demonstrates ability to work with people

The ability of learners to get along well with co-workers is a very important factor in their performance. They must be able to work cooperatively, undertake responsibility, accept direction and criticism, and maintain pleasant relationships. Supervisors should have no difficulty making this judgment as they regularly evaluate employees on this basis in the course of their duties.

Demonstrates understanding of psychological principles of training and adult education

This section on the form in Figure 13–1, as well as section 9 ("demonstrates ability to maintain an orderly training room") are specific to my college and involve one particular internship. But any evaluation form must be flexible enough to adapt to a variety of learning activities. One solution is to leave extra space in the form of several blank sections, to be filled in by you and/or the supervisor on a placement-by-placement basis with the relevant criteria.

Maintains ethical standards in personal and professional relationships

As problems on the worksite in workers' interpersonal relationships become more frequent and complex, and are taken more seriously, the ability of learners to conduct themselves in a professional and ethical manner is of utmost importance. In making judgments in this area, supervisors will need to consider sensitive issues, such as truthfulness, honesty, and sexual conduct.

Is punctual and dependable

This judgment is another simple one for supervisors to make as they do it all the time. Reporting for work on schedule and on time is an important part of learner performance and must be noted. Again, if reliability is a problem, the supervisor must contact you immediately.

Demonstrates ability to accept critcism

Supervisory personnel will be instructing and coaching learners from time to time. During these sessions, supervisors may have to tell learners that their performance is incorrect or inadequate, and inform them that there is a better way to do the job, or suggest they learn a different method from that which was mastered in the classroom. How learners received such correction is very important. Do they accept criticism willingly and try their best to improve their performance? Or, do they show negative signs of resentment and hostility, and argue or reject such correction. Supervisors must watch for these reactions in order to judge this matter.

Shows increasing interest in professional responsibilities and obligations

As time progresses and learners become more involved in their work, supervisors should watch for signs that these learners are adapting to the professional role required of them in their jobs. Do learners really demonstrate an affinity for the kind of work they are performing? If not, this must be brought to your attention.

In conclusion

There should be ample room on your form for comments regarding any of the above criteria. Encourage supervisors to record as extensively as possible as they will have special knowledge impossible to gain from any other source. Also, point out that providing details of specific incidents, discussions, reactions, etc., are very useful ways to convey how learners are getting along and what they are learning.

Finally, supervisors date and sign the form for your files. You must meet with them to discuss the evaluation in detail. The particular one-time evaluation in Figure 13–1 is usually carried out at the end of an experiential learning internship.

Evaluation follow up

Advise management and supervisory personnel of the procedures to be followed if problems occur with learners at work or if their attendance is unsatisfactory. Make it clear that you must be notified immediately in such cases so that action can be taken. Also tell the firm whether a simple phone call is sufficient or a written report is required by your college when trouble arises. In any event, a means of fast and direct communication must be established. However if you do this in your situation, the linkage between college and firm will be strengthened. A few of the possible issues worth discussing first and dealing with immediately if they become problems include work scheduling, work hours, appropriate dress, safety requirements, and degree of supervision to be provided to learners.

Dealing with Problems

A third purpose for visiting worksites is to address or alleviate learner on-the-job problems. Most cooperative education coordinators report that they spend considerable time with certain learners counseling them about work-related problems. Some learners have difficulty adjusting to the work environment: for example, problems can arise over taking direction from the supervisor or other workers, accepting criticism, arriving at work on time, focusing on the job, failing to observe safely precautions, refusing to follow company policy, etc. We must not forget, however, that cooperative education often offers learners their first legitimate job experience. Regard difficulties as opportunities for real-life instruction; some of the most important lessons for learners may arise from facing and settling problems on the job.

The faculty coordinator must identify any problems as quickly as possible. In order to do so he or she first must gather information about the situation in question from all persons involved. After ascertaining the nature of the problem and the facts of the matter, learners must be counseled so that their concerns and distress are resolved. Open, honest, non-judgmental communication with supervisors and other workers is also necessary to defuse most conflicts and prevent further problems from cropping up.

Some problems result from a lack of technical competence on the part of learners so that they are unable to carry out the requirements of the job and meet the objectives of the experiential learning activity. If this is the case, as judged and reported by the supervisor, immediately terminate the assignment and redirect the learner in question to a more suitable worksite.

Sometimes, difficulties are caused by personality clashes between learners and supervisors and/or co-workers. These cases can be very difficult to resolve as strong emotional reactions are engendered. However, discussion and counseling with all participants can be helpful. Learners must understand that they will need to get along with many kinds of people throughout their work lives and that solving misunderstandings or simply putting up with certain workers is part of their responsibility.

However, if outright prejudice, as displayed, for example, by racial slurs, is encountered, it must be dealt with firmly. With more minority and non-traditional learners entering cooperative education programs, it is not uncommon for them to experience unpleasant situations of this kind. It will probably be necessary to meet with the management and supervisor of the organization and alert them to the problem so that they can call in the worker(s) involved and make it clear that such behavior is completely unacceptable. Learners have the same full rights as all citizens and must be afforded a workplace free of racial or ethnic hostility.

Sexual harassment is another potential problem that is much more fully recognized today. While most colleges try to alert learners to problems that may arise on the job prior to their leaving the campus, it is impossible to cover every contingency or expect all learners to cope with all problems on their own. As with racial or ethnic harassment, it is mandatory that a faculty coordinator intervene on behalf of a learner. Talk to a supervisor in charge, describe the incident(s) in detail and whom they involve, and resolve the problem as speedily as possible.

Experiential learning is not intended primarily to provide an opportunity to learners to be gainfully employed, but is designed to be an educational experience. If the experience gained and money earned on the job become the learner's overriding interest so that the worksite activity begins to interfere in any way with the college program, then the job must be curtailed. Learners must not miss valuable class time, nor ignore academic assignments because of their work. If they assert that their absence at school or inability to complete college papers is due to the demands of the job, they must be informed that this is unacceptable. Keep in close touch with the employer, who can provide information on learner behavior on the job site. And observe how these learners perform in class for a full picture. However, when intervening and counseling, keep in mind that today many learners seek out experiential learning as the only possible way to get an education. They cannot afford not to "earn-and-learn."

Problems of this nature will defy solution without the full cooperation of the supervisors. They must be prepared to require the same quality of job performance from learners as they do from their regular employees. The supervisors should also be willing to use the job as a means of correcting learner problems in college work. In some cases, the employer may be reluctant to require job performance equivalent to that of regular employees. As a general rule, however, employers are more willing to accept this guideline than they are to use the job to enforce conformance with college policies.

Informing Worksite Personnel about College Programs

Another important purpose of visitation is to acquaint employers/ supervisors with the overall college program with which they obviously have little or no direct contact and in which their learners are enrolled. Maintain a close liason with the firm in order to accomplish this.

If possible arrange for the worksite personnel to visit the college in order to gain a better understanding of what learners are doing in the classroom. If this is not feasible, take them classroom materials, such as study guides, reference books, and completed assignments. These can serve as an excellent basis for discussion, as well as further acquaint them with the college curriculum. By visiting classes and/or examining assignments the employer and supervisor gain a better understanding of the overall college program and how it correlates with the work experience.

As well, in such reciprocal visits, you can make supervisors aware of any difficulties the college may have in providing adequate programming (e.g., lack of suitable equipment or reference materials). Employers may be able to donate technical books or trade journals or other appropriate documents not otherwise available to the college. If the problem is lack of money, they may be willing to purchase reference materials for their learners. Having personal contacts with faculty coordinators and an investment in learners may make them more responsive to such needs at the college.

In addition to keeping employers and supervisors appropriately informed about college courses and instruction, encourage them to supply additional information or suggest further areas of study relevant to the work the learner is doing. Once worksite personnel become acquainted with the course of study, they will be in a better position to advise the college and its program advisory committees where, in their opinion, changes, additions, or deletions to course content may be indicated. Experiential learning makes this kind of input possible, but only if the faculty coordinator works to maintain the relationship.

Another method of encouraging close contact and fostering the spread of information is to create actual exchange positions whereby faculty members spend a semester working in the organization while the supervisor takes over the faculty position for that period of time.

Coordinating Work Experience and College Programs

The best experiential learning occurs when the activities at the worksite closely match the formal learning taking place in the classroom. When this happens, learners are better able to put theory into practice. To achieve this educational match, there must be close coordination between the job and the classroom. Faculty coordinators must maintain frequent contact with worksite supervisors and employers, and be prepared to relate the work done in class to the work performed on the job.

On a routine basis, meet with supervisors, and review the training agreement and list of performance objectives to ensure that what is recorded and intended is actually happening. Inform employers and/or supervisors of the content of their learners' current courses. Point out opportunities for that classroom material to be linked to what the learners are actually doing. Emphasize that this is a particularly important part of the role of on-the-job instructors as members of the educational team.Work closely together to make sure that what is being covered at that point in the classroom is applicable to and reinforces the on-the-job experience. In addition, ask supervisors whether learners are attempting to apply the technical knowledge acquired in the classroom to the solution of problems encountered on the job. Always draw attention to the relationship between classroom instruction and on-the-job work experience so that supervisors will appreciate this special aspect of cooperative education and experiential learning.

Weekly or bi-weekly seminars, in which learners meet with their faculty coordinator, are a beneficial component of experiential learning. Here, in the privacy of the college classroom, away from the distractions of the worksite, explore both the technical aspects of the work experience that are of interest and/or need further explanation, and any problems that have arisen on the job and are appropriate for open group discussion. This is further discussed in Chapter 5.

After some time has passed, and after discussion with both employers/supervisors and learners, you will be in a position to make judgments about which aspects of a course or program are better delivered by worksite training and which by formal class instruction. Make any appropriate and desirable adjustments to courses when feasible.

Providing Corporate Training

Another excellent purpose for visiting employers is to discuss the possibility of the college providing educational services to the firm. The faculty coordinator should be on the lookout for any training needs or problems of cooperating employers and consider how to help. For example, discuss with the firm's manager how the college could provide customized training for either existing or prospective employees. These kinds of reciprocal arrangements cement relationships and give the college a higher profile in the community.

The Benefits of Worksite Visits

It is clear that visits undertaken for clear and definite purposes offer many advantages. Some of these include the opportunity to:

- observe the learner at work;
- check the general progress of the learner;
- identify areas in which the learner needs to improve;
- become aware of the general attitude toward the learner;
- sample attitudes of co-workers;
- examine the training agency environment;
- evaluate the quality of the on-the-job training;
- influence the thinking of the employer; and
- receive ideas and suggestions for related study.

These benefits can serve as an indication for what to look for during visits. As well, keep these ideas in mind when judging how successful a visit has been. You should gain some information about one or more of these points during each visit. If you do not, examine and improve your visiting techniques.

Visit Follow-Up

It is essential that a follow-up session be held individually with each learner after a formal visit to the worksite. During this time, inform learners about the results of the visit, including honest discussion of deficiencies, provide counseling and guidance when necessary, offer encouragement and praise for successes, arbitrate difficulties, and discuss issues or problems learners may with to raise with you. Thus, in your meeting, you should include:

- discussion of employer evaluation of work performance;
- review of accomplishments;
- suggestions for further skills development;
- analysis of any problems in relationships with co-workers;
- time for personal comments by learners.

Chapter References

Mitchell, E.I. (1977). *Cooperative Vocational Education*. Boston: Allyn & Bacon.

Chapter 14

Evaluating Cooperative Education and Experiential Learning Programs

Evaluation of experiential learning, like any other aspect of instruction, must be closely linked to the instructional objectives of the program that is to be measured. This chapter describes the Evaluation Step, part of the final *Product Phase* of the Experiential Learning Planning Process Model (See Figure 14–1 below).

Through evaluation, the instructional value and success of an experiential learning activity (what and/or how much has actually been learned) is assessed. This feedback is useful for assessing both the worksite learning activity and the classroom-based instruction. For instructors, evaluation results provide a yardstick against which to measure learner improvement and help ensure that training is on target for the identified audience and need. As for learners, evaluation can demonstrate progress, substantiate learning mastery, and ensure that they are capable of carrying out a job safely. From the cooperative education program developer's point of view, evaluation provides indications for improving current curriculum and planning future activities. Evaluation measures should be both formative and summative.

The Formative Evaluation Process

Formative evaluation is ideally an on-going instructional development activity conducted throughout the duration of the course or program. It is used to determine learner progress and/or detect strengths or weaknesses in programs, or specific courses, and at worksites. Formative evaluation should be conducted at all stages of program or course development and delivery. It involves asking questions—of yourself and others—before determining performance objectives:

- Why is this experiential learning activity being developed?
- What are its instructional objectives?

Figure 14–1

Evaluation of Cooperative Education and Experiential Learning Programs

INPUTS

✓ Feedback and comments on cooperative education and experiential learning program including individual worksite evaluations

PROCESS

✓ Analyze feedback

✓ Gather additional clarification as needed

✓ Interview learners and cooperating employers

✓ Repeat formative evaluation steps as necessary

OUTPUTS

✓ A report on effectiveness of individual worksites and overall program

• What type of experientially based activities are needed?

And while administering the learning activity:

• Are we maintaining the original instructional purpose?
• Is the activity suitable for our learners' needs?
• Are learners responding as expected?
• Are they learning?

Methods of Formative Evaluation

Types of formative evaluation measures that are appropriate for experiential learning include observations, oral questioning, worksite performance checks, and others. Be careful with these techniques! Observations, like all worksite anecdotal records, are only as reliable as the observer. This evaluative method is good, however, for getting a "gut reaction" to on-the-job instruction. Formative evaluation measures also include checking the outcomes of an experiential learning activity against the stated instructional objectives, conducting pretests, and field-testing a pilot activity or course. A three-step process of formative evaluation is discussed below.

Input: Collecting the data

Data which should be collected for program evaluation include:

• worksite visitation reports;
• employers' oral feedback and written reviews;
• classroom instructors' comments on learner progress and experiences;
• learners' comments via interviews and written reviews;
• advisory committee feedback, reflecting the employers' or community's needs, experiences, and expectations;
• data regarding experiential learning activities in a specific program; and
• future needs of learners and the business community, as well as of the college program.

Once these data are collected, the Cooperative Education Committee should convene and review them. This is often an annual procedure; however, for new programs this procedure can be carried out after as few as six months.

Analysis: Processing the data

Using the performance objectives of the experiential learning program as a basis, the data listed above should be analyzed in order to consider:

- Are learners afforded appropriate and sufficient worksite opportunities to master intended skills and develop appropriate knowledge?
- Are learners succeeding in their attempts to meet performance objectives?
- Are appropriate procedures in place to supervise learners adequately and support worksite supervisors fully?
- Are some worksites inadequate?
- Are more worksites needed?

In some cases it will be necessary to interview learners and worksite supervisors again to clarify further some of these issues. After this program evaluation is completed, any necessary revisions can be planned and carried out.

Output: Reporting the findings

The final action in the formative evaluation activity is to draw up a report on experiential learning activity effectiveness with recommendations for:

- revisions of performance objectives, if necessary;
- program revisions to better meet performance objectives; and
- worksite location and/or administrative changes.

Sometimes large-scale formative evaluation will take place after cooperative education programs have been in place for several years. In this case, different methods, including user follow-up forms, are developed to collect the data for each module systematically.

The Summative Evaluation Process

Summative evaluation is directed toward measuring the degree to which instructional objectives were met over time. Examples of summative measures include written final course tests and assessment checklists, as well as overall assessment of job performance at the end of specific periods of time.

Design, Development, and Use of Performance Tests

Depending on the experiential learning activity to be measured, tests are either written or performance based. Retention of information and cognitive processing are best measured by a written demonstration of knowledge. Physical skills are best measured by performance testing. Much of what is done in an experiential learning setting is performance oriented. Therefore, it is necessary to understand how performance tests are developed in order to evaluate cooperative education program outcomes.

Performance tests can be used to verify attained skills and diagnose areas where experiential learning can be improved. A well-designed and objective measurement tool can:

- classify new learners with related experience for training or placement;

- monitor the progress of learners throughout various stages of their learning;

- analyze training effectiveness by measuring knowledge retained by individual learners; and

- verify the status of learners being considered for advancement.

The processes described here will show the instructor how to write content-valid performance tests (i.e., the test measures what it is supposed to measure).

Performance test development has three distinct phases: (1) determining the test design, (2) preparing the test materials, and (3) validating the test materials. Each phase has its own requirements and records, and together they provide a trail for auditing content validity. Methods for carrying out each phase are sufficiently flexible to suit a variety of organizational constraints and resources.

Phase one: The test design

The test design phase specifies what is to be tested; it can itself be further divided into three parts, which will be discussed below. The first part involves defining the purpose of the test, using a written, self-designed test plan. Second is the initial analysis of the tasks, knowledge, skills, and abilities that make up the job or position to be measured. This analysis is an important part of establishing the content validity of the test. Although the source data for the analysis can vary, in all cases it must document the needs of the learner or job incumbent.

The third part of the test design is to determine the selected measurement points (specific skill elements) and methodology. Together, these parts make up a specification from which the test is written. Each test element should be related to a job or task.

Test design: Step one—the test plan

A cooperative education program/course developer should design and fill out the test plan. The information to be gathered includes:

* the purpose of the test;
* the planned test method;
* the scoring process;
* the approximate test time; and
* the subjects to be measured.

This plan is a working document that should be completed, reviewed, and discussed early in the development process and subsequently revised as required to reflect the purpose(s) of the test.

The purpose of the test should be clearly stated. Before the actual development of a measurement instrument begins, you must decide who is to be tested and how the resulting measurements are to be used. As a test designer, be sure that your instrument will make fully clear to the student the purpose and application of the test.

Ideally, analyzing the purpose of the assessment and the behavior to be measured will determine the best measurement approach, or planned test method. Constraints on administrative time or resources may dictate whether product or process performance testing is to be used. Any constraints or preferences regarding the planned testing method should be indicated in the test plan.

Most tests will be either pass/fail: measurement is based on an established standard or criterion, or diagnostic, in which the measurement will compare each learner's skill mastery or competency with the other learners. This second type of scoring reference is called "normative."

Be sure to note an approximate test time and length in the test plan, as well as any constraints on the time available for testing. Take into account the test purpose and subject matter to be covered.

The test plan also should indicate the subjects to be covered in the test. The test writer should determine these based on the performance objectives (see Chapters 2 and 3). The number of items or measurement points dedicated to each area should also be noted.

Test design: Step two—Initial task analysis

To identify the tasks, knowledge, skills, and abilities critical to carrying out the work associated with each experiential learning activity, it is necessary to analyze all appropriate areas in detail. This was described earlier in Chapter 2. Again, it is advisable to involve several qualified experts (possibly from the cooperative education planning committee) to review and agree upon the critical measurement points to be used. Establish a process for recording relevant work and training experience about the people who are asked to judge test content. There are no specific guidelines on how much experience is enough, but they should have recent and relevant experience with the task being reviewed. Often a mix of people who supervise the work and those who actually do the work is best.

Each expert should record the perceived importance of the various components of the task analysis data to the overall purpose of the test. The components include duties, tasks, task elements and knowledge, skills, and abilities.

For example, if a learner's performance on a specific task is to be measured (e.g., setting up a cardiac monitor), then tasks and task elements probably will be rated as more important to the end product and the analysis. If overall job performance is to be measured, then the knowledge, skills, and abilities will be rated higher. The level of detail in the analysis need only be enough to satisfy the intended purpose of the test.

Test design: Step three—measurement points and methodology

The task analysis serves to identify the general elements and potential measurement points, such as:

- the specific elements that should be measured;
- whether a performance test or a written test is most appropriate for the measurement; and
- the number of questions or trials needed to establish proficiency on a task or element.

Other initial considerations are the time that will be required to complete the test and whether drawings and documents will be used to assist the examinee in taking the test. Make sure the appropriate tools, machines, and materials are available if needed to support taking the test. Record all such decisions in as much detail as required to make the specification clear. Although this process of definition and review is time consuming, it is vitally important that it be carried out in order to ensure content validity. It also makes the job of the test writer much easier.

If the task analysis and measurement selection was done by a technical instructor, the resulting task analysis and selected measurement points should be reviewed by others actually working in the area, such as a supervisor at the worksite. If the analysis is done by a working group of technically experienced and competent people specifically gathered for the purpose, there is no requirement for external review.

Phase two: The preparation of evaluation/test materials

Evaluation and testing materials will always include a guide to instruct the employer how to administer the test, and the test itself. Also included are answer sheets, directions, and information sheets for examinees, supporting documents, drawings, tools, and other items needed to take the test. Some tests may require further materials to support written and performance-based components.

Written directions should always accompany performance tests and may accompany written tests if the employer/proctor of the test wants them. It is also important to include a list of procedures, materials, constraints, safety measures, and scoring methods.

Information sheets

When information on the learner's educational background and work experience is available, the analysis of the test results, in many cases, is more meaningful. This is particularly true when the test population is small or consists of people with specialized or technical knowledge and skills. It is advisable to have each examinee fill out a form specifically designed to elicit such information at the beginning of the session. File this information with the test for future reference.

Supporting materials

All materials necessary to support a performance test should be listed in the test guide, including a brief statement of the purpose, the people to be tested, and instructions for the proctor. Also included should be a list of materials required for the test and instructions to be read to the student.

Make a note of any task items or performance checkpoints that are governed or supported by documents, drawings, or directives. Use the test item form or evaluation checklist as appropriate. Also cite all matters of common industry practice. For instance, a technical standard might have an informational notation such as "all nuts are tightened to 57 foot/pounds."

Phase three: Validation of text materials

Of course, most written tests require more than one good test item, because most jobs or tasks demand competence in more than one central area. A series of items must be included in order to indicate mastery of the subject. To do this, two important concepts must be clear: validity and reliability.

Validity refers to the test's content and, simply put, means that a test should measure what it claims to measure. In the case of most performance-based tests, this means that it should measure the cognitively based knowledge, skills, and abilities required to function at a given level of competence in the job position. Any effort on the part of the test writer to measure more or less than this criterion diminishes the validity of the test.

The test must reflect the competencies identified as critical in the job or task analysis, the instructional objectives, and the content specifications. That's why it is important to review these documents at the outset. Make sure there is a test item for each of the critical aspects of the job. Once all items are arranged into a complete test, it's a good idea to have subject matter experts review your effort. They can tell if anything is omitted. Also, administer the test to some competent performers and their feedback will give a good idea of the real-world applicability of the test.

While validity determines *whether or not* a test measures what it claims to measure, reliability determines the *degree* to which it does so consistently. A written test, like any other measuring instrument, is useless unless it can produce results consistently.

Several factors influence the reliability of a test. The most important is the appropriateness and technical accuracy of the test items. They must evaluate realistic and practical aspects of job performance. The number of test items is also important; the more test items, the better the capacity of the test to measure competence. This is not a license for overkill, however; a three-step procedure doesn't warrant a 100-question test. Just make sure to test adequately and completely all the critical skills and knowledge.

Remember, too, that the order in which the items are presented can affect test reliability. Just as improper distracters can cue the correct response, improper sequencing of items may give away answers. Make sure question 1 does not tip off question 2. Also make sure the correct answer to question 2 does not depend on knowing the correct answer to question 1. Each item should present an independent problem.

It may be impossible to control some of the factors affecting reliability, but be aware of them. Try to create a consistent atmosphere for test taking; uniformity of the examination environment is important. The same test administered once in a noisy and poorly lit factory area and again in a quiet classroom will probably yield very different results. Also, realize that cheating will skew test results. Arrange for as much test security and exam proctoring as is necessary.

In Closing

I believe that I am safe in stating that representatives of both business and industry, and community colleges and institutes, fully realize the necessity for cooperating in the education and training of a productive workforce. To accomplish a joining of these forces, this book has provided suggestions and guidance for developing and delivering experiential learning activities. It will be through cooperative education that well educated and trained learners will enter the workforce and serve in a productive and self-satisfying manner, and thus enable the organizations for which they work to grow and prosper. The end result is true economic development.

Chapter References

Cantor, J.A. (1987a). Developing multiple-choice test items. *Training and Development Journal,* (May) 85-88.

Cantor, J.A. (1987b). A systems approach to instructional development in technical education. *Journal of Studies in Technical Careers, IX*(2), 155-166.

Cantor, J.A. (1988a). How to design, develop and use performance tests. *Training and Development Journal,* (September) *42*(9), 72-75.

Cantor, J.A. (1988b). The training effectiveness algorithm. *The Journal of Educational Technology Systems, XVI*(3), 207-229.

Index

A

C

D

O

P

R

S

T